RIDERS TO THE MIDNIGHT SUN

RIDERS TO THE MIDNIGHT SUN

MARC LLEWELLYN

FROM THE BLACK SEA TO THE RUSSIAN ARCTIC

First published in Australia in 2000 by
New Holland Publishers (Australia) Pty Ltd
Sydney • Auckland • London • Cape Town

14 Aquatic Drive Frenchs Forest NSW 2086 Australia
218 Lake Road Northcote Auckland New Zealand
24 Nutford Place London W1H 6DQ United Kingdom
80 McKenzie Street Cape Town 8001 South Africa

National Library of Australia
Cataloguing-in-Publication Data:

Llewellyn, Marc.
 Riders to the midnight sun.

 ISBN 1 86436 641 9.

 1. Llewellyn, Marc—Journeys—Ukraine—Sevastopol.
 2. Llewellyn, Marc—Journeys—Russia—Kola Peninsula.
 3. Sevastopol (Ukraine)—Description and travel.
 4. Kola Peninsula (Russia)—Description and travel. I. Title.

914.71304

Publishing Manager: Anouska Good
Project Editor: Jennifer Lane
Editor: Sophie Church
Designer: Nanette Backhouse
Cartographer: Guy Holt
Printer: Griffin Press, Netley, South Australia

Typeset in 10pt Bookman ITCLt

CONTENTS

Leave thy home, O youth
And seek out foreign shores:
A broader range of things begins for thee.
He who disembarks on far-off sands
Thereby becomes the greater man

Marco Polo

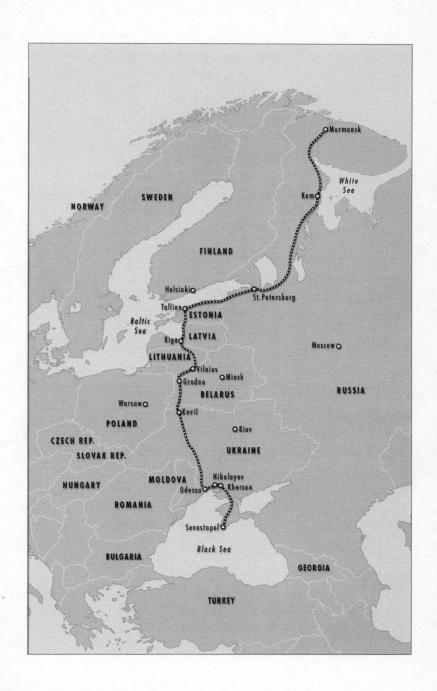

PROLOGUE

THROUGH THE BOTTOM OF A BOTTLE

All good things begin in the bath. When immersed in bubbles, and preferably half cut with whisky, the most outlandish ideas spring to mind. I read somewhere that two bicycle mechanics, named Orville and Wilbur Wright, first conceived the idea of flying 35 metres in a huge, heavier-than-air contraption after one of them was almost paralytic in the tub after consuming an entire bottle of Jack Daniels and pretending his hand was a seagull with an engine attached to its backside. And it's said, mostly by resident drunks in seedy bars, I admit, that Napoleon got the idea to invade Europe after losing the soap between his legs and coming to the conclusion that if you made yourself slippery enough nobody would ever catch you (the British at Waterloo were the exception as most of the lower classes, who did all the work, habitually refrained from washing and were therefore immune to the concept).

Fortunately, most people fail to adhere to plans made while lounging around in the nude and towel themselves off to emerge spanking clean in the same course of life they were on before they immersed themselves. I, however, was at the mercy of an idea that refused to budge with even the most brutal rub down.

As I wallowed in the bath, attempting to imitate a whale by squirting water from my navel with my finger, a particularly unsettling thought came to mind: I was thirty years old. I had achieved little in my life except an expensive spare tyre around my waist. Almost every girlfriend had left me for another man, citing the pressing need to be rid of someone who kept losing his contact lenses while being violently sick in pub toilets (I remain proud that I always retained the composure to flush afterwards and never tried to fish about in search of them). To my parents' delight, I at least managed to make it to university—although my psychology lecturer soon advised me to take some time off to 'find myself', after I presented an idea for my final year's dissertation concerning the combined hallucinogenic effects of lager and LSD.

Following my debut into the world of work I was thrown out of jobs for calling in too frequently with a hangover, or, more commonly, for just being infuriatingly incompetent. I felt I had been hard done by in all this, of course, and felt confident that one day I would show them all and do something so remarkably outlandish that they would all slap themselves on their foreheads and berate themselves for failing to foresee the fact that I was not a loser after all.

The problem was finding something that no-one had done before. It didn't help that I had previously shown passing competence at only two things: drinking and escaping respon-sibilities. I was born too left-handed to invent anything, and I didn't have the patience for a long-term goal. No, what I had to do was something that combined my strengths. I began racking my brains: I could climb a mountain, but I got all itchy when I grew a beard, so that was out; maybe a trip somewhere that nobody had done before—that was more like it. But where?

I dried myself off. I turned on the radio. Someone was banging on about how Russian vodka distillers were being bought out by western businessmen. I'd always meant to go to Russia, but the only contact I'd ever had with the Russians was through my grandfather. Through the fog of my drunkenness I remembered sitting on his knee as a small child, listening to his stories about when the lamps went out, the whistles blew in a heaving swell, and the ack-ack guns spun in their turrets, roaring angrily as they lit up the night. He'd been part of the convoy delivering supplies through the iceberged sea to northern Russia, from the Firth of Clyde to Murmansk and back. His tales of engines droning, seaboots filling with ice cold water and orange mackintoshes floating off unworn had sent shivers down my spine. He garbled between sobs about periscopes, ships' engines stopped and friends lost at sea. Not soon enough he made it back home with frost-bitten feet and a twitch which stayed with him until the day he died.

Long after his funeral I had come across a journal scratchy with faded ink. It touched on Murmansk. He wrote of an unreal world, where concrete buildings crumbled beneath a leaden sky and crawled up the hills to be swallowed in mist; where down on the jetties women and political prisoners unloaded the ships, their overseers in astrakhan caps forbidding help from sailors from faraway ports; where it always seemed to be raining, and everyone felt the Russians might turn upon their helpers at any time.

Then all at once I hit my teens. One night I found myself locked in a nightmare: I was sitting in my grandmother's outhouse, wrapped in the odour of potato sacks, old flattened shoes and damp laundry. I watched the timer counting down: ...three...two...one. The needle fell to zero. For a moment all was silent, yet magically bright. The blast, when it came, threw me squirming wildly back into bed. I was rattled. What did it all mean? It was The Bomb all right. I had even made out the hammer and sickle on its side. But why did they want to kill me? I hadn't even met a Russian, let alone had the opportunity to get an insult in. But it wasn't just me of course. Hundreds of millions of us had awoken in a Cold War sweat. Generations of us, especially in Europe, had lived with the fear of The Bomb, and truly anticipated the yell of the siren— warning us too late that the Russians were coming, missiles first. Once I even stole cans of baked beans from the pantry and sneaked them out to a home-made shelter in the depths of a nearby wood, piling them up beside comic books and my penknife before settling down for the final show.

Nostradamus certainly foresaw our destruction, or so I was warned by the television one evening. It was due to happen just before my final school examinations. I remember it vividly: I put down my exercise books and strode downstairs.

'That's it!' I informed my parents, 'the world's going to end. I'm dropping out of school. There's no point in studying. I'm going to live life while I have the chance.'

Meanwhile, as far as you could get from my native Wales, my future Australian girlfriend, Rohan, was spending fitful nights awake with terror. She was sure of it too. But the fateful day came—and went. The exchange of warheads had been postponed, and I was strangely comforted by the familiar annual procession of android guards and their missiles rolling through the streets of Moscow for the May Day parade.

Now, as I dried my toes and pulled on my socks, I quickly forgot the dark thoughts and contemplated travelling through a land of buxom women ladling out vodka by the bucket load. I poured myself my fourth whisky for the night. And then another. The more I drank the more feasible it seemed. I could avoid the big cities and slip through villages in the guise of a local, with a sack thrown over my shoulder and a tobacco tin for my roll-your-owns in my pocket. But walking as far as the local shop gave me the shits, so that was out.

I thought briefly of doing it by car, but as I had failed my driving test four times already—and was so uncommonly scared of roundabouts that more often than not I jumped out at their approach and handed the wheel over to Rohan—that idea flitted away as quickly as it came too. No, what I needed was something in between, some way that I could travel faster than a painful amble, but which was not quite as disconcerting as tearing around the countryside in a thin metal box. I took a final gulp and reached for the bottle again.

Suddenly, the haze parted and it came to me. It was obvious. I should do it by bicycle—one of the simplest, least polluting and most efficient of human inventions. What's more it reached across all classes. People rode bicycles whether they were rich or poor. It would also mean I could interact with the scenery without standing out too much. The fact that I had last ridden a bicycle nearly ten years before didn't even cross my mind. My body had spread like a maturing brie, it was true, but I was sure I could get fit enough. Yes, it was certainly an interesting notion. I poured myself another drink and lit up a cigarette. Of course it would mean cutting out the fags, but what better incentive was there to give up smoking than a few thousand kilometres on a saddle.

When I sobered up I was still intrigued. I found myself trawling local libraries and devouring the little I could find about the people newly released from behind the Iron Curtain. The more I learned, the more obvious it became that they had suffered on a scale unique in world history. The human tragedy of the masses was too huge to grasp. Ceaseless ideological and military clashes had turned their lives into epics. But as individuals I couldn't quite put a finger on them—they were ghosts, spirits, things that went bump in the night. All that came out of the vast, featureless abyss of the former Soviet Union were vague tales of gangsters and radiation, and Western bankers making it rich quick. It was like living in a house with a room closed off. And in the end I knew I was too inquisitive not to try breaking in.

'It's a ridiculous idea,' Rohan huffed when I broached my plan some time later. 'If you want to cycle why not ride around Spain or somewhere? Why do you want to go there?'

There were a million reasons why it was a foolhardy plan, but I tried to explain nevertheless that the time was right, and babbled on about my grandfather, and finding out more about the people who had threatened us all with mutual destruction since we were kids. But she knew me too well, and it didn't take her long to winkle out the truth: I was afraid that what I was now might be all that I'd ever be. Rohan shook her head sadly. If I couldn't even make it through a roundabout in a Toyota, she didn't fancy my chances of getting from one end of the former Soviet Union to the other on a pushbike.

I continued working for a daily newspaper in Australia. Weeks slipped by devoid of inspiration. I tried to convince myself that life was meant to be like this; trudging to the office, coming home with a headache, ironing shirts I didn't want to wear, sleeping away much of the weekend and getting suddenly older. Then, before I knew it, I found myself reading Gogol and Tolstoy on the bus to work. I began to escape my desk, to lock myself into toilet cubicles, and began to plan my trip on the walls. With the help of an old atlas, the entrails of a route began to emerge. Though bicyclists had ridden from west to east across the former Soviet Union, as far as I knew nobody had ever ridden from the south to the north. Sevastopol, at the tail end of southern Ukraine, seemed the obvious starting point, and Murmansk, at the top of Arctic Russia, was where I would finish. Ominously, it seemed both had navy bases crammed with nuclear warships and submarines.

The local library supplied me with another map, this time splattered with the symbols of Soviet industry. Amongst the triangles, squares and circles of coal mines, mineral deposits and major industries were the familiar yellow and black tags of nuclear power stations. There was a whole horseshoe of them, standing out like beacons right along my route. A theme was emerging which I didn't particularly like the feel of. One always needed an erudite reason for going on a long excursion and I had hoped mine would have simply been the glorious pursuit of vodka. I swallowed hard, but pencilled in an auspicious starting date in my mind—May Day.

By the end of October, fate and my big mouth had led me by the nose onto the nuclear trail. I lapsed at work and found myself confiding in colleagues about my upcoming trip, and in the end I think I convinced myself. At home I worked underhandedly, teeing up a harmless extended Christmas holiday in Berlin with Rohan's mother, Susanne, who had taken a brave decision, I thought, to emigrate back to her homeland to marry a gynaecologist. The time came and we booked our tickets. I packed in my job. Rohan got suspicious. She packed in hers too.

I walked back from my last day at the office with my ears sharpened to the cries of birds and shouts of playing children. Freshly cut grass hung in the air more pungent than I ever remembered. I bounced up the hill to my apartment and shouted a cheery hello to the cockroaches nibbling at the remains of last night's dinner in the sink. It was comforting knowing that I wouldn't need to wash up in months. Ah yes. It's one of the most liberating and vivid times in life—the evening before the great adventure.

1 MUTTLEY AND KATOSHKA COME OF AGE

Berlin was suffering its coldest winter on record. Susanne and her husband Kurt met us at the airport swaddled in thick coats and bespeckled with snow flakes the size of postage stamps. Even their German Shepherd seemed pleased to see us, and insisted on grabbing me by the arm and increasing his grip by calculated degrees, squeezing tears from my eyes and presenting me with the dilemma of either making a good first impression with my girlfriend's mother or immediately smacking her dog in the mouth. Fortunately, my watery eyes were seen as a sign of honest emotion at our meeting, and as the dog let me loose to pad off for a meal of a compatriot's faeces left steaming in the snow, we kissed and hugged and plodded with our luggage through the car park. Despite the teeth marks on my wrist I managed a smile beneath my borrowed scarf: I was in Berlin—one step closer to Russia and the East.

At ten the next morning the sun rose lazily and took to loitering just above the horizon like a boiled egg. Sensing we should stretch our limbs to stop them hibernating until spring, we dragged ourselves away from the radiator and out into a nearby forest. Soon we were forging our way past the crumpled remains of frozen bracken stalks and up a ridge kerbed by the mossy trunks of fallen trees. We continued on, ploughing through clouds of our own breath, stopping when we came to a fenced-off area housing a few wild boars. From where I stood there was not much between them and the bulky middle-aged Fraus in fur coats smacking their lips and drooling over the thought of pork on the hoof.

It was here that I let slip my plans. Eager to find out what Kurt thought of the Russians, I was happy when conversation turned so naturally, as it nearly always does in Germany, towards the war.

It turned out he was born in Breslau, the capital of the coal mining province of Silesia. At nine years old he had fled with his parents, and millions of others, westwards in advance of the Red Army surge, and had ended up in a small village in Saxony, not far from the charred remains of Dresden. Soon afterwards the Potsdam Agreement gave Silesia to Poland, and those Germans who had remained in Silesia were expelled and replaced with Polish refugees from further east—from cities like L'vov and Vilnius which Stalin had claimed as his own. Kurt's family finally made it to the West in 1949, the same year the Soviet Union exploded its first nuclear bomb in Kazakhstan.

'You must feel a little bitter about it all,' I noted. 'You know, being kicked out of your homeland and everything.'

'No. The Russians and Germans have no dislikes now,' Kurt responded matter-of-factly, like the trained gynaecologist he was. 'The old ideas have gone. It's time to forget.'

It struck me that if I were Russian I'd still be more than a little bit miffed considering more than fifty million Soviet citizens had been massacred on the back of German nationalism, but I had the sense to keep quiet. I wrapped my mouth up with my scarf and crunched on through the snow with my thoughts to myself.

That evening, over the entire German culinary repertoire of sauerkraut, potatoes and herring salad, Susanne told of her own experiences with the Russians. She had been eight, and living in a small village to the south of Berlin when the invaders came.

'We were told they ate children and would boil us in big pots when they found us.' She spooned out another helping of limp pickled cabbage. 'As a child that was the most gruesome thing you could think of: being put in a pot of boiling oil and being eaten by a hairy Russian.'

I could only guess, as I played with the food on my plate, that the Russians had shared the same overwhelming urge to devour anything apart from the locally accepted diet as I did.

The troops finally entered her village in early May 1945, she continued, and the villagers were rounded up—but not before many of Susanne's young playmates were murdered by their own parents after Nazi propaganda had insisted the Russians would do the same anyway, but with a slathering of torture on the side.

'We were terrified! When the first Russians came and searched the village, a giant of a man with a huge red bushy beard picked up my sister and brought her towards his mouth. She screamed—she was sure he was about to eat her.'

'What happened?' I piped up, always the lover of an offbeat ending. Rohan jabbed me in the ribs. Susanne clapped her hands together.

'He just laughed out loud and kissed her. Kissed her! All over the face... '

The last remark, delivered without drama, made me lose interest and I began idly forking herring around my plate.

'But you see, even then the adults still didn't understand them,' she went on. 'All through the occupation we were told by our parents never to stray after dark. The Russians would be hiding in the alleyways, they told us. But as a child I thought they were wonderful. They fed us their own rations, and played games with us... '

But childhood is soon choked by prejudice—and in no other country I had visited was this so obvious. In the coming weeks, Susanne referred to everyone living to the east of her as pimps, gangsters, car thieves, or just plain stupid. Vigorous nods from other Berliners I came across affirmed the East Germans were ungrateful; the Rumanians were robbers and gypsies; and the Czechs, well, one good thing had to be said about them, they made damn good waiters. As for the Russians—they were barbarians who washed their potatoes in the toilet. Even Kurt's Polish housekeeper assured me they were all drunks, and that they'd steal my bike and I'd be murdered and left to rot in the forest. And the roads—well they were the worst in the world: I'd have a puncture or a buckled wheel in the first five minutes. Then there was the radiation... Finally, to assure myself, I rang the only English-speaking expert on the former Soviet Union I had heard of: the chief Russian analyst at the BBC World Service. 'You're totally mad,' he said. 'I don't think you've thought it through at all.'

✶ ✶ ✶

With a frightening resolve I began searching the city for maps, finally coming across a 1:2 000 000 scale plan of the whole of the former Soviet Union. It would do for a start. I carried it home like a new-born puppy, checking the bag now and then to make sure it was still there, opening up a corner, picking out a name at random and rolling it on my tongue, repeating it over and over again: Smolensk; Zitomir; Novgorod; Murmansk. Once home I rushed up to our bedroom, unfolded it gingerly on the floor and stuck sticky-tape over the creases to stop them tearing. Then I took a long, gluttonous look.

The Crimean peninsula dangled like a chunky earring from the Ukrainian Steppe, only the width of two fingers from top to bottom. Ukraine, Belarus and all three Baltic states together were a finger's length each. Russia, on the other hand, was a monster, reclining across the unfolded segments, and squashing its neighbours into tight little corners. I moved my finger down to the far south of the Crimea, to Stalin's 'Hero City' of Sevastopol, the main stage of the Crimean War and the main port of the Black Sea Fleet. I traced a route across the thin grey ridges of the Crimean mountains to the Ukrainian grasslands and westwards to Odessa, before wheeling north-west through Belarus to Lithuania. I could cycle through the Baltic capitals and then onwards to St Petersburg, swinging due north deep into the Arctic and the Gulag Archipelago. Finally, my road would traverse the snowy uplands to Murmansk, ending with the nuclear submarines hidden away in the fjords. The width of my middle finger nail represented 100 kilometres on the map's scale. That made my route more than forty-five finger

nails long, or 4500 kilometres. I shrugged my shoulders.
Three months. Tops.

✳ ✳ ✳

Winter ended abruptly, leaving no time for spring.
Temperatures shot up from freezing to 30˚C in a week. Berlin
emerged like a seedy drunk. The trees began spitting out
catkins. Snow drops, crocuses and daffodils all struggled to
flower together, their usual linear progression upset. The
German Shepherd began raiding grassy strips for defrosting
snacks of shit it had squirrelled away in bleaker times.

February moved into March and we still showed no sign of
going back home. Then one sunny day, when I had been
caught out for the umpteenth time sighing dramatically at a
passing bicycle, Rohan finally pinned me down.

'You're not still thinking of this Russian thing, are you?'

'I think I am,' I said, desperately unsure. We walked on in
silence.

'But you've heard everything people have been saying. Are
you totally insane?'

I had to admit the thought had crossed my mind. 'It's just
something I have to do,' I said peevishly. 'I don't really know
why, but the whole thing has got a will of its own now.'

It was weird. I could no longer have packed the whole idea
in as the dog could rid itself of its instinctual truffling
expeditions along the kerb side. Something was dragging me
onwards. Whether it was fate or stupidity I didn't know. But it
was futile to think about doing otherwise.

'Then I'll have to come with you,' she said at last. 'I just can't
trust you to take care of yourself.'

'Thank God,' I thought, and a huge weight slipped off my
shoulders. There'd be no chance now of buxom Russian
wenches having their wicked way with me after pouring vodka
down my throat, but at least I didn't have to do the whole
thing on my own. On a purely practical level Rohan comple-
mented me well: whereas I was more likely to jump in boots
first, she calculated her risks carefully; while I had some
vague idea of us whisking effortlessly through the Steppe,

she visualised each painful kilometre with a wince; I was satisfied with not thinking about what we would find, Rohan expected trouble. In the light of that, her decision to go was far braver than mine.

We started learning Russian with the alphabet. I scrawled out each character on its own square of paper and we tested each other in the bath over bottles of Moët—presents for the gynaecologist for all those babies he helped see through to term. Rohan sipped and revised; I knocked it back Cossack-style and forgot everything.

The planning stepped up. We would both need visas for the Ukraine, Belarus and Russia. Rohan, with her Australian passport, would also need visas to cover the Baltic states and to transit through Poland. My British one would do the trick in that department. All roads, it seemed, led to a travel agency in the former East Berlin—a poky little place with a pathetic collection of matt brochures. I picked out one which made Kiev as inviting as a weekend for two in the Glasgow slums of the thirties. The owner, a frizzy-haired young woman tagged Frau Dein, announced that she could arrange everything.

'We are the only ones,' she added with an unnerving smile. I knew then it would be expensive.

Both the Ukrainian and Belarus visas would take about a week, she told us. To get the Russian visa we would have to book every night's accommodation along our route.

'But that's impossible! We won't know where we will be every night,' I spluttered. 'On bicycles anything can happen.'

'Did you say bicycles?'

'Yes, bicycles. We want to cycle from the south of Ukraine to the north of Russia.'

'Impossible,' she hissed, replacing her biro pointedly on her desk and sitting well back in her chair (for a moment, I half expected her to put her feet up on the table and light up a cigar). 'You will not be allowed. You must understand. The former Soviet Union is a bicycle-unfriendly place. It is illegal for foreigners to cycle in the big cities. If you cycled in Kiev you would be arrested. You can only cycle if you go with a tour group.' She lunged towards us menacingly. 'We can arrange everything.'

'I'll bear it in mind,' I said, but nevertheless we left our passports and money behind, held to ransom.

Our next task was to buy bicycles. At Berlin's largest cycle emporium we apprehended a spotty-faced youth who croaked that we would be mad if we bought anything other than a top-of-the-range mountain bike. Then, with a straight face, he launched in German into the benefits of double-butted tubes, machined brake-surfaced rims, and indexed shifting.

'Whatever you do, don't buy a racer,' he concluded solemnly. 'It will damage your spine irreparably.'

I baulked at the thought of surviving the cycle trip only to end up a hunchback but I needed a second opinion. Across town we were accosted by a pimpled clone who insisted we consider something with aero wheels and 'sixteen series alu 853 steel', before wandering off into a cookery lesson involving carbon-fibre forks and heat-treating your tubing at 850°C for eight hours until done.

'How do I pump up the tyres?' I asked, trying to look as if I knew what he was on about. He stopped mid gush.

'Are they cheap?' Rohan added innocently.

'What exactly were you after?'

'Something not too expensive' she responded more nervously.

'And that, um, goes up hills easily,' I threw in.

Realising he was faced with a couple of idiots, he warned us to get the idea of mountain bikes out of our minds for a start. Such small wheels and thick tyres would never do the distance.

'What would you recommend then?' I asked. He manoeuvred us towards the most expensive racing machines.

Finally, two weeks before we were due to leave, we found them: unpretentious, dull-grey Korean contraptions, with shiny steel wheels, medium-sized tyres and 21 gears— hybrids between a mountain bike and a racer. They were the cheapest in stock. We snapped them up, and an oily salesman led us to a courtyard stacked with boxes.

'You have to put them together yourselves,' he said. 'Come back in a few days if you have problems.'

'Ourselves!' we echoed open mouthed.

'What do you expect for 400 deutchmark?'

We built them in the garden. The pedals sheared off thin slivers of aluminium as we screwed them into their shafts. Our bells broke on their very first ring. The seats twirled around unfettered. We found a similar problem with the handlebars, so that each time we rounded a corner they stayed facing the same direction we had originally turned them, causing us to fall off repeatedly. By the end of the first day both bikes were so badly dented that we felt too embarrassed to take them back.

✳ ✳ ✳

Our passports finally arrived—with the wrong dates stamped on the visa for Belarus. It meant we had just six days to cross the country. I filed away the problem on a long mental list. As for the Russian visa...

'The rules have changed,' Frau Dein announced as she scraped a handful of purple nails through her hair. 'You can now only get them from your own countries.' She leaned back in her chair again. 'But we can do you a special favour. I know the Russian Consul and I've told him about you...' My neck prickled. Thoughts of men in long mackintoshes with stiletto knives crossed my mind. 'I will be meeting him at a cocktail party on the weekend. Maybe I could ask him to do you a special favour. It would cost you more money.' She quickly added the figures up. 'Visa fee...invitation...consulate charges...courier fee...our expenses...that extra charge...' Finally, she came up with some astronomical figure. Even then, the Consul could still refuse us and keep the money, she warned.

'I'm sorry. It's impossible. We just can't afford to go to Russia,' I said calmly. 'Please give my thanks to the Consul when you see him.'

'There's nothing for it,' I said, after closing the door behind us with the realisation that sometimes in life fate has a knack of making it difficult for itself. 'We'll have to try and get the visa somewhere along the route.' No doubt, when or if we finally got our Russian visa, we, like Napoleon before us, would feel like burning Smolensk too.

'Maybe we could take a stack of American dollars with us and if the worst came to the worst we can bribe someone,' Rohan prompted. I smiled. She was catching on quickly.

* * *

I wanted to travel eastwards by train, through Poland and into Ukraine, to see the countryside Stalin's troops might have seen as they flooded westwards to invade Eastern Europe. It would also give us an idea of the kind of place we'd have to cycle through later. In six years working at one of Berlin's major train stations, the ticket inspector had never heard of anyone trying to take bicycles to the East. Nevertheless, she checked her books and computer. The only way to do it was to hand over our bicycles a week before we were due to leave and pick them up in Warsaw.

'Then you can put the bikes on the Polish train to the Ukrainian border,' she said. 'But as for Ukraine, I think it is safer if you did not go at all. The bicycles will probably disappear before you arrive at your destination.'

I nodded politely, then asked her how long it would take to get to Sevastopol, just the same. She tapped away at her keyboard and referred to her atlas of Europe. 'I can't be sure, but perhaps five days.'

'Five days! You can't be serious... '

Less than an hour later I was holding two one-way airline tickets to Kiev in my hand. Our departure point was the tiny Tempelhof airport, the site of the Berlin airlift. We would have to take our chances in getting from Kiev to Sevastopol.

* * *

A week before we were due to leave we still hadn't ridden our bicycles further than the end of the road. Kurt was concerned.

'You must train,' he yelled, banging his fist on the table during our third bottle of chianti. 'Tomorrow we go to

Potsdam with Werner, he can tell you all about Russia and Ukraine. He was there for a long time.' At last, I thought, someone who can really give me an idea of what to expect.

Early next morning, a sprightly man with candy floss hair arrived on a ram-horned racing bike. He was in his early eighties, but from the look of his calf muscles I knew he could out-ride me any day. He shook my hand warmly.

'I have heard zo much about you,' he said, bubbling over. 'You are kvite simply mad,' he added. 'I vould love to come.'

'I hear you have been to the Ukraine,' I said.

'Vait a moment.' He walked over to his bike and took out a tatty map from his single back pannier. He unfolded it carefully and spread it between us. I noticed a large greying swastika to the west of Russia. 'Here, here and here and, ya, here too,' he said, pointing out locations with jabs of his index finger. 'Ya, a vonderful place. A vonderful experience.'

'When did you go there?'

'Vell, in the vor of course,' he said, his eyes wide in surprise.

'In the war? Oh, I thought you had gone there on holiday or something.'

'Nein, nein, nein,' he said, delighted at my ignorance. 'My dear chap, I bombed it!'

My jaw dropped. 'Yaaa,' he continued, jabbing at the map again. 'Here, here, here unt here.'

Werner told us he had spent most of the war making movies for Josef Goebbels' Propaganda Ministry, filming Russian and Ukrainian towns being bombed by the Luftwaffe, and the tanks as they moved along the road to Moscow. He had earned the Iron Cross twice and had ended the war in an American field hospital after being shot in the back by an Allied machine gunner. He proudly showed us his wounds as Kurt disappeared to fetch his bike from the shed. I was rapidly coming to the conclusion that my experience with the effects of illegal substances had been invaluable.

Shortly afterwards Kurt appeared again, with a carthorse of a beast beside him, complete with a barrelled back-wheel hub which acted as a brake. He mounted like a Prussian cavalry officer. My bike flicked its chain off in timid response. I slipped it back on, messily oiling my hands and gloves.

'If this thing makes it then it deserves a medal,' I thought to myself. And there in a flash it was christened. I would call my bike 'Muttley', after Dick Dastardly's mongrel sidekick who demanded a medal every time he saved his master. Rohan laughed. She expected it might earn a few citations before all this was over.

We took off unsteadily, with Rohan tailing the rest of us as she struggled with her gears. She had insisted on stuffing her panniers full of books to gauge what it would be like to cycle fully equipped. It looked tough going. I was having none of it—biding my time.

Bunching together, we pedalled through the suburb of Wannsee, where in January 1942 Hitler had ordered that the Final Solution should commence with the eradication of Poland's Jews. At the old East German border Rohan called out breathlessly for a rest break. She pulled up beside me, almost toppling under the weight of her overstuffed mount, and breathlessly announced she had found a name for her bike too.

'I'm going to call it "Katoshka",' she said. 'Russian for potato.'

I had to admit there was certainly a resemblance.

We continued on, buoyed by the thought that at least the bikes had names. It was all coming together. Then the roads of the West fell apart and a rash of cobbles and tree roots began rattling our teeth. If this was a taste of what we were likely to expect then I doubted if we would survive a couple of days in the saddle before calling it a day and checking into a clinic specialising in reconstructing buttocks. But there was little else to do now but ride onwards under the creaking eves of a woodland, trying to distract our minds from the bone-jarring track with disguised 'oohs and aahs' aimed at the Painted Lady butterflies which were twirling through the air. Thankfully, it was not long before a row of mansions appeared, reflected on the surface of the River Havel, and Kurt pulled over to take a better look.

'Most of those houses belonged to the great actors of Berlin,' he pointed out to a largely unenthusiastic audience. 'And that one,' he gestured to a ramshackle Gothic structure, 'was where Truman lived when he came to Berlin for the Potsdam Conference.'

There, behind that gloomy façade, the American President had warned the Japanese they faced utter destruction from the atomic bomb. Looking back on it, I would have expected a shiver to have run down my spine. But I felt nothing. The day was too sunny; the trees so full of life. I was in too much pain.

We were forced on, and a little later the forest thinned, ending in a bald patch of English-style gardens. On one side menaced a row of former KGB cottages, and in its centre a palace sagged beneath a pastry crust roof and twirled brick chimneys. Here—amid the belongings of both Frederick the Great and Voltaire—Truman, Churchill and Stalin had divided up the spoils of war. While at the same time, in a New Mexican desert, scientists and dignitaries were holed up in their bunkers. There was a flash, a wave of heat, a roar, a ball of fire and a mushroom cloud. The sand all around fused to glass. When Truman, in an aside, mentioned the Americans were going to use their new bomb on Japan, Stalin ignored him. Truman later wrote to his mother:

'You never saw such pig-headed people as are the Russians.' The Germans were just as bad, I cursed, as we set off again with Kurt determined to step up the pace and get some real exercise in.

By the time we arrived home we had covered nearly 50 kilometres. I was so thoroughly exhausted I could barely stand up, and had to support myself against a tree in the front garden—with a kink half-way up where a Russian tank had collided with it as a sapling. I desperately tried to summon enough strength to wobble towards the door. Werner, on the other hand, looked as fresh as if he was just starting out, and gave us a cheery wave as he set off across the city for a swim in his local lake. Kurt wanted to drink schnapps. Rohan wanted to cry. I limped bravely upstairs to bed.

The next day there was news from Chernobyl, the scene of such disaster back in 1986. A fire had started in the grasslands north-west of the power plant, inside the heavily contaminated 30 kilometre exclusion zone. The flames had spread quickly and engulfed five deserted villages before crossing the border into badly irradiated Belarus. Plumes of radioactive particles had been pumped into the air. Hundreds of former residents, who were making their annual pilgrimage to their ancestral graves, were being evacuated. On the same day a United Nations report warned that the areas surrounding Chernobyl had become a 'radio-active powder-keg'. A huge amount of fuel had built up in the forests and fields since the evacuation of villagers, it stated. There were now more than two thousand fires in the area annually. A serious one would send radioactive ash and smoke over hundreds of thousands of kilometres. Now, a giant radioactive cloud was moving towards our first stop in Ukraine—Kiev.

There was news from the nuclear power station itself the day before the tenth anniversary of the disaster. Workmen had 'failed to package' some highly contaminated filters they had been replacing at one of the plant's two working reactors. Instead, they were left lying around on the floor, and employees were forced to step over them, sending up invisible streams of dust as they went. Radiation levels inside the plant had increased seven-fold.

Next morning, a letter arrived from Rohan's father in Australia. It contained cuttings from the local press, referring to the latest radioactive cloud, and the lingering effects of Chernobyl. 'Avoid this place at all costs,' his message read tersely.

★ ★ ★

We spent our last evening in the West listening to the National Symphony Orchestra of Ukraine playing Prokofiev's 'Romeo and Juliet'. Scattered around in piles were enough packets of dried potato, soup, pasta and rice to take us through Ukraine and Belarus to Lithuania, where we hoped to stock up on more from a Western-style supermarket we'd heard had opened in Vilnius. Food from the badly irradiated areas was turning up in the markets and restaurants all across the former Soviet Union, so the more we avoided eating local produce the better. And anyway, we couldn't rely on meals being available whenever we were hungry.

As well as the food, we each had a pair of shorts and a couple of T-shirts for the road; a couple of pairs of jeans; a sweater; thick socks; underwear; and thermal long-johns for the Arctic. I insisted on a pair of sturdy working boots to cycle in; Rohan preferred a pair of cheap gym shoes, which hurt her toes from the start. She was to carry bicycle tools and spares, including a couple of inner tubes, while I took responsibility for a hefty first aid kit containing everything from syringes and sutures to hangover remedies. I tried on my helmet—a sleek, black, bullet-shaped thing. It fitted more tightly than was comfortable, but I persuaded myself it would stretch. There were cameras and lenses, diaries, a pile of books for the road, and a primus lacking its fuel of methylated spirits, which we had been warned we couldn't carry on the plane. Sprawled out too was an aluminium cooking pot set; plastic plates, cups and cutlery; a couple of good quality sleeping bags; and an expensive green tent to hide us from axemen who obviously haunted the forests. Then there was the map, hefty locks and chains and four water bottles—two cheapies for our bikes and two larger ones made of durable plastic, which claimed to be indestructible and which began to split as soon as we hit the road.

We had luxuries too—a miniature short-wave radio for me: which I hoped would pick up the BBC World Service and which ended up demolishing a set of batteries in a couple of hours—and for Rohan a book of Chekhov's short stories and some crayons in a metal cigarette tin to satisfy a latent desire to become a great artist. In the end, each pack weighed about as much as a small cow.

Late that night the telephone rang. It was Rohan's father. He was desperate.

'You don't seem to realise how dangerous it is,' he pleaded with me. 'It's different for Rohan with all that radiation over there. She could have real problems if she wants to have children. Sperm get replaced every day. If they get damaged by radiation then they are simply substituted by others, but Rohan has had her eggs in her body since before she was born. If she goes there is a real chance of her having deformed children!'

I passed him over to Rohan. She broke down almost immediately, and eventually had to hang up on him.

'He's begged me not to go,' she sobbed. 'He said he would give us all the money we had spent on arrangements and tickets. I don't know. I think I shouldn't go. I've been worried all along. Oh God, it's all been such a waste of time.' She began clutching at straws. 'Maybe I can meet you in Lithuania or somewhere and cycle with you into Russia, as long as I don't go to the Ukraine or Belarus, they're the worst...'

I hugged her tightly. She was trembling uncontrollably. The tension of the last few days had finally been unleashed.

'Look. He's not an expert,' I whispered as calmly as I could manage, 'but neither am I. You'll have to make your own decision.' She pulled gently away from me, wisps of her dark hair sticking to her tears on my face.

'I'll pack things up with you anyway,' she said. 'I'll have to sleep on it. I'm really sorry.' Suddenly, I felt very alone.

We continued our tasks in silence and by two in the morning both sets of panniers were straining at their zips, and the sleeping bags and the tent were stowed away in plastic garbage bags to be tied on top. Muttley and Katoshka themselves now looked like wounded horses, their frames liberally strapped with brown package tape to prevent them being damaged in transit.

The clock was set for six, ready for the cycle to the train station and the journey onwards to the airport. I collapsed into bed and fell asleep almost immediately. I began to dream, but the images of friendly peasants and the Steppe full of wildflowers eluded me. Instead, I saw only missiles and gulags, bombs and the KGB. I was fighting a pig-tailed Cossack when the alarm clock jolted me awake. Rohan was already up and dressed in her cycling gear. She had come too far to back out now. It was time to go.

2 BATTLING GALINA

I have never entirely trusted a country which keeps soldiers on its international airstrips. Kalashnikov semi-automatic machine guns make you feel far less welcome than a smile from waiting ground staff and a shuttle bus, I find, especially when you know the soldiers haven't been paid in weeks and you've got an expensive camera in your hand luggage. No-one pestered us though, and we made our way nervously to the baggage collection shed, where our bikes and panniers duly appeared and we were processed along with returning Ukrainians who were loaded down with TV sets and videos from working stints in the West.

Ten minutes later we were in a decrepit taxi, ploughing down an even more decrepit road towards the centre of Kiev, with the promise from the driver that he knew a hotel which was licensed to take visitors—the whole point of the place, I would have imagined, but you never know.

Eventually, the tenement blocks rattled through the taxi's windscreen as the city engulfed us, and we swung towards a neon sign fizzing a disconcerting carotid red: CASINO. NIGHTCLUB. HOTEL MIR. A giant pink flamingo half way up the wall cast us all in a sickly stomach-lining hue. Evidently the driver had made a bad mistake and delivered us to a place more suited as a haunt for street walkers than for innocent young cyclists. But there we were, with me fumbling through my pockets for a stack of grimy bank notes we'd managed to change at the airport, and Rohan quickly taking charge as she realised I was staring at the money with no idea about what set of zeros on one particular note meant compared to the zeros on another.

As she paid the driver I climbed out, just as the sky rumbled ominously and spat out a fork of lightning. In a macabre portrayal of an electrified zombie, our driver then swivelled his bald patch around to reveal an unshaven chin.

'Skolka stoit, vilasipyet!' he growled.

'What?' I mumbled. Rohan handed him an extra note.

'Nyet, nyet,' he spat, taking the offering anyway. 'Dollar, dollar. One hundred, two hundred?'

'What?' I repeated.

'I think he wants to buy our bikes,' Rohan guessed. It wouldn't be the first time I'd wished we'd accepted such a sensible offer.

Uninspired by our refusal to sell, the driver wrenched Muttley and Katoshka out of the boot and dropped them roughly onto the pavement. They certainly didn't look well. Their handlebars were twisted like strangled cows, and Muttley's rear lamp had been smashed in transit. For an anxious moment it struck me that the frames were probably snapped in half too and only holding together because of the wrappings of sticky tape bound around them. But as I lifted them up one by one they seemed to be still intact and faith was restored in the Korean apprentices who had no doubt put them together.

Then, with one last leer and a screech of tyres we were left adrift. It was late. The moon was the colour of beaten copper. I rolled my shoulders, took a deep breath, and almost choked at the sight of a bright red, open-topped sports car which roared up beside us. It disgorged a tuxedo and a young peroxide-blonde in a mini-dress and heels. Miniature flamingos reflected in gold cufflinks as they linked arms. Then, without a glance in our direction, they drifted towards the casino with the practised ease of the idle rich. It struck me that not only had I never thought I would come across anyone in Ukraine who could afford a Lamborghini, but that I hadn't actually thought about what I would come across at all. Reality wasn't a strong point of mine. I had planned the whole trip without a glimmer of thought to what I might really expect. It was a worrying trait, but at least it meant the trip would be full of surprises.

'Shall I ask about a room or will you?' Rohan asked.

'What?'

'Never mind. I'll do it,' she sighed.

The reception hall was gloomy, and clattered with the knitting needles of three blond beehives sitting behind a wrap-around desk. Rohan strode towards them, with me shuffling up behind. A beehive acknowledged our presence with raised eyes and shoved over a set of forms. They had to be joking. It was bad enough that everything was in Russian let alone it being too dark to read anything at all. Rohan took a stand and gestured for the darkened lights to be turned up.

'Nyet.'

'Pazhalsta?' she pleaded. But the beehives were immovable.

There was little option but to tick boxes randomly. I probably singled myself out as a married female metal worker from a commune out the back of Ternopil, but if the beehives noticed they didn't seem to care. Though I guessed we weren't your average type of visitor, our visas went through the standard procedures of being checked and rechecked, signed in triplicate and rubber stamped. Rohan counted out a stack of one million kupon notes to cover the bill. Finally, we received a slip of paper with our room number neatly printed on it.

We crammed everything into the lift, the bikes up-ended on their back wheels like rearing show ponies. A floor lady met us on the sixth floor, dressed in nightgown and slippers. I wasn't sure if she was rubbing her eyes because someone downstairs had rung to say we were on our way and had woken her up, or she was simply astonished to see us pile out onto her floor. Either way, she held out a key then turned on her heels and quickly scuttled off down the corridor towards our room.

It was good to lock out the world and be by ourselves. Once we had emptied everything from our panniers onto the floor and trashed the place it felt like home. As Rohan sipped from a water bottle I washed my face in a dingy bathroom with caustic-smelling hot-pink soap, and brushed my teeth with a dribble from the tap. The familiar experience of toothpaste and saliva pouring over my bottom lip and splattering into the sink, filling in the cracks and chips, was made intensely dramatic by the rosy flashing flamingo light and the thought that the water I'd just swilled my mouth out with was probably swimming in radionucleoids from Chernobyl.

* * *

A dust devil played among a keloid strip of withered grass outside our hotel the next morning, before whipping across a concrete path to cling to our skin like cinders. Blocks of flats semaphored a morning's washing. An old woman lay sprawled beside an empty bottle beneath a concrete bench, her legs poking from a grimy skirt, half her face plastered in mud, her chest twitching almost imperceptibly. I felt a surge of hopelessness. I didn't even speak enough Russian to ask if she needed help.

Turning away, we put our minds to brighter things. We were here to explore. And to look for fuel for our primus and tickets to Sevastopol. It was all best done on foot, what with the police pouncing on roving bicyclists. We set off down an impressive boulevard shaded by spiny acacias, following a hastily-scribbled map badgered from a beehive. Passersby came mostly in pairs, exchanging stoic, long suffering looks at each other. But they completely ignored us and frankly their lack of interest began to unnerve me. Bizarre as it might seem, I had an overwhelming feeling that they saw us as aliens: dangerous creatures from another ideology. Whether they were just being polite, or didn't want to get themselves mixed up with us, they stubbornly refused to acknowledge it. I stared into their eyes, willing old communists to stop and point an accusing finger and shout out at the top of their voices: 'Halt! Reactionary! Spy! Send them to the gulags!' But instead they averted their eyes. I suppose, looking back on it, that with all my frantic glances and full-on stares they probably thought I was either a lunatic, or about to rob them. Either way, none of us felt comfortable.

Continuing on we spotted a market place, where triangular stumps of women with rectangular bosoms and legs thick and bulbous like the trunks of ancient, pollarded oak trees guarded makeshift stalls. In amongst it, the air smelt of fish and straw and of cabbage leaves wilting in the sun. We edged past a coal-eyed pike, its sharp little teeth glinting in the sun as it guarded a dried-up lump of cheese. A crone held out a solitary tulip. Further along, others offered bunches of spring flowers picked from the country or an ice-cream box wriggling with crayfish. There was a box of tiny stock cubes, a lone bread roll, a pair of socks, and no fuel for our primus. More women stood like forlorn soldiers outside the subway entrance, the wealthier and plumper among them armed with a box or two of American cigarettes, the majority with just a handful of singles. They reached alongside the queue outside the ticket booth, pestering people with downcast looks and weak smiles.

We were obviously in the middle of nowhere, so we figured that taking the subway would get us closer to the city centre. Queuing is not my idea of indulgence and, in general, I'd rather do without what was at the end of a line than put myself through the abject boredom of standing in one. But it was either that or no fuel, and I didn't fancy the idea of cycling through the Ukraine subsisting on dried spaghetti.

To my great relief we slowly inched forwards. Then, fifteen minutes later, just before we reached the head of the queue, the babushka inside pulled down her shutter. The man in front of us turned away and disappeared in the crowd. I couldn't believe it. We had queued for nothing. I didn't care if that was the local way of doing things, they should get their act together. How did this country ever expect to get on if it didn't even respect the end game that queuing represented? I banged on the hatch. Strangers began gathering around to watch the scene develop. One started eating lunch. Another looked as if she was about to unfold a picnic chair for the occasion. I banged again, more feebly this time. There was no answer. Rohan cautiously pointed out another ticket booth across the road. I smiled sheepishly to the assembled throng and ambled over to start all over again.

At last, with metal tokens in hand, the crowd sucked us through recessed blast doors and turnstiles, and we were shunted past a mosaic of Lenin onto one of the longest wooden escalators in the world. Once onboard, the acoustics were disorientating. Voices seemed to be whispering in my ear. I looked around, half expecting to find my conscience sitting on my shoulder. Then I realised the conversations were coming from people riding on another escalator a few feet away, separated from ours by a wide wooden central slide studded with two-foot-high regency-crowned lanterns, every other one unlit to save on power.

The longer I stood there, the more strongly I felt like I was being drawn down into the underworld. All around me the damned babbled, or kissed, while others read, or tapped their fingers on the moving rail. At long last, our steps were eaten up from below us and we passed a bent old woman in a tiny glass office, who was waiting patiently for a ring from an old brown phone and a message from above to press the red button and stop the world around her.

I was glad to get off, but so far below ground I felt claustrophobic. I began to sweat. It didn't help to know that the platforms were large, modified fall out shelters with collapsible edges which became steps to allow people to seek refuge on the tracks in the event of a nuclear war. I knew I had no chance of making any sense of the Cyrillic signs that ran across the walls, so I left it up to Rohan. Thankfully, she picked out the platform that corresponded with the drivel on our map almost immediately.

Once on the train I began to relax, and to examine my companions more closely. There were sandy-haired Slavs and dark-skinned Mongols, and northerners with alabaster skin and cyanic eyes. The dowdiness which I had expected was missing. Instead, they dazzled each other with tangerines and limes and iridescent stripes. Men of all ages wore Hawaiian shirts and baseball caps, and younger women flaunted their bodies in mini-skirts and see-through blouses which showed off their lacy bras. It passed my mind that at last I was seeing the fruits of new-found Capitalism, but I found out later the Kievans had always dressed like this—it was just that you had to catch them in season, like cherries. It made me, in my chaffed-knee jeans and crumpled travelling shirt, feel like I'd just popped into the city from the farm.

The train slowed and stopped. The doors opened and closed again. I now found myself standing opposite three conscripts splattered with acne and camouflage. They showed gold teeth as they yawned. Like the Jew who keeps a suitcase ready packed beneath his bed in case of trouble, these people kept their inheritance in their mouths. And it wasn't hard to understand why the Kievans were on their starting blocks. Tartars, Khazars, half-breed nomads, Lithuanians, Poles, petty Russian princes, Fascists, Comm-unists...they had all ravaged and plundered this ancient city, long called the 'Mother of Russia'. During the Revolution Kiev had changed hands five times. Soon after, millions of its inhabitants had been shovelled into the gulags, while tens of thousands more were carried away by horse and cart in the morning round-up of corpses caused by Stalin's famines. At the end of the Second World War, three-quarters of Kiev's population were dead, or living as slaves in Germany. The city had been flattened. Black Marias motored around, their passengers picking over the ruins like crows, pecking out the eyes of anyone who had come into contact with the West—especially ideologically-tainted prisoners-of-war returning home in search of what was left of their families. Then, just when things seemed to be getting a little easier, the hex returned—in the form of Chernobyl.

✷ ✷ ✷

'This is pathetic,' I spluttered. 'Why can't anyone just help us. It's bureaucracy gone mad.' We were stuck in our sixth queue to buy tickets to Sevastopol. So far each had ended in a shrug of shoulders from the clerk. Rohan was forced to plead at last for at least an idea of where we should go next.

'You're wasting my time,' came the gruff reply. 'Can't you see there's a queue behind you?' I hated that word.

Suddenly I felt someone tapping my shoulder. I turned to find a woman in her early fifties, wearing a printed fruit-patterned blouse tailored above a sensible green skirt and matching shoes. A small patent leather handbag hung from her wrist.

'Can I help you?' she asked in sing-song English, her nose twitching as she spoke.

'We want to buy tickets to Sevastopol,' I said. 'For us and two bicycles.' She looked perplexed.

'Bicycles?'

'Yes.'

'Then you definitely need my help. Please, I will get you the tickets for Russian price. It is much cheaper than foreigner price.'

We already knew from our hotel experience, where we had paid ten times as much as the locals for our room, that foreigners were ripped off when it came to settling a bill.

'My services cost five American dollars,' she said, narrowing eyes the colour of walnuts. Rohan handed over the money.

A short time later the woman, who identified herself as Galina, returned with our tickets.

'There is no problem with your bicycles, they will go in your compartment with you,' she said. 'But I will come with you tomorrow to make sure. I charge five American dollars.' Rohan and I looked at each other. Anything to make things easier, we both thought.

'Good. Now, perhaps you would like to stay with me. I charge only ...'

'Five American dollars?' our voices harmonious with hers.

'Yes,' she said with a look of astonishment in her eyes. 'Have you stayed with me before?'

'Just a lucky guess.'

She opened the clasp on her handbag and scrabbled around for a pen and a scrap of paper to draw a route to her house. When she had finished we realised it was on the far side of the city.

'I don't know,' I said shaking my head. 'What about the police?'

'What *about* the police?'

'It's just that I heard they might pull us over if we cycled.'

'Pah! This is Ukraine. Where did you hear such a thing? Of course you can cycle. The police stop expensive cars for money. They do not stop bicycles.' My cheeks flushed. Galina broke out into a laugh that sounded like high-pitched cow bells. We agreed to check out of our hotel the following morning.

✶ ✶ ✶

We set off early, and soon found that Kiev's roads were purposely designed to make cycling difficult. Cratered and split by trenches, they forced us thudding into holes and jolted us back out again, ensuring frequent stops to check for buckled wheels. It was smoother going along the concrete banks of the Dneiper River, where women in sun hats and flowered dresses promenaded with dapper men, ignoring the bronze statues of workers still caught in the struggle for the Revolution.

Almost everyone we saw was munching on the ultimate barometer of changing times in Ukraine: the banana. For decades, if you had a banana you had connections. Since the fall of communism they were shipped in from Equador. But one still peeled them with a flourish, sucked on them slowly like an ice-cream and tossed the skin at the feet of the statues in a decadent display of abandon. And when one wasn't chomping fashionably on bananas, the done thing was to sunbathe on the beaches on the river's far side, standing up the Russian way to get an even tan, or to wade up to your waist in water and sludge drained from the lands further north.

The river edged away, and before long we were skimming down boulevards doubly-rowed by chestnut trees aflame with candelabras of flowers. There were few cars, but plenty of red flags, fluttering Coca-Cola in the warm breeze. Every few hundred metres a pair of traffic police with white striped batons methodically pulled over the BMWs and Mercedes. They refused to even catch our eye.

Then we were mugged by the suburbs—kilometre after kilometre of cobbled apartment blocks, set back from the road by concrete paths split with slivers of grass. In Galina's street the black clouds that had been gathering all day decided to burst, sending us racing for the tattered awning of a bakery clogged with customers already steaming like puddings.

While Rohan consulted Galina's map once more I noticed a number painted on the side of a block of flats just across a grassy strip. Rohan checked the address again. To our surprise the numbers coincided. We decided to make a dash for it and dived into the rain, splashing through the already forming puddles before ducking into an alleyway smelling of cats. In front of us was a black padded door, its leather covering ripped to expose rotting wooden planks. I pounded on it with dripping knuckles. A few seconds later Galina answered, dressed exactly the same as the last time we'd met her. As a Ukrainian she was very used to wearing her Sunday best on a daily basis.

Inside, the living room's uneven floor boards creaked threateningly, while the walls peeled cream paint. A cheap table balanced in its centre alongside a broken-down television spewing its wiring. It had spontaneously combusted, I was informed—a common problem with Soviet-built TVs.

I rested Muttley against a wall and introduced myself to Nadia from Moscow, who sat up to her mini-skirted hips on a saggy bed.

'Are you staying here too?' I enquired politely.

Nadia scowled through her lipstick. She only spoke Russian. As all I could say in her language was 'Hello, I'm Marc. I don't speak Russian', I intuitively concluded I wouldn't be up to speed on the suitable small talk and left Rohan to scour through her phrasebook while I went off in search of Galina who had taken it upon herself to slink away.

I found our hostess fussing around a steaming kettle in the kitchen. Four mis-matched tea cups sat on a linoleum-covered bench beside her. Two battered pans hung from nails hammered into a wall. A tap dripped incontinently. Galina handed me a tin containing a scraping of thick, yellowing condensed milk and a sticky glass jar with a few teaspoons of damp brown sugar in the bottom. She placed the tea things on a tray with a scratched picture of the Winter Palace on its surface, and I traipsed through the living room after her. I took a seat. Nadia slumped opposite me, plucking her teeth tunelessly with a pink-varnished nail. In that oppressively dismal room her short, dyed-red hair was the brightest thing around. I noticed her sunglasses, which she insisted on wearing despite the gloom, still curiously had the little plastic '100% UV' sticker attached to the middle of a round lens.

'Sorry it's not Indian,' Galina chuckled as she poured the tea. 'It's Russian. Not real.'

'It's a nice place you've got here,' I lied. 'Very homely.'

'It is very simple place. It is my mother's apartment. Now she is old and she stays with me.'

Galina informed us she lived with her husband and mother in a suburb even further away from the centre. Nadia was camping down with her until she found a place for herself in Kiev. She was looking for work. Her husband had left her for another woman, some tramp from Novgorod. I produced some peppermints and passed them around as consolation. Nadia popped one into her mouth and began crunching noisily as we blundered through our cycling plans. Nadia looked blankly into thin air, then scoffed another peppermint.

'You must like exercise,' Galina noted. 'I myself swim every weekend in the Dneiper.'

'Aren't you a bit worried?' I ventured. 'I've heard reports that there are radioactive particles in the silt, still coming down from Chernobyl.'

She paused for a moment. 'If you worry about things like that everyday...' she sliced with her hand at her throat. 'I have a house only here and I don't have a possibility to go anywhere else. You heard about Chernobyl in Australia?'

'Of course,' I said.

'Well, after all that,' Galina scoffed, 'less than six weeks later, the government was telling us that Chernobyl's reactors would be operating again before the end of the year.'

'That's madness,' I said. But I guessed it stood to reason— just. The station had supplied 45 per cent of the country's nuclear-generated electricity, and the authorities wanted it back. The trouble is, since then more than 90 per cent of its experienced workers have died or left the plant, and safety improvements have largely been abandoned. Wackier still, the international community proposes building two more nuclear reactors in its place, in return for Chernobyl being closed down altogether. The Ukrainian president wanted five more, though, to add to the fourteen already producing electricity in his country. This irrepressible drive towards nuclear energy— despite Ukraine having huge coal reserves, an abundance of under-utilised coal power stations, and the technology available to build cleaner, more efficient conventional power stations—was perhaps the ultimate measure of powerless-ness felt by people like Galina.

'Now our parliament says give us more money. So now they have big money, and it very good for him. But for us no money.' Galina banged her fist over-dramatically on the tabletop, causing Nadia to spill her tea down her front. 'I finished the Moscow Physical Engineering exams in 1970. I'm an engineer in nuclear electronics!'

Tickled at the surprise on my face, she raised her shoulders and stretched out her arms in emphasis. 'Yes. I worked in the Institute for Nuclear Research near Moscow! I worked there for a year until they told me to go because I was a woman and it was too dangerous. So I came to Kiev to work in a research institute for microelectronics. Then we have independence and everybody said things will be better and then my company have no more money to pay the telephones or electricity. They closed. Everything closed. So I have no job!'

Despite her education and evident intelligence, Galina had been reduced to spending seven days a week in the train station to occasionally bag a migrant worker from somewhere out on the Steppe. A foreign tourist was a rare and lucrative catch. From us she had received more than she would have earned in two weeks on an average Ukrainian salary. To me it seemed as if she had adapted well enough to the new political circumstances. But then, she could either survive or go under—and the Slavs had a habit of making do and getting on with it.

Galina finished her tea. Rohan, too scared of radiation to drink hers, was still pretending to sip.

'My government. Just money, money, money. Democracy in Kiev, in Ukraine, is impossible,' Galina went on. 'When the land has no laws there is no democracy. Nothing has changed.'

'But haven't there been good things?' I asked.

'For me, no.'

'Well, isn't there more food in the shops?'

'Less food! Food only if I have money! I go to market where there are women from the village and they have almost nothing, or to the shops where everything has big price. If I have no job I have no money and I...' she made the sign of a hangman's noose, before breaking out into a grin. '...or vodka.' She saw my eyes perk up.

'No, really. Everywhere they are dying. Old men. Old women, dying in the street. The government says die. No, it makes them die. That is the policy of our government. To make us die. An old man needs sugar, needs tea and the rent is very large for a small place. With all his money he can buy less than fifty loaves of bread in a month and nothing more.' That reminded me, I was hungry. I thought of the biscuits stashed away in our panniers.

'What do you think should be done?' Rohan butted in.

'First we need laws,' she said after a studied pause. 'If we have good laws and policies, we will have good lives and industry will rise. I go to my small land and dig potatoes like everyone in Kiev. But when we think only about our small potatoes we have no time to go to the Soviet and demand laws.

It's impossible to demonstrate when you are too hungry, or have to worry about where your next food comes from.' She stood up to leave. Time for dinner then, I thought, and rubbed my hands together unconsciously.

'But we have hope,' she said, smiling again as she did up her coat buttons. 'After all, we cannot fall any further.'

'That must be the famous Russian optimism,' I said.

'We are very good at it, aren't we?'

After they had left I put half my trip's supply of Darjeeling tea bags in Galina's caddie. I knew it was only a gesture. Tea bags wouldn't solve her problems. But freeze-dried flavoured rice would go a long way to solving mine. I cooked it up on the stove while munching on a packet of custard creams. After all, you can't rest the world's problems on your shoulders. You have to muddle through the best you can.

After dinner, I took a shower from the large iron kettle and stomp-cleaned my T-shirt in a discoloured enamel tub in a bathroom smelling of cabbage and urine. Later, in bed, Rohan clung to me tightly, sure the dust from the bush fires had come with the rain.

We performed the first of our regular bicycle checks the following morning, squeezing the tyres and checking that screws and bolts were tight. After strapping on panniers and plastic bags, we finally pushed Muttley and Katoshka out onto a road behind the flats. Tram lines led us directly towards a major highway filmed with soupy puddles stretching across the unmarked lanes. We splashed through them at speed, lifting our legs up to save our trousers from a soaking, as all around us concrete blocks grew like mushrooms, the product of the post-war drive to build pre-fabricated dwellings for the tens of thousands made homeless by the war. The tram lines increased as we cycled into the centre. The train station appeared. People milled around in haphazard groups. Smokers puffed away beside huge piles of luggage.

We waited for Galina outside the station's lock-up, eyed suspiciously by gun-carrying police. A procession of drunks, stumbling and unshaven, were bullied past into the holding cells by their comrades. One drunk swayed as he approached us, almost barging into the bicycles. A policeman savagely punched him in the stomach, then smiled at me. I struggled to grin back. He winked. Ukrainian justice was seen to be done.

Galina finally scurried up, her handbag swinging wildly, panic on her face.

'The train is going. Hurry, hurry,' she puffed. 'I find your carriage and tell the attendant you have bicycles.' She flapped us up a flight of steps and down again like a chicken with her brood and egged us on towards a stout female official, wearing fluffy slippers and dressed like a caterpillar in a pale green running suit, who was waiting on the platform. Our tickets were checked while we lifted off our packs, unscrewed the front wheels and separated them from their forks. Quickly, we lugged frames and wheels and packs and bags, helmets and mirrors down the corridor and into our compartment, stowing them all in a rack above our heads. Fluffy slippers warned Galina the train was about to leave. It gave a jolt. Galina yelped and stumbled out just in time. I waved her a kiss through the window, and we slipped out of her life forever.

We slept fitfully that night and awoke at dawn just as the six nuclear reactors of Zaporozhe power station were passing by our window. The largest in Europe, it was a great showpiece of Soviet nuclear technology, put together in record time. It also has the worst safety record of all the Ukrainian plants, clocking up to thirty-five malfunctions a year since the first reactor went on line in 1984. From the start there was extensive pilfering of materials and shoddy workmanship. The plant lacks skilled personnel and frequently runs out of fuel. An extreme lack of nuclear waste storage space has even led to the station's manager threatening to close it down. Meanwhile, there is not even enough money for essential maintenance work. Yet, despite more than 90 per cent of local citizens voting against it in a referendum, a sixth reactor was switched on just a few months before our arrival. It was a building that couldn't help but inspire anxiety, and I was relieved when the train picked up speed and began putting distance between us.

The morning wore on. I lay on my bunk staring out at the relentless Steppe, picking out shacks and farm houses, the odd startled cow in a field of mustard, last year's birds' nests smudging the tree branches, and women bent double as they picked through the potato fields. Rohan's relief grew the further we got from Kiev and its goitre, Chernobyl.

It's a funny thing when you know someone well. You often only notice they've changed when they've returned to normal. Rohan had her smile back. She told me that at last she could breathe properly. In Kiev she'd felt the radiation all around her. She'd even taken to consciously breathing as little as possible, hoping that way she'd inhale less that would harm her. Although I knew what she was talking about, I hadn't really shared her fear about our health being damaged. But now that she'd confessed her worries they began to affect me too. As the sun climbed above the carriage and grape vines began cracking their knuckles beside the tracks, I found myself tormented with thoughts of the road ahead of us, with its side-swiping cars, the axemen in the forests, and that bloody fallout everywhere.

Officially I wasn't even sure if we could enter Sevastopol. We had heard it was still closed to foreigners and that we were likely to be chucked off the train by military police, who would most likely board soon after the Crimean capital, Simferopol. Our only chance if they got on was to pretend to be asleep when they came through the carriage and hope they would take us for locals and not bother us. But there was little chance of that—with our bikes we looked absurdly conspicuous. If we were found out the only option was to cycle northwards from wherever we ended up. I just hoped that the police didn't think our impertinence was worth a night or two in the local lock-up. But in the end the increasing heat got the better of my worries. I dozed off, though my internal voice murmured on, until, at last, a military um-pa-pa marched into the carriage from the tannoys of Sevastopol station.

3 UNTO THE BREACH

Sevastopol was up to its oilskins in paranoia. At its centre a cubist, granite-chested Hercules warded off tank shells with a giant outstretched hand. Beneath him, two pairs of teenage cadets in blue and white naval uniforms goose-stepped towards each other, the boys with rifles and the girls in miniskirts. Two old women approached, their thick winter coats shielding them from the unseasonable cold snap, their chests a squall of hammers and sickles, red stars and ribbons and shiny profiles of sailors above flukes of Sevastopol anchors. They stopped. On the cenotaph in front of them, carved in limestone, were the names of the Red Army and Navy divisions which had defended their city during the Nazi siege. The cadets each brought a robotic arm to their chests, their fingers curled to a fist. Left leg forward, right hand to the chest, right, left...the two couples sniggered as they passed each other.

The sea lay as calm as slate. Pigeons jigged in the salty breeze. Sailors in bell-bottoms and thin-striped T-shirts strolled purposefully back and forth. Apart from soldiers of invading armies, few Westerners still alive had seen this place. For decades it was a closed city, highly sensitive, the main port for the Black Sea Fleet. It had been 'open' for only four months, but it still seemed to be cut off from the rest of the world. This was a warrior city-state—a modern Sparta—its people purely engaged in the cultist worship of a thousand monuments, sown like dragon's teeth and dedicated to the courage and resistance of the people, each looking ready to crack apart and spew out armed men to spring to the city's defence. In front of us, silhouetted against the bruised sky, was one of them—an eagle on a column immortalising the ships of the Black Sea Fleet which were scuttled to block the entrance to the harbour at the beginning of the Crimean War. And, in the mist on a cliff to my left, was another—a giant memorial to the fall of Sevastopol to the Nazis. This was a Hero City, honoured so by Stalin for its gallantry under siege. There had been brave revolutions and glorious victories here and everywhere the idols wouldn't let you forget: 'Remember the Revolution,' they boomed. 'Remember the Occupation.'

But though they bellowed and squabbled for attention, they were obviously only minor gods, for, standing on a hill above us all, in a terraced garden of trees and daisies, and pointing a massive bronze finger seawards, was a modern-day Zeus, a Jupiter, a Sanskrit Dyaus, an Odin—the immortal Vladimir Ilyich Ulyanov Lenin. Four heroes were guarding him: a sailor, of course, with bandoliers wrapped around his body and holding a bomb; a peasant carrying giant sheaves of drooping wheat; a soldier with a rifle slung over his shoulder; and a blacksmith, sitting on his anvil, his strong right arm resting on an up-turned hammer. Supplicating themselves at their leader's feet they turned their heads to follow his gaze across the Black Sea, which the Turks had named for its storminess and Jason and the Argonauts had sailed across in search of the Golden Fleece.

We cycled behind a packed trolleybus, its grimy windows unevenly lined with squashed noses, until the first of the masts of the Black Sea Fleet emerged from behind a hillock. We had been climbing a steep hill, the first of the trip, and I was gasping for breath, each revolution of the wheel bringing with it a chesty wheeze. A better look at the Black Sea and the ships below was a good excuse to rest. And my backside hurt like buggery.

We chained our bikes to the legs of a concrete bench and descended a steep track towards the harbour. At the bottom we found ourselves on a bitumen path dwarfed by a scribble of hulls, rigging, masts and cranes. In front of us the decks of warships were strewn with potatoes, onions, drying fish and lumps of meat. A woman on the dockside was haggling over a bucket of offal with a sailor standing, hands on hips, on board a hulking, rust-streaked mine-sweeper. On the next ship along another sailor in a blood-spattered vest hacked at a dead cow with an axe, the back half of the carcass still slumped over the chopping block, the rest piled in chunks around his feet. More customers appeared, mingling with the stray dogs looking for scraps. A quarter of the former Soviet Union's navy, and for decades the counterbalance to the US Sixth Fleet based in the Mediterranean, had been reduced to little more than a floating market.

Since Ukrainian independence the bickering over the rightful ownership of the port and its fleet has inflamed local politics. Most sailors (70 per cent of them are ethnic Russians) sided with the Russia claim. The Ukrainians, on the other hand, hijacked ships, threatened Russian officers at gun point and refused to pay wages or supply rations to 'renegade' crews. The conflict soon spread to land, and the Crimea, more staunchly Russian than anywhere else in the Ukraine, claimed independence. Fearing trouble, Russia rapidly removed the fleet's tactical nuclear weapons. Ukraine in turn offered the Crimea greater autonomy. Finally, after years of threats and counter threats, both countries eventually agreed to split the fleet. Sevastopol was to be rented to Russia for twenty years. In exchange, US$100 million would be wiped off Ukraine's gas and fuel bill.

I felt uneasy around the wharves, conscious that if we were caught down here, with cameras in our back-packs, we could be in trouble: others, I had heard, had been detained for much less. I tried to act as casually, as Russian, as possible. I scuffed my feet, looked bored, despite feeling exhilarated, and peered into the water whenever a sailor walked by. I noticed a sheen of oil dancing on its surface. Jagged tin can tops, corroding iron and sodden cardboard littered its shallow fringes. Walking on I passed more ships, mottled in rust and shedding paint like dandruff. Half these hulks could barely float, let alone be combat-ready.

Across the harbour I spotted a submarine tied to a creaking berth. It lurched, half sunk, slowly being licked away by a briny tongue. Nearby, a team of sailors were spraying water from hoses over four more subs, lashed together like a team of slugs, and each flying red and white stars and their hammers and sickles. Around us the air was sooty, engines murmured on idle and hammering bounced between hulls. A sailor gestured to us with a dog-eared fan of playing cards. He wanted us to play. The fleet was busily going nowhere.

✷ ✷ ✷

The banana seller's deep brown eyes sparkled from below overhanging lids. She wore a brown, home-knitted jumper, a sack-cloth skirt and thick skin-coloured stockings. Chestnut curls snaked from a striped head scarf, dusted with golden braid. She looked to be in her sixties, but the smoothness of her skin made it hard to tell. Two rows of golden teeth caught the sun as she handed me half-a-dozen bruised fruit, with which we planned to supplement our dried food for the next two days. Noticing my unfamiliar accent she asked me where I was from. In turn, she introduced herself as Urie. Urie the Tartar—a descendent of the Golden Hoarde which, under the leadership of the grandson of Genghis Khan, had galloped westwards from the plains of central Asia. These Mongols, as we know them in the West, nourished themselves on the blood and milk of their wild-eyed ponies and came armed with iron darts, two-edged swords and long bows. They met little organised resistance as they tramped across the marshes and rivers frozen by winter, slaughtering their way to Kiev. They spared no one. The traveller, Plano Carpini, visited Kiev soon afterwards and later recalled: 'Everywhere we saw the scattered sculls and bones of the fallen and killed. The once large and populous city had shrunk to a mere nothing. Hardly 200 houses remained.'

The Tartars surged onwards, crushing Hungary and Poland and eventually reaching the Adriatic, where they looked across the sea to Italy. Over the years most trickled eastwards again—they missed the dry, hot air of the eastern plains, they moaned. But Urie's ancestors in the Crimea had decided to stay. There was still plenty of booty around. They regularly besieged Moscow and plundered throughout western Ukraine, Russia and Poland. According to Giles Fletcher, the ambassador to Russia for Queen Elizabeth I of England in 1588, they specialised in capturing 'young boys, and girls, whom they sell to the Turks or other of their neighbours [and] to this purpose take with them great baskets made like baker's panniers to carry them tenderly—and if any of them happen to tire or be sick on the way, they dash him against the ground or some tree and so leave him dead'.

Some captives were ransomed, while others (some 200 000 in the first half of the 17th century alone) were auctioned off to end their days chained to the oars of a Turkish galley, or as sex slaves in Ottoman harems. So notorious were the Tartars that their savagery was enshrined in the Russian lullaby:

'Tartar here, Tartar there,
In the darkness everywhere.
Sleep my baby, sleep my bairn,
Tartar comes for other men.'

In short, they were evil bastards.

Talking of evil bastards: 'Stalin!' Urie cleared the name from her throat like phlegm, pulled at the air and whistled through her teeth.

'She says she was taken away,' a voice behind me said in surprisingly good English—a short, stocky, blond Russian in his early twenties. He introduced himself as Yuriy.

'Can you translate for me?' I asked.

'Sure. Stalin accused them of conspiring with the Nazis during the occupation.'

The Tartar eyed him suspiciously. Her people had welcomed the German troops following a twenty-year Soviet policy of mosque-burning and purges. Tartars had hurried to don German uniforms, thousands even slipping on the black arm bands of the SS. In revenge, Stalin filled cattle trucks with nearly half-a-million of them, and deported the lot to the

Soviet far-east. Among them was seven-year-old Urie and six members of her family. Around half those transported died before they reached their destination—including Urie's grandfather and grandmothers. Back in the Crimea, Tartar villages were destroyed, cemeteries bulldozed and tens of thousands of ethnic Russians moved in. Urie ended up in Tashkent, the earthquake prone capital of Uzbekistan.

'We had two days to leave,' she said, her looped earrings bouncing off her bronze cheeks. 'Others had one hour, with the NKVD standing outside their houses with guns to shoot them if they tried to escape. The train was very crowded. There were lots of ill people. People were dying. Twenty-two days. Only salt sprats and herrings to eat and no water. Only what we took from our house. At every stop we had to throw out the dead.' She spat in the dust. 'Stalin was a sadist. He destroyed our people. Tell the world, tell everyone what he did to us.' Rings flashed from her fingers. The air was sliced with the banana knife.

'Please put that down,' said Yuriy nervously.

'You think this Tartar is going to stab you?' she whispered hoarsely, leaning closer. It crossed my mind that she just might.

Since the collapse of the Soviet Union more than a quarter of a million Tartars had made their way back to the Crimea, many to live in mud huts and temporary buildings made of boards. They face the highest level of unemployment in Ukraine and crippling discrimination, particularly from the Russians who had replaced them. But none of them would return to the east.

'I miss Tashkent. I love it,' Urie confided. 'Very beautiful buildings. Good climate. Good job on a collective farm. But this is my motherland. I had to come back. My mother came back with me to be buried here. Some who returned died very quickly because they were old. My son-in-law was killed in the Crimea by a thief trying to get into his car.' She swallowed me up in her eyes. 'But now we have formed our own militia. We are preparing to fight!'

★ ★ ★

UNTO THE BREACH | 39

There was no way out of the Crimean War. We agreed to meet Yuriy at the white-washed, circular building which stood at the centre of the gun emplacements. We would cycle—it was just up the road. He would take a trolleybus.

'Ukraine is very different to Russia,' he announced as we stood in line a short time later. 'I think I speak for most Russians living in Ukraine that life was much better when we were all together in the Soviet Union. We had quite enough to live and we could afford to eat different meals. Now we have to forget about luxuries. All people are angry and cross. I notice it every day, people just quarrel, there's no real reason.'

But Yuriy wore expensive clothes, and his perfectly mani-cured finger-nails and muscular frame to me betrayed a vanity hard pressed to keep up in poverty. He noticed I was looking him over. His family had survived the changes well, he admitted. Both his parents had jobs: his father repaired buses and his mother sold clothes on a market stall. They had made enough money to send him to a private academy to learn English and to help him fly to the United States within the month. He was going to work as a sports instructor for Camp America.

'The USA is like an obsession for me,' he continued, as our tickets were checked. We climbed upwards, with Yuriy talking effusively about a seven-year dream inspired by Arnold Schwarzenegger. 'I decided to devote my life to body building and I made my muscles,' he rambled on, glancing down to admire his body. He had also studied English intensely and written hundreds of letters to American companies asking for work. Finally, he had received a job offer and was about to follow in Arnie's footsteps. 'I think life in the USA is much better than here,' he noted simply.

'Better than Ukraine or the Soviet Union?'

'Perhaps both. But better than Ukraine certainly.'

He then went on to reveal an astonishing naivete about the country he adored. His face dropped when I told him of the racial problems in the United States—he had no idea that black people even lived there. He dismissed the murder statistics as propaganda and insisted that unemployment, health care problems and inequality did not exist. 'You must be crazy to say such things,' he interjected darkly. 'We must stop this conversation.'

I shut myself up, struck by his ignorance of life outside his own country. Funnily enough, he reminded me of the average American.

We reached the top of the stairs. The panoramic defence of Sevastopol, all 900 square metres of it, wrapped itself around the walls in front of us. It was a diorama of the Battle of Malachov, during which the Russians successfully repelled an attack from a superior French and British force in June 1855, and where the only allied troops to reach the outskirts of Sevastopol alive were a small band of Irish, who found some Russian women, got drunk and eventually staggered back to their lines dressed in bonnets and aprons. This was a serious Russian victory. There were painted cannons and clouds of smoke, cavalry charges, full-scale heroes, death and dirt. Over by the sandbags lay an officer in crisp, bloodied regimentals, attended by half-a-dozen soldiers. On a hilltop in the distance I fancied I could make out some specks. Perhaps they were the sightseers who had followed the allied troopships off to war: British army wives, gentlemen travellers, reporters, salesmen and souvenir hunters, who had picnics on the heights overlooking the battlefields and played cricket; while the French had bathing parties, went fishing and held race meetings, every now and then issuing a cheery 'oo-la-la' whenever a shell landed on their own soldiers or the citizens and defenders of Sevastopol.

One of my favourite stories from the Crimean War comes from a self-described 'observer', the gentleman traveller, Jeffrey Bushby. As he strolled around the British camp he noticed the generals, field officers and their staff performing their ablutions in their imported enamel baths and basins (I would have done the same in their situation, no doubt) while a military band played 'Rule Britannia'. Bushby probably came across Colonel Darby Griffiths, who went to war with a

French chef and provisions supplied by Fortnum and Mason; Lord Rokeby, who brought along a patent water closet; and perhaps Hubert De Burgh, who arrived in a yacht loaded with cases of champagne. (I really like these people.)

Yuriy interrupted my musings, announcing he had visited this shrine to the defence of Sevastopol regularly during his school years. It was a monument to Russian glory, he said. It was nothing to do with Ukraine. It was the symbol of resistance and of bravery and had inspired Russian Black Sea sailors during the Second World War to throw themselves into the flames to save the burning canvas after a bombing raid and rush the remains to the destroyer Tashkent, the last ship to escape the besieged city and already loaded up with 2000 refugees. It was nationalistic fervour like that, I thought, that had caused all the trouble in the first place. But I didn't say anything. By rights, I felt, the whole city should be packed up brick by brick and carted away in a straight jacket.

✷ ✷ ✷

Later that afternoon we joined the belching trucks on the main road north. The longest slopes of the Crimean Mountains were to the east of us, but still the going was gruelling. The top of the first hillock saw us stretched out in the dust, with Rohan groaning in agony and the base of my spine feeling like metal shards had been hammered into it. But before long we were freewheeling downhill at a fast pace, whooping with exhilaration; the vibrations of the handlebars drumming my finger tips; the wind cracking my lips; the tyres skirring and the breeze thick with Crimean oak and pine. I felt intoxicated and couldn't contain my happiness. The journey really had begun now. We were on our way. I whooped and whooped again to let it out. I didn't want to think: the road was all that mattered now, as it whizzed beneath us, stretching out in front for as far as we could go, with poplars and pink cherry trees and picket-fenced houses with shiny tin roofs blurring in the corners of my eyes. Another hill. I slipped into the hard shoulder in time to receive a face full of grit from a groaning truck, its driver leaning out of the window, gawking like a Spaniel. A woman pulling a goat on a line clicked her tongue as we struggled past. An old man appeared, and then another, both sitting in front of their rickety dwellings. The first had limp-topped radishes for sale, the second a jar of milk on an up-turned wooden crate. I avoided their gazes, unsure of how I should meet them, ashamed of the wealth my shiny new bicycle suggested.

After another hour I had to stop, letting Muttley slip like a hippo on its side below heavily folded cliffs of dark clay shale. I was staggeringly tired and felt physically unable to overcome the difficulties that appeared before us. I had a crick in my neck and my legs felt like jelly. Rohan's prone form swam wearily in the grass as I tried to focus. I wrenched my drink bottle from its frame for the first of a thousand times and sucked greedily between gasps at warm water tinged with iodine and plastic. I crumbled in pain onto the grass and lay staring weakly at the sky. A fly buzzed and landed on my cheek. I felt each one of its tiny feet, too tired to brush it away. Then it crapped on me. I tried to budge, but my body revolted and refused to obey. Already I felt like giving up, but we rode on anyway, like monkeys grinding a couple of organs.

4 THE STEPPING STONES

The knack of looking sorrowful is indispensable to the traveller. Rohan was a genius at it. Her bottom lip would pout mournfully, her head would hang to emphasise her tearful eyes and her face would flush to such a miserable hue that remorse would jump between bystanders like a yawn. The two Sunday-shift babushkas at the Hotel Sportivnaya in the town of Simferopol stood no chance. 'But your visa is inadequate,' one insisted, holding weakly onto her resolve. 'You have no Crimea stamp. It is impossible.'

Standing your ground is another travelling necessity. Besides, we knew she was wrong. Technically, tourists could now travel all over Ukraine without the old requirement of having each area visited pre-stamped on their entry visa. But news travelled slowly and dealing with foreigners still meant a lot more work. 'Please...' Rohan mooned, testing their tolerance to the limit.

The babushkas conferred. A telephone call was made. Then another. Finally, they relented. We could stay, but they would have to keep our passports to pass on to the local police chief. As I'd previously put two passports through a washing machine and left another behind in a hotel room in Canada, followed by a night in jail on the American side of the border after trying to sneak in through the woods, I didn't feel too worried about entrusting my latest one to a policeman for the night. As for now, forms had to be translated and filled out, once more in triplicate. Finally, an hour later, we had the keys. What's more we paid the local price.

The room was on the third floor, with a balcony looking out over a graveyard. There was no water, which was no great loss as our priority was beer. We quickly unloaded our bikes, wheeled them back downstairs to the foyer, and once outside got back in the saddle. Out on the road again Muttley fretted and champed at the bit, feeling unfeasibly light beneath me now that it was unburdened by panniers. And it was just as well that I had more control of the thing than when it was loaded up like a mule, as the first car I encountered dusted itself off on my knee, forcing us up onto the pavement.

'Bastard!' I called out, giving the driver the two-fingered salute and regretting it immediately when I realised the driver could easily be a distant descendant of Genghis Khan.

We rode on, winding carefully around pedestrians, swarthy types with the broad and flat visages and the olive skin of the Tartars. Some were stocky with cruel looks, others were natural horsemen: short-legged and nimble. All of them seemed a little nervous, as if they too half-expected their fellow tribesmen, wedged inside their metal ponies, to mount the kerb and chase them down the street with a flashing sabre pointing out the side window.

In the centre of town we came across a bar with plastic tables and chairs shaded by a chestnut tree. Men in suits and gold chains drank whiskies on the rocks, while fake blondes dived for peanuts. We chained our bicycles to a surrounding fence and walked over to a shed serving drinks and snacks. A heavy set man stood in front of us, his suit sleeves rolled up to reveal bulging, tattooed forearms. He reached for a couple of wrinkled dried fish and carried them over to his painted escort. I turned to see her wrench off a head and suck out the brains.

Rohan ordered two beers. They were expensive—Western prices. We took them over to a table near the street, sat down and regretted it almost at once. Passers-by eyed us enviously. Each drink cost the same as half a day's work. I felt uneasy with the company around us too. Dressed in crumpled clothes, with greasy hair and me unshaven, we felt like toads trying to croak with the frogs. So, we rapidly drained our glasses and slunk away.

We took to cruising the streets instead, circling a huge statue of Lenin, lonely in his barren square, as we searched for a restaurant. In the end we ended up on our hotel balcony with the moon glimmering over the headstones and soup simmering on the primus.

✲ ✲ ✲

Early next morning we bought a loaf of bread from the back of a baker's truck and set off northwards again. The traffic was already heavy and unpredictable, making up its own rules as it went along. Cycling on pavements and road-side tracks as often as we could, we flew by breeze-block houses dripping with cement, and chickens and geese pecking around in the grassy verges. After two-and-a-half hours the road forked. Our map sat on the fence, unwilling to commit itself.

In the distance I saw an army-green petrol tanker pulled over in a lay-by. As we approached, the petrol man flicked his half-smoked cigarette into the grass, grunted up the engine, and directed a greasy nozzle into a hole in the side of a car. A few minutes later the pump was reholstered and smeared notes were counted out as change. The petrol man wiped his hands down his oily thighs and turned again to search for his smouldering cigarette. I moved closer with the map. Tobacco smoke escaped his lips as he clasped it in his tarred fingers. The left prong was ours, he said at last. He stretched out his arm and waved his wrist: keep on going for a very long way. Bastard.

✲ ✲ ✲

I am lying under a dappling acacia now, an oasis in an enormous crop of winter wheat. Campions, thorow-wax, saxifrage and St John's wort tingle among the grasses. The road is blistering to itself. I roll onto my back and lie for a while, my body feeling both peculiarly light and heavy after a long morning in the saddle. A nightingale warbles. I raise myself to my elbows. A sunburnt arm has flumped over Rohan's face. A fly which was preening itself on her elbow reels drunkenly as my movement shimmers across its eyes. I stand up woozily and stagger towards my bicycle. I rummage through my panniers for plates, cutlery and packets as the sun bastes my scalp. Here in these bags is everything I need. Too many possessions, I have found, tend to maroon me. Then I become anxious, knowing deep down that one day's travelling is worth more in memories than a hundred days of drudgery at home. So I abandon everything from time to time, and when I come back after a while away I find I have strangely forgotten those things I had once thought it impossible to live without.

A bumble bee is humming around my red-gloved hand, attracted by the brightness. Dried slivers of pasta schlurp into the iodised water. I put a match to some sticks. Fatigued by the effort in this heat, I meander back to where Rohan lies, noticing her shoes have split and her red T-shirt for the road is already fading to pink. I sit down beside her. Buttercups are reflected on her cheek. I breathe deeply. This place resonates with me, like a wineglass and an opera singer's voice. We share the same harmonic frequency, we reverberate in sympathy with each other. Whereas others prefer eating outdoors, or walking into a piazza for the first time, I favour lonely, secluded places, where I can bury myself and just glimpse the sky. The times I have experienced this, and they have been few, I have left feeling more aligned with myself than when I had entered. It's important not to forget you're alive.

✳ ✳ ✳

We mounted up again, riding for the next four hours in the same gear, at the same speed and on the same hard shoulder sheltered from the steady run of traffic by a slippery white stripe, the sun beating down mercilessly, stretching out my shadow as if it were on the rack. It was early evening by the time we entered the village of Vojkove, both exhausted and with our water bottles drained. We pedalled wearily towards a small roadside café. A painted sign outside said it sold beer. A doorway led into a small concrete yard quartered with wooden tables and covered by camouflage netting. At the far end a shabby booth with a flat, corrugated iron roof and tiny windows tempted passing travellers with coloured bottles and chocolate bars.

We slapped the chains around the bikes and I swaggered painfully up to a pair of hands flexing themselves in the gloom of the waist-high opening. I ordered two beers. The hands disappeared and emerged again with two warm bottles frothing from their caps. I carried them over to Rohan, who was simmering in her own perspiration in a plastic bucket-chair. As we drained the bottles a figure staggered into the yard.

Kola was a drunk—a blur of himself. Somewhere in his fifties, he possessed that beet-red face and swollen nose which are the hallmarks of heavy boozing. His beer belly bulged above a pair of hanging-crotched, ragged brown trousers. His arms hung limply at his side, but waggled like broken wings as he spun towards us. He blinked purposely like a lizard from beneath a shock of dishevelled white hair. With an effort, he managed to find his lips with two trembling fingers. He wanted a cigarette.

'I'm sorry, I don't smoke,' I said in English.

He muttered in Russian.

'Yeah, they're all idiots,' I said. He nodded his head, apparently in agreement. It was a cruel and mercenary world.

'Still, best to have another drink and forget it, hey?'

He stopped, his face contorting in bewilderment as he searched his fuddled brain for the reason he was bothering to converse with someone who made no sense at all. Suddenly a smile crawled up his face. 'You're Po-lish,' he slurred, again in Russian.

'Nyet.'

I had answered in his language but was obviously foreign. But if I wasn't Polish then what was I? His face reddened further and I thought he was going to cry, but Rohan saved the day by breaking in and telling him where we were from. He shook his head in disbelief, prodded bluntly at his chest and said the only thing that made sense any more: 'Vodka?'

'Nyet Vodka,' I replied.

He thought again, then waggled a stubby finger at us, placed his hands to the side of his head as if in prayer. Then he snorted like a pig.

'I think he's offering us a place to stay,' Rohan whispered.

'I think he might be. Would you take it if he was?'

'Would you?'

Travelling is as much about the chances you take as the places you visit. If we followed him then something remarkable could happen, if we didn't then we would end up just spending the evening in a tent in the bushes. I was sure there would be plenty of opportunities to do that ahead of us. Anyway, it wouldn't harm us to just take a look at what he was offering. I motioned to Kola that we would follow him.

It was then that one of those strange turns of events, that pop out of nowhere, occurred. A Lada stopped in front of us, followed by another. All the doors opened and the driver from the first car flung open the bonnet as the other occupants from both vehicles gathered around. I saw a cloud of steam spew from among them, then heard reels of laughter. I pushed Muttley over and took a look for myself. The driver was holding up a dead, white-feathered chicken. Whether it had been put there on purpose to be slowly par-boiled, or had been sucked up from the road, I would never know. Kola had already weaved his way to the other side of the road and was beckoning for me to come. The ruckus over the chicken obviously held little interest to a man who with two half-Polish cyclists in tow had now seen it all.

We followed him into a rutted mud lane and past a row of several whitewashed shacks with blue-and-white striped gables, each separated from the next by a paling fence. Kola halted outside one of them and pulled open a creaking, slatted gate. I went first, bowing my head so as not to bang it on the low lintel, and entered into a yard of hissing geese, bundles of goslings, a cat and a yelping terrier tied by a chain to a home-made kennel.

The house itself was divided in two by a crumbling concrete path which careered around the back to a corrugated-iron water closet and pens imprisoning a sow and a milking-goat. On either side of the courtyard were two fenced-off garden patches and in one, more goslings, larger and scruffier than the first, flicked gobs of oaty goo at each other as they pecked at the contents of a metal bowl. We rested our bikes against the side of one of the buildings and I bent over to take a closer look. Sadly, I realised I had never been so close to geese before. The city sucks for geese.

Ushered across the path, I stepped over a pair of worn slippers and the wooden frame of the building itself, and found myself in a dingy outhouse floored with linoleum and covered in places with hessian rags. Piles of unfolded clothes and twists of dried-up meat were scattered all around. An antique side table next to a window stood out like a courtier in a medieval market place. Suddenly, an old woman with a face like ship's biscuit and a forehead glistening with sweat appeared from a side room. She thrust out her aproned chest and clamped her hands to her hips. I spun around expecting to find Kola to introduce us, but he was gone.

'Um, do you live here?' I said, feeling foolish. She stared, hard. I repeated Kola's sleeping charade. She looked doubtful.

Suddenly I remembered Galina and I fumbled in my pocket. I found a five-dollar bill and held it out. The confusion was cleared up immediately. She took the money, folded it carefully, stuffed it into her cleavage and grinned. She introduced herself as Ola, then reached out and clapped her hands on my shoulders, before moving past me to squeeze Rohan's sunburnt arms. Seeing the yellow imprints she had left behind, Ola poked at her own.

'I worked in the fields today,' she said in a flash of silver. 'I was planting and I'm red from the sun too.' Ola laboured on a communal farm with some forty others from the village. At the moment there was lots of weeding to be done and soon the wheat had to be harvested.

As we continued staring at each other and smiling gormlessly, I became aware of the sweet stench of vodka behind me. Kola had returned after freshening up with his bottle.

'He used to drive the buses,' Ola said, pointing dismissively at her husband. 'From Simferopol to Sevastopol and sometimes to Odessa. But he preferred vodka.' I must say, I couldn't blame him. Obviously reading my mind, Kola's head made an involuntary backwards jerk. 'Vodka?' he asked, his question half aimed at me and half, pleadingly, at his wife.

'No. No more vodka,' his wife chided and wagged a finger in his face.

Vodka had been a scourge since before Ivan the Terrible. For centuries, women in labour drank it to relieve the pain and children were said to stop crying if you dabbed it on their lips. Today, festivals and transactions are not complete without a bottle or two. But formalities apart, drinking for the heck of it has always been popular. Adam Olearius, a traveller in Russia and Ukraine in the 1630s, noted: 'The vice of drunkenness is prevalent among this people in all classes, both secular and ecclesiastical, high and low, men and women, young and old. To see them lying here and there in the streets, wallowing in filth, is so common that no notice is taken of it...none of them anywhere, any time, or under any circumstances lets pass an opportunity to have a draught or a drinking bout.'

The Communists banned the spirit soon after the Revolution, but the people were drowning in it again following the Second World War: Russians were braver when they were drunk. By the 1980s, being out of your skull at work was normal: vodka had taken the place of ideology. When Gorbachev shoved his oar in by reducing the opening times of liquor stores, banning alcohol from official functions and ordering the ploughing-under of hundreds of thousands of acres of vineyards, the price of alcohol went up and 11 000 people were poisoned by home-made spirits as a result. Gorbachev's popularity never recovered. Some say it may even have led to his downfall. He had tried to change the very essence of the Russian and his kin. While we in the West see our bodies as the transport system for the soul—and as such most of us try to look after it and keep it ticking along for as long as possible, sheltering it as much we can from the ravages of excess, the Russian sees the spirit as the ultimate reason for being alive—and vodka is as important to the spirit as family, or friends, or the changing of the seasons.

Outside in the yard again, Ola handed Rohan a small plastic bowl of corn and motioned to her to feed the geese while she prepared some food. Around us, feathers and goose droppings, straw and torn sackcloth littered the concrete yard. Bell jars were skewered out to dry on the fence palings along with a large rusting iron pan. Goslings pecked around a cherry tree, among the dead heads of daffodils and a sprouting rose bush. It reminded me of the picture book farmyard of my childhood, an image I had treasured so much in my early years. I liked it already, and I wanted to stay.

But by now Kola was resting his weight against my shoulder. I scanned sideways and noticed his eyes were closed. I needed to think long and hard about this. Obviously the correct response was a well-timed shuffle to the side, while slowly manoeuvring his head upright with my palm. Being pissed out of your head can sometimes leave you unfathomably stable, but this guy was so gone that in the circumstances I didn't entirely trust him to keep standing. Still, what else was there to do? I decided to risk it and gingerly eased his chin off my shoulder with my right hand and began inching sideways. Caught off balance he began swaying like a bottle. Then in slow motion he fell backwards, as stiff as a board, and crashed straight through the garden fence. I clenched my eyes shut, expecting to open them again and find him with his head split open. But like a toddler he had bounced, and was left sitting up bemused on the flattened palings. He pointed meaningfully to the side of me with a crooked finger and blurted out what could only be a pitiful: 'Shit.'

I hauled him up, his breath sour in my face. I took my arms away and he swayed again. In the end I was forced to flatten my hand between his shoulder blades and hold him there. If I attempted to remove it he simply waned backwards, following my hand as if it were magnetic. Hearing the commotion, Ola had by now emerged from the kitchen to investigate. She helped me manhandle him to the outhouse, and forced him down onto a short, three-legged stool. To make sure he stayed there she tied his shoelaces to the legs. Notwithstanding, he thrust out a heavy paw to smooth her hair. 'Sweetheart, sweetheart,' he drooled. His wife giggled. Remarkably, to her it was just a joke.

'Look how men are today,' she said. 'Good for nothing.' I felt embarrassed for her, but said nothing. Rohan was looking at her feet.

Ola closed the outhouse door on her husband and directed us into the kitchen. A dim electric bulb emphasised the shadows. As my eyes adjusted I noticed a pot of goose pieces bubbling on the small wood-fired stove in the corner of the room. On a huge solid dining table, covered in blue-flowered linoleum, were several bowls and plates, loaded up with thick strips of herring, boiled potatoes mixed with browned onions and chunks of pickled gherkin and home-made bread. It was food we might just as easily have come across in Berlin.

Ola showed us how to wash by scooping up water from a bucket with a plastic ladle and pouring it over our hands into a metal bowl swimming in thick, grey scum. Then she served three cups of tea from a samovar and stirred in a thick layer of fat from a jam-jar full of milk, as Kola called out plaintively from his cubby-hole.

At first, meaningful communication between us was difficult. Rohan especially was quickly picking up Russian, but Ola talked in such a monotone voice, without gestures or emphasis, that we found it virtually impossible to know whether she was asking a question or making a statement. On our part we tried our best to converse in a language of hands and nodding heads and screwed-up faces. Ultimately, though, it really didn't matter what was said. For me, the most remarkable thing was that we were having contact at all with a being who was living a life so different to our own.

What we did find out was that Ola was as steadfastly committed to work as Kola was to drink. She saw to it that the two of them didn't starve and was proud of her achievement. The little money she brought in from labouring on the farm was spent on basics like sugar and tea, fish for special occasions, and clothes when the old ones were too ragged to fix up any longer. She exchanged food, usually in the form of goose eggs, for vodka, which turned Kola into the child they had never had.

Later we showed her our bikes. She patted Muttley on the saddle, like some prized cow. Rather us than her, she said. The troubles of the world were caused by people wanting to move around all the time. But I couldn't help thinking that here we were in a single day having more adventures than they would in a whole year. We were moving on and they were staying put. But I hoped our arrival was an adventure for them too.

✳ ✳ ✳

The sun set sickle-red that night. We left Kola asleep on the outhouse floor and followed Ola into a tiny second bedroom. There was just enough room for our panniers on the floor beside a single bed with a gleaming brass headboard. Ola went off to unbutton her husband's eyes and scuffle him away to bed. She would spend the night amid the geese on the kitchen floor.

I crawled into bed and immediately smelt the scent of someone there before me. Rohan turned off the light and jumped in. A while later I heard footsteps outside our room. Someone stumbled against the door. The bedroom light was switched on again. Kola rolled pugnaciously above us.

'Go to bed. Leave us alone,' Rohan moaned to herself under the covers. But I saw the crazy look in his eyes. Thoughts that take on a life of their own when the moon is out pounced upon me, tightening around my windpipe. What if he were an axeman after all? I tried to calm myself. No, he was just a drunk, a harmless old drunk. Kola brought a hand up to one shoulder and held out the other. It looked to me as if he were aiming a rifle. I started to panic. Adrenalin rushed through my body. 'Gun?' I asked in English, as bravely as I could muster. Kola nodded gravely. Heavily-built and ugly above me, his bulbous nose and wet lips peeked through his shadowy face.

'Bang bang, Avstralia.' He stared at me menacingly and pointed towards the curtained off window.

'Outside?' I gulped.

'Da.'

My mind raced. There were obviously more of them, outside. All those things I had been warned about were true. How stupid could I have been? It was obvious. This had all been a set up. Now we would be murdered and our bodies buried in the vegetable patch. What would Rohan's father say? What was worse, Susanne and the Berliners would have been right all along.

Kola prowled towards the window. The curtains flinched as he reached behind them. He grabbed for something, and turned again to face us. His hand shot out and I recoiled, banging the back of my head on the wall. I saw a gun, pointing at me, but then as suddenly as it came it vanished. I blinked. Then blinked again. It wasn't a gun after all. It was...a portrait. A haloed and gilded Russian Orthodox Christ! Kola moistened his lips with his tongue and brought the image to his face, kissing it wetly. 'I love him,' he said, starting to sob. The tension flooded from me, leaving my body drenched in a cold sweat. Kola staggered towards our bed and handed me the portrait. I took it in a damp palm. He approached the window again, retrieved a mug and a large jar, similar to the ones drying on the garden fence. It was a quarter full of what I was sure was vodka. He poured some out and offered it for me to try.

'Um, nyet, nyet. Thank you. I have to cycle tomorrow,' I said and held onto imaginary bicycle handles and twirled my feet on make-believe pedals under the covers. He looked even more confused than normal. 'Pazhalsta,' he implored.

The last thing I wanted now was to offend him. I still hadn't entirely shrugged off the fact that I was in bed and this drunk might have a shotgun out in the shed. Funnier things happen. A sip wouldn't hurt, I thought, as I raised the rim of the mug to my mouth. I sucked in a teaspoon's worth and exaggerated a gulp. It tasted like fetid water. Suddenly it came to me. It was water: *holy* water. But then what was all that about the guns and the shooting?

'Tasmania,' Rohan uttered suddenly. 'He's heard about that massacre in Tasmania, where that guy went crazy and shot all those people.'

And there it was. Kola, who was attached to the Ukrainian grasslands like a barnacle to a rock, was miming the shooting dead of thirty-five people by a maniac in far away Australia. He had seen the aftermath on television, a peasant's only concession to the modern world. I was astounded. If a world like that arrived so vividly on the Steppe, no wonder Ola didn't feel like she needed to travel anywhere. As for Kola, he remained wagging his head feverishly until Ola rescued us by pulling him out and wishing us a good night's sleep, followed by a trail of tutting.

✳ ✳ ✳

Breakfast was fist-shaped pancakes and sugary tea. Kola refused to eat. Ola tutted, shook her head, pushed her hand into her cleavage and pulled out a key on a string. In a cabinet behind her chair was a flagon of vodka. She filled a chipped teacup to the brim. By the time we cycled off, with our water bottles filled with tea and two pickled gherkins the size of small cucumbers wrapped in a sheet of Pravda, Kola was on his fourth.

✳ ✳ ✳

That very morning in Moscow, 7000 service men filed past Boris Yeltsin to mark the anniversary of the end of the Great Patriotic War against fascism. The President stood on top of Lenin's Mausoleum with Russia's flag fluttering behind him. Elsewhere in the city the communists were having their own parade. Most people ignored them all, preferring, like us, to get as far away from the cities as possible and to take advantage of the unseasonably hot weather. Meanwhile, in the village of Voislavichi the men were suffering the wrath of their wives, who had for too long put up with their drunken brawling and their foul-mouthed ways. Since January they had refused to feed their husbands when they were drunk and had resorted to shaving off all their hair as they lay unconscious after a long day on the vodka. They had even convinced employers to send their men to clean the village pigpens whenever they turned up drunk for work.

We, on the other hand, were soberly emerging onto the road which connects the Crimean peninsula to the rest of Ukraine, and by the amount of oil and the number of bolts we encountered, it was obviously as hard on the steady drizzle of box-like cars as it was on us. The junk soon took its toll and Katoshka came down with a slow puncture. In the end we decided to blow the tyres up every 20 kilometres or so, rather than stripping off panniers and bags and trying to fix it by the side of the road.

By now we had slipped into a steady rhythm. We'd cycle for around 10 kilometres and have a 10 minute break, then another 10, then a longer break and a bar of chocolate to boost our energy levels. After a third 10-kilometre break we would push on until the daily odometer read 40 and then we'd stop for lunch. The afternoon passed similarly. Eventually I hoped to increase the day's riding average to 90 kilometres or more, but in those early days, all loaded up with heavy packs, 80 was more than enough to turn us into wrecks.

As we pressed on, the full glory of the Soviet agricultural system revealed itself. Stout-shouldered women toiled in the fields in generous sixties-style bikinis, or lugged water from wells in large metal milk urns. The men were generally drunk, or conspiring how to go about it. Every now and again we would pass a giant concrete cow head, or chiselled-out sheaves of wheat, carved peasants, and always the hammer and sickle pre-empting the next collective farm. Sometimes fields were so large that trees were mere brush strokes on the horizon, and occasionally a pre-war tractor would clutter towards us, followed by farm hands on bicycles with tiny wheels and long seat shafts and handlebar necks, which showed they had grown up together. Towards lunchtime the first lake appeared, lined with spines of reeds and rippled with screaling gulls. The land bridge to the Steppe could not be far off.

We rested under a tree. I boiled some tea and pasta as swifts twittered and dived for flies around us and children squealed past on their bicycles, the younger among them hanging off side-saddle while their friends pedalled furiously. After lunch we skirted the last city in the Crimea, across a flyover and down a street signposted to Kiev. The road arrowed onwards, over a bridge teeming with half-naked people lined up to dive from the metal struts into the cooling river below. Further still the land took on a parched maroon hue, bleached at times with dried-up lake beds. Eventually, we found a canal and followed it northwards.

By now it was getting late. Somehow I still had the dregs of energy left, but Rohan was taking it badly. She had slumped down over her handlebars, her face drawn. The thin white line on our map which would take us over the estuary had still not appeared. I began to think we must be lost—or the map was telling lies.

We heard the village well before we saw it. Raucous singing, high-pitched giggles and roars of laughter emanated from a huddle of red-brick houses. We stopped outside the first. Rohan volunteered grudgingly to ask directions, while I held onto the bikes. She reappeared a little while later with a pneumatic young woman with large eyes rimmed with thick green mascara, wearing a tight black skirt and blouse. They were followed by her tanned and bare-chested husband. Neither wore shoes and both were obviously drunk. The woman took hold of the map, turned it around several times to get her bearings then laughed at the idiocy of trusting such a thing. We introduced ourselves. Sergei demanded to know where we were going as Natalia prodded our bicycles.

'Over the bridge,' I said. The bridge? Oh, that was too far, Sergei responded with a rueful smile, his top front teeth glinting gold as they caught the sun. I told him we hoped to make it to Murmansk. His jaw dropped. Like so many peasants we were to meet, simplicity and honesty shone in his eyes. The gauze which we in the West learn to cover our gaze with, fearful that someone may see us for who we are, was absent. My defences fell too as I looked at him. Suddenly, he burst out laughing. Our ocular handshakes had made us firm friends.

'Please, please. You must eat. Stay with us for a couple of days. It's a holiday. Come and have some vodka,' he said.

'But we have a long way to travel. I want to make it over the bridge before night-time.'

'My home is your home,' he implored and put his arm around my shoulder. 'Food, vodka, sleep. Don't be crazy. Murmansk. Murmansk! You're crazy. Come drink.'

I could feel myself weakening and Sergei sensed it. To Rohan's alarm he took hold of my handlebars and wheeled Muttley down his driveway and into the open garage. He rested it against a German sedan covered in dust. It hadn't worked in three years. There were no spare parts.

'Are you sure we should do this?' Rohan appealed. 'They stink of vodka.'

But we had little choice—Katoshka was following its twin down the driveway with Natalia at its horns. We were shepherded over a hearth lined with shoes and into a large living room, bare except for a four-seater couch, a television, a stereo system and a grey, balding underlay carpet. Sergei advanced on the stereo and filled the room with pulsating rap, while Natalia led us to the couch. She plumped herself between us and said loudly in English: 'I Tartar.' She puffed out her chest. Her bust threatened to break through the buttons on her blouse.

'And him?' I asked, pointing at Sergei who stood above us beaming.

'Him Ukrainsky. And him...' she pointed at an ancient man in tatty green who had just then wobbled through the doorway. 'Him father. My father.' The old man smiled a stubble of blackened teeth. Across his chest were lines of medals and red ribbons. There's nothing quite as dejected and careworn as an old soldier, especially when he's vodka-sodden and dressed up in his old regalia. He reminded me of an ancient, musty actress with smeared lipstick and caked-on make-up to fill in the wrinkles. I found I had to look hard at him to see what he had once been, and only then could I respect him, instead of passing him off as a rather ridiculous relic.

'DEUTSCH,' Natalia shouted at him.

'ICH SPRECHE DEUTSCH,' he yelled back and made towards us, spluttering and spraying spittle with an imaginary machine gun. Natalia flew into hysterics.

'Forget him,' said Sergei, gaining my attention with a flap of his hand. 'He's crazy.'

Natalia heaved herself off the couch and pushed the old man through the doorway and into the garden. She returned, tapping her temple conspiratorially. 'He was a partisan. He killed Germans in their tanks. But now his mind has gone.' She motioned for us to follow her and led us into a small kitchen and sat us down. Plates of cold fried eggs, chunks of home-made bread, slices of salami, gherkins and a dish of melting butter were produced. Natalia picked up a slab of pig fat still attached to the skin and began tearing at it with her teeth. 'Eat. Eat,' she demanded.

I picked, not feeling hungry despite the long ride. Rohan, entirely exhausted, looked as if she were about to be sick. Sergei was concerned. If we refused to eat properly, he would have no choice but to teach us to drink. He reached into a cupboard and produced a large jar swashing with murky liquid. He levered off the cap. Orange juice glasses were found and filled with warm vodka. I had learnt that vodka should be served ice cold and drunk in small, barely perceivable mouthfuls, each sip accompanied by a mouthful of food. Sergei taught me the Ukrainian method: knocking back the whole giant glass full in a gulp followed by a lunge at a chunk of bread. Natalia followed his lead while I took a sip. Sergei frowned. Natalia shook her head and slewed over to sit on Rohan's lap.

'Drink. Drink,' Sergei entreated.

'Cheers,' Natalia slurred and lurched over to my lap with a lushy grin. I took a mouthful, swallowed and involuntarily screwed up my face. I was unused to drinking spirits straight and, ever the vigilant traveller, the last thing I wanted was to lose control of the situation. Natalia waggled a finger in my face. 'No, no, noooo.'

I drank more. My throat smouldered. Rohan, left out of the contest, winced as she sipped. Natalia hugged me tightly, the ripeness of her bosom pillowing my chest and pinning my free arm to the chair. 'I love you. I love you. I love yoooo,' she woozed in English, as Sergei, with a static grin, refilled my glass.

As the vodka hit home the scene around me turned into a Brueghel painting. Drunken neighbours showed up to fight over which one of them we should stay with. Rohan was led off by a woman's fleshy arm, down the street and into a house where she was sat on a chair and leered over by a creepy, mustachioed husband. Meanwhile, meaty hands were swallowing mine and podgy faces greasy from pig fat and sun plunged into my vision and were withdrawn again amid waves of belly laughs. More vodka followed. With my throat anaesthetised, it slipped down easily.

'I love you, I love you, I love yoooooo.' Natalia had grabbed me by the arm and began tugging me towards the living room. I knew it was useless to struggle, and anyway she wouldn't be able to understand my protestations if she even noticed them. The music was turned up full blast. Natalia grabbed my hands, rubbing my knuckles brazenly with her fingers and squashing herself up to my chest. The walls pounded and the old man's medals shimmied around his chest as he sneaked back in. Rohan followed in behind him and was forced into an embarrassed waltz with Sergei. Natalia slapped a fat hand against my cheek, looked up into my eyes, stood up on tip-toes and tried to kiss me. I managed somehow to slip out of her embrace and glimpsed Sergei gesturing with hand tunnels in front of his eyes: no more drink for her.

The room swirled. Natalia had me by the arms again, swinging me round and round. I found myself facing an open door leading through to the bedrooms. Pinned behind it on his back was the old man, his khaki legs stretched out like a corpse. Natalia doubled up with laughter at the sight, and held onto her stomach as if to stop it rolling away. Swivelling on her heels she pounced at Rohan, grabbing her between the legs before slowly falling to her knees. With one last bibulous 'I love yoooo', she was slapped in the face by the carpet. I helped Sergei carry her to their bedroom, where we laid her out on a zebra-striped quilt cover.

'She wanted to sleep with you,' Sergei said. 'Or with your girlfriend. It didn't matter.'

The cassette clicked off. It was late, Sergei said quietly. There was a party tomorrow, could we stay? I thought not, I said as he guided us to our room. Pity, there'd be plenty to drink.

A television set garbled in the corner of our bedroom. One wall was entirely fortified with shelves stacked with delicate china cups and saucers, a few leather-bound books and photographs of the family in ornamental frames. A double bed took up much of the remaining space. Sergei turned off the television and showed us how to lock the door from the inside. It was better, he said. It would stop his wife from barging in during the night. I took his advice and bolted it behind him, ripped off my clothes and fell into bed, still filthy from the day's long ride. I drifted off in a haze of alcohol.

Sometime later Rohan shook me gently back to my senses. 'I have something to tell you,' she said quietly. 'I haven't told you before because I wasn't sure.'

'Ummmm,' I mumbled.

There was a pause. 'I think I might be pregnant.'

My eyes jolted open. I was sober in a second. 'What?'

'I didn't want to worry you. But I've already missed one period and the second hasn't come either.'

I was silent. I didn't know what to say that would come out not sounding stupid.

'I'm worried with all this radiation and stuff. What if... ' She didn't have to finish the sentence, the look in her eyes said it all.

'Look, I don't think you should start thinking like that,' I said, shaking inside. 'Anything could have caused it.' I stammered that I had read somewhere that female marathon runners quite often missed their periods. Then there was stress. There had certainly been a lot of that around before we left Germany.

'We'll go back if you feel we should,' I said.

'No. You're right. It could be anything.' But I knew the truth as firmly as she did.

✶ ✶ ✶

Natalia was wrapped in a scruffy robe and the fumes of stale perfume the next morning. She moaned a headachy greeting and disappeared to be sick in the kitchen sink. The old man on the other hand seemed entirely unaffected. He was a veteran in more ways than one. He greeted me warmly as I wandered into the backyard, and showed me to a tap above a ceramic basin full of dirty dishes. I splashed my face and brushed my teeth. He watched intently. Finally, I asked about the medals he was wearing on his crumpled suit.

'Bogdan Khmelnitsky,' he said proudly, pointing at a gold ten-pointed star hanging from a pale blue-and-white ribbon. A portrait of the Ukrainian hero glinted from its centre. He jabbed at the red star of the Order of the Patriotic War and then a silver Partisan Medal on a bright green ribbon. I reached over and turned it in my hand. Stalin and Lenin eyed me suspiciously.

To his family, this man was a sorry tale long worn out from the telling—a hero of the Soviet Union, but nevertheless an embarrassment. He had fought alongside the communists against both the Germans and others fighting for an independent Ukraine. Now people like him were regarded by some as virtually traitorous. Fighting Nazis was one thing, but fighting patriotic Ukrainians, well, that was unforgivable.

Like most, he had welcomed the Germans as liberators from Stalin's terror. He helped house and feed them, showered them with flowers, serenaded them with balalaika music and offered salt and bread, the traditional gifts to invading armies. Within days, Jews, gypsies, insane people, Asiatic inferiors and Communist Party functionaries and officials were rounded up and slaughtered. Ukrainian civilians started dragging Jewish neighbours to the execution spots, sometimes bringing their children and picnic baskets along for the show. At Solibor and Treblinka most of the guards were Ukrainian, and at a ravine called Babi Yar, Ukrainian machine gunners, under the direction of the Germans, mowed down more than 100 000 Kievan Jews. In all, some three-quarters-of-a-million Ukrainians signed up to serve in the rear-echelons of the German army (the Nazis considered them too brute-like to fight like men in the front lines), and thousands of Cossacks, who were identified not as Slavs but as descendants of the Goths—an Aryan race— began riding with SS cavalry divisions. But to Hitler, Ukraine was a mere geographical term stocked with sub-humans. The Ukrainians were to be shipped out or eradicated; their land would make good living space for the German people.

The brutal Erich Kock set up shop in the western Ukrainian town of Rovno. Known for such one-liners as: 'If I find a Ukrainian who is worthy of sitting at the same table as me, I must have him shot,' Kock instructed his subordinates 'to suck from the Ukraine all the goods we can get hold of without consideration of the feelings or the property of the Ukrainians. I am expecting from you the utmost severity towards the native population'.

With Nazi Party officials in place, the crackdown started. In the Crimea alone more nearly 80 000 people were executed. Food was diverted away from the Ukrainian cities to feed the invaders, curfews were enforced with summary executions and nearly three million able-bodied young men and women were pressed into service for the Third Reich and sent as slaves to Germany.

The old man had fought back, hiding in the forests with his fellow partisans and emerging to strike at checkpoints and stragglers. When the Red Army eventually made their own push into the Ukraine, he re-stated his allegiance to the Soviet Union. The country rose in civil war, but the power of numbers won in the end.

By the time the Nazis had been driven from the country, over seven million Ukrainians had perished. It was left to the forebears of the KGB to hunt down the remaining rebels, who had fled westwards to join Ukrainians displaced by the war. Everyone—refugees, prisoners of war, partisans—were rounded up. Those who survived immediate execution went to the gulags.

✳ ✳ ✳

The whole village waved us off. Natalia hugged us and kissed me on the chin. Sergei, still bare-chested, wished we would meet again. I knew we never would. It's a sad fact of travelling that we meet and share our lives so intensely, yet as soon as our journey moves on all that is left are memories.

The village grew smaller by degrees until all that was left was a smudge which wavered for a moment in my mirror before finally dissolving into the Steppe. After a couple of kilometres we stopped and dismounted. Rohan laid out a sarong amid the ragged waist-high shrubs and we ate a breakfast of bread and cheese. I took a healthy draft from my water bottle.

'This is what I came here for,' I remember saying as I tied the bottle back onto my panniers. 'The sun, the freedom of a day ahead of us and not having a clue what will happen or where we will end up.'

'Pity about the cycling bit,' Rohan said, rubbing suncream into her arms.

The Steppe arched with the horizon. The shade trees of the previous day had gone. Ahead of us the road was just a thin chalky slash. Our tyres shushed as we pedalled and stones shrapnelled between our spokes with a ping. Apart from that, there was silence: no cars, no voices, no machinery of any sort, not even a breeze or the call of a bird. The world meditated. After a while I pulled over to the side of the track and dismounted. We stretched our backs with the smell of crushed lavender wafting up from beneath our feet.

By eleven that morning we had reached the Sivash Lagoon and the wooden-slatted bridge levelled on a dam of boulders that would take us out of the Crimea. A large red star tacked to a concrete obelisk nearby commemorated the dead of the Great Patriotic War. Tiny knobulous succulents had turned the land a spectral blue, while the sea on one side of the bridge glared a bright pink.

'Don't touch it,' Rohan warned as I lay Muttley down on a patch of grizzled grey grass and began walking towards a small pebbly beach. The sea lapped weakly like an old cat. I bent down and looked into the water. I moved closer and squinted. Suddenly I realised what was causing it: brine shrimp. Hundreds of millions of them, each smaller than an eyelash. I could just make out a pair of pin-prick eyes on a sliver of flesh. All were dead after frantic mating, their specks of eggs massed in clouds on the surface. The bridge wall had cut them off from the Sea of Azov and Mother Russia across the waters.

5 TAILS OF MINCED ZEBRA

In a land where summer is short, most time is spent preparing for winter. Beside the road, scythes whistled through heavily scented air as peasants, slick with sweat, cut swathes of broad-bladed grass as high as their knees, or hewed thick slices of wood into triangular blocks to be stored in lean-tos attached to their homes. One peasant we passed, a teenage boy in a broad-brimmed, floppy straw hat, sat bareback on a compact mare as his small herd of cattle, whipping flies with their tails, rummaged through a field of ripening wheat. Later, car loads of farm hands pulled off the road in front of us and drove abreast through another field of crops to picnic in its middle. I was reminded of Levin in Anna Karenina who had struggled for years against the 'elemental force' that was constantly evident in his farm hands' ineptness. But, in reality, why should they care when they had been freed by politics from any attachment to it? Traditionally, the Collective would always get the same amount however much they produced—the excess would be carted away as part of the quota anyway. You only need work as hard as it took to produce the minimum. As a result a general malaise had settled onto the land, and it was certain that anyone who worked harder than was necessary was a traitor to the rest in the group and put unwelcome pressure on the others to do more than they needed to get by on.

As for us, just before lunchtime we parked outside a shop to stock up on mineral water and bread and cheese. It was like all the others we would visit in Ukraine: a squat, simple white-brick structure, cool and ill-lit inside; its windows guarded by a blue, arched gate of iron; its floors a dusty grey and its walls washed in storm-cloud patterns. Well-spaced bell jars of pickled cabbage, gherkins, tomatoes and carrots, and others of apple juice, preserved cherries and red currants, stood on wooden shelves like science class exhibits. Beneath a glass counter crouched pats of butter the size of rabbits, and behind it were bottles of mineral water and vodka, hardening loaves of dark bread, flat tins of sprats, Mars bars, a comb, a pair of scissors, a knife and a fork and some bobby pins. Stored in tea chests on the floor were loose, damp biscuits and flour and rice and sugar. Sometimes, though not that day, you could find chunks of gristly meat. Hardly anything had changed in a hundred years. When English traveller F.J.Wishaw had passed through this particular part of the Ukraine in the 1890s he found the shop's counters 'covered with a disorderly array of small bottles of vodka, piles of black bread, many of the loaves half cut, a keg of herrings…some dishes of black-looking biscuits…and a tub full of Finnish butter'.

Of course the West offered more choices, more luxuries, and more colourful packaging but there was something comfortably wholesome about the simplicity of what we came across here—it was garden produce, farmyard cheer; free, we expected, of the artificial additives that made me wince every time I scoured the ingredients list on a cellophane packet of Western convenience food. If it wasn't for the constant threat of Chernobyl fallout we would certainly have eaten as heartily as peasants, if not kings.

The shopkeeper, an ample woman in an immaculate white apron, interrupted our browsing and asked us where we were from and where we were headed. She shook her head in disbelief at our answers, the loose skin beneath her chin flapping like a turkey's wattle. 'Take these,' she said, handing over a bag of biscuits she scooped from a plastic bucket, refusing payment. We were a phenomenon.

★ ★ ★

The country is as flat as rolled dough. We are out of the parched plains and riding through greener lands singing with larks and smelling of the dry bite of wild oat pollen and fairy flax. The call of a cuckoo reminds me of English country churches and cricket matches far away. I turn my nose up at the sweet stench of another corpse on the breeze; yet another, a thrush perhaps, or a yellowhammer, a hedgehog, a mink or cat, rotting pungently in the sun. In stark contrast to the cars that had killed them, we are rolling through the countryside in harmony with it. Even beetles and caterpillars on the road ahead of us are in no danger as we effortlessly swing around them with a turn of our handlebars. And if we wish, we can count each and every dandelion flower and moo a greeting (as we occasionally do) to bemused-looking cows tied to wooden stakes by the roadside. As for the noise we make as we slip through the Steppe, well, that's no more intrusive than the preeps of grasshoppers from the verge. This ability to fit so well into the scenery makes the bicycle a far superior form of transport than anything I can imagine. There is just enough speed to shorten the times of little interest, and just the right pace to be able to interact with the world we are riding through.

I am climbing a rise now in my lowest gear with the weight in my panniers clawing at my back. My mirror is knocked out of place, so that instead of the grey road over my shoulder, I see my face in the enamelled sky where Michaelangelo would have painted the cherub. And I glare into my own fixed eyes and see the wrinkles beneath them and the scruffy tufts of hair and the unshaved chin of a man sweating over one last stab at youth. And as I ride I realise I have no worries, I'm enjoying getting there and not worrying about my final destination or how long it will take to make it there. Worrying is wasted on youth, there's too much time in later years—when the body has decayed to a state of unreliability—to dwell on such things; and then it's probably not worth the effort.

On the road traffic is rare. Sometimes I feel lonely on these long straight stretches, when Rohan is just a squint against the sun in front of me, or far behind and stuck with the fears of her pregnancy—thoughts which fall on each other in tedious repetition like so many layers in a sandstone rock. I refuse to think about it and concentrate instead on more mundane things, like counting down each hundred metres as they pass, or hypnotising myself on the blur beneath my feet. But now the road is running out, disintegrating into a ribbed, dark mud track through a ploughed field the colour of spat tobacco juice, sending Muttley pouncing upon its own shadow and billowing up dust until I am forced to stop.

✳ ✳ ✳

The sun sat heavily on the upper branches of a sash of trees: a windbreak for a field of young maize. We had been cycling for seven long hours, for much of the time on thin tracks across dusty fields with little shade and rationed sips of water. The copse of oaks was the first we had come across so near to the road in hours. I knew from the map that there was a largish town not far off. It was best to rest the night here. We pulled over. A grassy path, furrowed by cart tracks, led off into the bushes. I took a closer look and noticed the grass shoots had begun to reclaim them.

'It doesn't look as if anyone has been here for a while. I think this is probably just as good as we'll get,' I said.

We unstrapped our panniers and bags, and erected the tent. Rohan crawled in to make up our beds, while I hid the bikes in long grass beside our home for the duration and locked them together against prowlers in the night. We took it in turns to wash away some of the day's grime with handfuls of water from my water bottle, and used most of what was left in Rohan's to cook up a mess of beans and powdered potato. There was little else left to do then but move our panniers inside, climb in after them and settle into our sleeping bags, trying politely to avoid each other's sticky, hot bodies. Stretched out was an unusual position to be in after so many hours cramped on a saddle, and it always took us a while to wrench ourselves up again from the luxury of lying flat. But soon the energy from the meal would kick in and we'd try to make the best of our second wind. This time, I hunted out the map and traced the route we had covered so far. It seemed a minuscule distance in the grand scheme of things.

'I think we should take this white road,' I said at last, pointing at a colourless capillary which skipped across a fold in the map. 'It's more direct than this yellow one. We'll save around 15 kilometres.'

'No way. I'm not going on any more tracks,' Rohan declared firmly. 'We'll just end up going slower and it'll end up far longer.'

I knew she was probably right and dismissed the scenic route without a fight, and settled down to listen to the radio. A Liberian tanker was adrift off the coast of Africa and in danger of sinking with its cargo of refugees...I drifted off to the setting sun and the sounds of howling dogs in the distance.

'What if someone comes?' Rohan croaked, elbowing me back to my senses with a jab in the ribs.

'They won't. Why should they?'

'Perhaps someone saw us putting up the tent.'

'Let's take turns in staying awake, then,' I suggested. 'I'll take the first shift.'

'OK,' she said, and we both promptly fell asleep.

We packed up rapidly the next morning and used the last of the water for half-a-cup of tea each. While I was sipping mine I noticed a tight ball of tiny yellow spiders in a nest suspended between strands of grass. As I watched, the nestlings swarmed outwards like an expanding universe. An ugly wolf spider was tapping on a silk thread with a black, spiky leg. It swooped, grabbing a little one between its mandibles and manipulating it slowly towards its mouth. I couldn't help thinking of Stalin.

✳ ✳ ✳

Something was seriously wrong with Askania Nova: for a small town the cemetery was huge. Groups of people huddled around freshly-dug graves, while burial humps marked the resting places of the recently interred. With the town's population standing at only around 8000, its recently dead would soon outnumber the living. Our road ended in a highway that foraged through the Steppe towards Kiev, the intersection patrolled by a silver Mig fighter captured in take-off by a metal pole spearing its rear end.

I wanted to visit the Askania Nova wildlife reserve, the best known of all those in the former Soviet Union. With more than twenty-seven thousand acres, it is the largest area of untouched Steppe in the world and home to several endangered species, including the indigenous Steppe Eagle and the Bobac Marmot. But there are animals, too, which are truly out of place. In Ukraine, of all places, thousands of zebra, American buffalo, llamas, gnu, Indian nilgai, ostriches, emus and South American rhea wade through the feather grass—all thanks to Friedrich Falts-Fein, the great-grandson of a German immigrant who had made a fortune by taking Catherine the Great's advice and raising Merino sheep on the Cossack grasslands. The exotic animals arrived in the 1880s, and Falts-Fein was determined to breed up their numbers enough to feed and clothe the world. He crossed zebras with horses and domesticated the scimitar-horned eland, with which he planned to replace tsetse fly-prone cattle in the tropics. He tried zebra steak and found he quite liked it, but the problem was the winters were far harsher than those on the African plains and each spring was a desperate attempt to breed just enough to replace those which had frozen to death in the cold snaps. More recently, a scientific institute had set up intensive breeding schemes to boost the numbers of endangered Central Asian species, like Przewalski's horse, the markhor (one of the largest members of the goat family), and a type of donkey called the kulan. It is also busy improving the genes of sheep and, at a price, can supply the best eland steaks this side of Botswana. Unfortunately for us there was no signpost to direct us there. We sucked at our drink bottles, wondering which way to go.

'You are lost, I think,' a voice called out in English. It came from a willowy young man, dressed in jeans and a red-and-white checked shirt. He sat on the ground, his back against a metal pole missing its sign. 'You need help?' he asked.

'Uh, yes. We were looking for the Askania Nova park.'

He pointed to a turn off just to his right. 'It is down here,' he said matter-of-factly. 'You can ride your bicycles through it.'

It struck me that a load of wild animals might be a little surprised by a couple of cyclists hurtling through their patch, but we sauntered off following his directions anyway. Through the gates we entered an arcadia of larches, silver birch and pine, blossoming lilac and chestnut trees, rhododendron forests and meadows sparkling with spring flowers. I went first, creeping around corners, my head darting from side to side to catch a Gnu off guard, or a startled herd of grazing zebra. But I saw none, and after an hour or so we decided we were wasting our time and cycled back out the way we had entered. I was convinced the animals had ended up on the dinner plate, victims of the Soviet collapse.

'Are you lost again?' The drollness in his voice was unmistakable.

'Oh, hello.'

'Did you see the animals?'

'No.'

'Did you go to the zoo?'

'The park?'

'No,' he said gravely. 'The park is for the people, the zoo is for the animals.'

'Oh. That's where the zebra are then.'

'No. They are on the Steppe. The Steppe is different to the zoo and the park.'

'Can we see zebras on the Steppe?'

'We can see them only with binoculars.'

'What about the townspeople?'

'They are everywhere.'

'No. I meant can the townspeople see them?'

'With binoculars...' He was beginning to look bored. 'It has always been that way. Only the scientists can see them closely. Would you like to go to the zoo? You can leave your bicycles in my apartment and you can meet my sister. She teaches English at the school. My name, by the way, is Andrew. I would prefer it if you did not use my real name. That is Andrei. We are speaking English, not Russian.' He set off, giving us little option but to follow him across the road and through an alleyway edged with red-brick tenements. He stopped outside the entrance to the last in the line. 'Ah. My room is on the sixth floor. It is too far for you to carry your bicycles. I will ask my neighbour if you can leave them with her.'

It was agreed. We wheeled our bicycles warily into a stranger's living room and promised to be back within the hour. Meanwhile, Andrew's young son skipped off to find Ludmilla at the school. She arrived a short time later. 'Good afternoon. How do you do?' she said all too properly, holding out a porcelain-white hand and gripping mine forcefully. I guessed she was about thirty-four. When she smiled I realised she was virtually the only woman I had seen so far who still had all her teeth. For that I found her quite attractive, not that I'm superficial or anything.

Ludmilla had been a teacher for nine years, but had not been paid for three-and-a-half months. She still turned up to school every day though; she had no choice. 'How can I leave the children? Who would teach them?' she pondered aloud as we wandered slowly towards the zoo. At least the government had promised to pay the teachers some money within two weeks. There was always hope. 'I think they are afraid now,' she continued. 'The exams are coming up soon and it will look very bad for the country if the teachers go on strike.'

It was the same all over Ukraine, she informed us. Some people had gone up to a year without money. They had no choice but to keep working. If they threw down their tools and walked out then when the money eventually arrived they would get nothing. 'When we complain to the authorities they just tell us to finish our jobs if we don't like it. They know that we can't...'

Lessons at school were taught in Russian—despite the fact that immediately after independence classes had been instructed in Ukrainian. That was soon put to an end when the parents, mainly Russians working for the Institute, kept their children back from school in protest. Ukrainian was a foreign language, they reasoned, even if they were all living in Ukraine. In true Soviet-style, a compromise prevailed. All lessons were to be taught in Russian, including four hours a week of Ukrainian language and literature. However, examinations were still to be taken in Ukrainian. Needless to say, few children in Askania Nova continued into further education.

I asked Andrew what he did for a living. He was restoring the old Falts-Fein mansion, he said. It was voluntary work. He didn't have a paid job. Both he and Ludmilla lived at home with their parents, and depended on food grown in their cottage garden. It was a big family—eight people in the one house, living in four rooms. There was no hot water, and cold only in the evenings.

'People here breed pigs, cows, ducks and hens to live,' Ludmilla said. 'They all help each other. After work they work to live. We get nothing from the collective farms. They take it all away, everything.' She shook her head, flouncing her hair. 'The only money in town is to build the first Christian church! But that is good, isn't it?'

I nodded, out of sympathy. In my experience a place to pray for money for food was always worth spending the cash on.

We had arrived at the zoo's entrance. An old woman in her booth folded her meaty arms across her chest and turned up her bottom lip when she heard our accents. We were forbidden. There was a heated exchange.

'It is a problem because you are a foreigner,' Andrew said finally, trying to appear calm. 'She said foreigners can only come into the zoo in a tour group.' I laughed aloud. I was sure that at least this hangover of the Soviet Union would have been cured by now.

'She says she doesn't trust you,' Ludmilla said, a little embarrassed.

'Why, do they think the foreigners are going to eat the animals or something? I asked.

'I will ask her,' Andrew said seriously. And he did.

She didn't laugh, but warily the babushka relented, on the promise that our hosts would personally take responsibility for our actions. After a struggle with Andrew I paid, and the babushka waved us through with a sideways roll of her eyes.

The zoo, as it turned out, was surprisingly good, with birds and animals from all over the world. It would have been a popular tourist attraction in the West, but that day we were the only visitors. 'Your government could make a lot of money by advertising the zoo and having organised safaris on the Steppe,' I commented.

'But the Russians and Ukrainians are very impractical,' Andrew replied.

'It is true,' Ludmilla butted in. 'We are not accustomed to thinking. We are accustomed to people thinking for us. And what can we do when the local authorities will not make decisions?' We strolled past a series of duck ponds. 'My husband saw many places in Europe as a sailor,' Ludmilla said softly as we leant on a railing watching a black swan float gracefully by. 'But he was given no money to go ashore. Everything was forbidden for the Soviet sailor. They were given enough money only to buy an ice-cream.'

She listed the countries he had excited her imagination with: France, Germany, Hungary, Spain, Czechoslovakia and then there was the Danube River...

'I want to travel so much. But how can I ever have money? Soon I will be old. But maybe my children will go.' She smiled sweetly. Ludmilla seemed to be completely untouched by self-pity and only once during our conversation did her happiness fade. It was when she remembered Chernobyl.

She had gone to Kiev on that fateful May Day, taking her six-month-old son with her. They were to stay with her husband's parents. 'We had heard something on the radio on 27 April that there was something wrong. But they said it was a small accident, so nobody took any notice. They lied to us and my son was there! I can't forgive my government. We only heard there was a serious accident five years later!'

Now Ludmilla saw cancer in every minor illness. She asked me if I knew that most of the energy produced at the power station had ended up not in Ukraine but in Poland. I said I hadn't. That was the final irony, she responded. The people most affected by Chernobyl never even benefited from it being there.

As for Andrew, Chernobyl had taught him not to trust the newspapers. The media he grew up with would never have attempted to describe reality as seen by the people it preached to. If they had then it would have been treasonable. 'You have to talk to people and hear their stories,' he said bleakly. 'It took nearly ten years of talking for me to find out what really happened in Chernobyl, but now I know everything, and I must tell you, I know that it will happen again. Very soon.'

'How do you know?' I asked.

'Everybody knows. The workers who work there, the management, the government, the old men, the old women, the West. Of course it will happen. There is nothing to be done.' The famous Russian fatalism, I thought. 'Where were you at the time of the disaster?' he asked me.

I thought back. The explosions caught up with me in a tin-roofed concrete box in Delhi, where I was sweating through the last racking chills of malaria in my year-off from college. The cloud, my newspaper told me, was already over Britain. At once I was terrified for my friends and family and thankful I was where I was.

'I don't believe it,' Andrew murmured.

'You don't believe what?'

'The cloud did not get to England.'

'But you can't eat sheep from certain hills in Wales even today.'

'That's impossible.'

I asked him if he had heard about the reindeer in Swedish Lapland getting cancerous tumours after the explosion, or that Munich had more radiation dumped on it than virtually anywhere else outside the exclusion zone around the station. 'No. Of course not. It's impossible. The cloud did not go that far.' I asked him too if he was aware that the cloud had passed right over Askania Nova on route to the Crimea, following fleeing Kiev schoolchildren; that it had turned the Crimean Mountains radioactive. But no. This man who read between the lines had heard none of this.

'Your newspapers lied to you,' he said.

My mind fuddled and I changed the subject, aware that my questioning was making me look foolish. I asked him instead about the graveyard.

'There is a chemical factory on the edge of the reserve. It produces titanium for the airforce. A lot of people die of cancer. If you look at the graves you will see that most people die in their fifties.'

'It must worry you.'

'Of course not. We are young.' I kept my tongue.

At the exit gate an old man met us with antelope milk for sale from a iron pail.

'Buy some here,' a cardboard sign instructed. 'It cures everything.' Somehow I doubted it.

✱ ✱ ✱

We covered more than 50 kilometres that afternoon, sustaining ourselves on a lunch of dried bread and a tin of herrings. Telegraph poles edged our route, chained to the horizon like decapitated crucifixes. In the fields, irrigating machines clanked their rigging and bobbed around on their wash. The road hurried west, running so straight, so keen, that with the wind behind us we covered as many as 20 kilometres in an hour and sometimes flew at double the speed. Every now and again we would skim through the corrugated high street of a village, its neat little houses pinned to the road to stop it escaping. Chubby old women in tan stockings, summer dresses and scarves made doubly sure of this surveillance by plonking their weight behind buckets of potatoes.

Towards evening, we slipped down the steep banks of a river glimmering with reflections of Ladas and Zaporozhets and stripped off, plunged under and washed the dirt and sweat away in the coolness. It was our first real wash in over a week. Revived, we continued onwards into the setting sun, with Rohan silhouetted upon Katoshka in front of me. We camped in an orchard of plums.

6 THE CUCUMBER COAST

The old man spat on his finger and pressed it onto the valve. He nodded his balding head and squeezed the tyre again. It would do, he said and beckoned for the dust cap. Rohan's back inner tube was welted with repair pads from my ineffectual patch-up jobs. Our German hand-pump had turned out to be as hopeless as me, and however much I put my back into it, the tyre refused to get harder than a bruised orange. The irony was that if we had paid more for our bikes, we would have ended up with more modern valves and no chance of getting help. As it was, a car's foot pump fitted ours perfectly—though it gave us about four hours before Rohan would be rumbling along on her wheel rims again.

On the Steppe it was far from perfect cycling weather. The road sweltered in front of us and the sun washed out the fields of stones and coarse grass which stretched to the horizon as far as we could see. It was an empty land, desolate and cracking as it toasted. As we whirred ever onwards the dust thrown up from Rohan's tyres in front began to get up my nose. I dug deeper, ramming at the pedals and sped past her at a furious speed, watching her clinging on grimly to her handlebars in my mirror until she shrunk to the size of a fly. I pulled over a kilometre or so later and waited for her to catch up while I chewed on a Mars bar. As she approached, Rohan swung her handlebars towards the verge a little too aggressively and, courting bad luck, saw her front wheel rebel and stay pointing forward in typical Katoshka and Muttley style. She tumbled onto the kerb in a thunder of expletives and lay there pinned by her panniers, not bothering to extricate herself. Too tired myself to help her, I remained in my own sprawl, my mouth chewing indulgently on chocolate. Eventually she crawled from beneath her steed and lay on her back, smothering her eyes from the sun with a sweaty arm. We didn't speak, we were too hot and bothered for that. Instead we both brooded silently as the dust settled on our weary bodies and caked to the wet dribbles of our hair. Ten minutes later I managed to squeeze out the last remnants of the water bottle attached to Muttley's frame, before collapsing back into the dirt. Another ten minutes went by, then another fifteen.

'How are you doing?' I eventually managed to ask.

'Fine,' she said bitterly. She was as remote from me as the coolness of evening and the crawl into the tent we both yearned for.

We hadn't seen anybody beside the road all day, and few cars on the road. Everything was flat and featureless and in a landscape like that it's difficult to even gear up your imagination to get you through the long hours, let alone any enthusiasm for the company of a riding partner. We could have sung songs together to relieve the monotony, but our throats were too dry and we felt drugged by the heat and blinded by the glare of thousands of rocks in the fields; we could have talked and planned for the future, but when the present is so draining and so unrelenting it was difficult enough to get sufficient air in your lungs to keep on riding.

Rohan, crooked and silent, made no movement as I unscrewed the dust cap on her wheel and pumped her tyre up once more, bleeding sweat onto the baking rubber. When she finally made it to her feet and clambered into her saddle she glared at me as if this was all my fault; as if I had purposely sucked up the moisture from this endless land and ignited the sun and turned this ocean of mud into leather.

We had no choice after all but to lurch forward once more, slowly picking up pace, but were faced now with a burning head wind. I spurred myself on with the thought of my next swig of water from the leaking bottle strapped to my panniers. Barely a kilometre on I stopped again to let Rohan catch up, then took off again almost at once with my ears plugged full of grit.

By past lunchtime we had covered less than half our usual distance, and Rohan was lagging behind again. The intense heat was making me irritable. My head felt like a stewed apple under my helmet. I stopped and pulled it off, riding on with my hair flipping at my scalp. After a while I checked my mirror; Rohan was further behind than ever. Not long after I pulled off the road and onto a dirt track between a ribbon of trees; the first all day. I followed them to a pond, where a fisherman stood behind a bamboo rod among a patch of reeds. I gulped at my water bottle with my throat convulsing, then reached for our primus and poured almost the last drops onto a dusting of dried soup powder. Rohan pulled up, her face distorted, as I lit the flame. The storm that had been gathering all day had no option but to break.

'If this keeps up we'll never make it to Belarus,' I said tersely.

I felt the hardness in her eyes through the back of my head.

'You're obsessed with kilometres,' she blazed. 'My back hurts and you keep racing off. I can hardly cycle at all. It's impossible!'

'Look, there's no point just sitting back and saying it's impossible,' I said pompously. 'You sound like a Russian.'

'Well, it is impossible. I hate this. I hate having to reach a number every day. It just makes this whole thing a chore. I shouldn't have come!' She slung Katoshka to the ground and decamped into some bushes. I gritted my teeth. She emerged a while later, her eyes puffy from crying. I crouched beside our boiling soup in silence.

'OK,' she said solemnly. 'Let's look at the map and work out exactly how many kilometres we have to do.'

'Look, I'm sure things will work out,' I mumbled into the saucepan. 'I know it's hard, but we have to keep going. How would we feel if we gave up?'

'Maybe relieved. No. I didn't mean that. It's just, well, sometimes I find cycling easier than you, but I try to stay behind with you. We both have our bad days. Today's mine.'

As usual she had a good point. There had been plenty of times when she'd been bowling along singing to herself while I sat crunched up on the saddle, feeling morose and breathing heavily. But then she'd slow and keep pace with me patiently for a while, before her thoughts distracted her and she'd pull away again. It always seemed to be me who was running on a short fuse in our relationship; though we were as stubborn as each other and would never let the other win a fight if we could help it. I swallowed my frustration and began studying the map. The route ahead gloated back at me, slapping its lips in the breeze. Things were tighter than even I had suspected. My sloppy planning was catching up with us. We had already spent two days longer in the Crimea than I'd planned, and it didn't help that the distances gleaned from our paper guide had no real relevance to that on the road. It quickly became evident that there was no other option: we had to up our daily average. From now on we had to ride at least 90 kilometres a day. With the extreme heat, and the fitness that was still eluding us both, it would be barely endurable. I felt like the kilometre-fascist Rohan had accused me of being.

✳ ✳ ✳

We took the back way to the town of Kherson, almost instinctively finding our way to civilisation on dirt tracks through a prairie where nothing moved except us. We were almost riding on our bellies by the time we reached it, weighed down by the intensity of the afternoon sun burning through our backs. By the time we arrived, my eyes were rolling like ball bearings in their sockets and my thigh-muscles quivered uncontrollably, like beheaded chickens. I pliered myself from my machine and limped like a cripple towards the water's edge. The Dnieper oozed into Kherson from the Donbas, streaked with oil and grease and polished to a sheen with industrial acids. I stood for a while, my face flushed, creaking my back slowly straight while staring across the estuary. The tug *Vostok* grumbled in to be moored next to her wasp-striped sister, the *Komkov*. A jaunty breeze blew the staleness of the Steppe dust out of my nose, then flicked my hair against my brow. I felt a spit of rain.

Partly recuperated by our delight at being here and at the cloud which had plunged itself moth-like at the sun, we slid away towards the main boulevard—a good road, strewn with catkins, Ladas and the winged fruit of witch elm. Lenin glared disdainfully above us as we rode chapped-lipped and mucky into the central square. His trench coat had been pulled open as his right hand fumbled for something deep in his pocket. Bird droppings had built up on his shoulders. Outside Sevastopol no-one seemed to clean them off any more.

The locals beneath him stomped straight-backed and confident, picking carefully over market produce and arguing with feudal peroxide-blondes behind their stalls. Mounting the kerb we toed our way slowly through the crowd, passing a colourless medley of cheap clothing and detergent, loaves of dusty bread, dried fish and withered apples. A woman, as wide as she was tall, blocked our route as she haggled over a mangled beetroot. At last she flung down the vegetable in disgust and moved on to huff over a mixed-bag stall of bras, sunflower seeds, three-headed carrots, hair dye and horn-buns sprinkled with poppy seeds.

We used the last of our kupons to buy a slab of Russian chocolate, a couple of dry cakes and a gallon of fizzy orange which we guzzled down, drowning our thirst. Seeking a place to demolish our food we followed a side alley into a patchy grass square, where the stench of communal rubbish bins hung sweetly in the air. We'd hardly finished eating when we fell into an exhausted sleep. We were woken an hour or so later by a drunk grunting as he defecated in front of us. He held out a begging bowl as he crouched there, enticing us to hand over a few coins. Not impressed by his act we left him to concentrate on the brown-black braids sagging onto the grass.

Our next task was to change money at a street kiosk. The government had outlawed direct transactions in US dollars, but an absurd inflation rate meant that as soon as anyone had kupons they swapped them for a harder currency. When they needed to buy something they exchanged them back again. Money-changers were now a fact of life, like mouth ulcers.

We also desperately needed some fuel. Sticks gathered from beside the road were fine in the sunshine, but any rain and we'd be in trouble. There had been no sign of methylated spirits anywhere along our route and the trip was developing into a constant search for anything combustible. The town's department store at least held out some hope. Rohan went first. She came back with a cheap red T-shirt.

'There's hardly anything in there worth buying,' she said. I went to have a look anyway. It was like a sarcophagus inside: dark, with trestle-tables sectioned off by vertical boards. One stall had ten rolls of film and a few long-snouted Russian cameras. Others were loaded with crockery, household cleaners and more cheap clothes. I wondered where the sophisticated Ukrainian city folk got theirs. Under the counter, I expected. Again, there was no fuel.

It was dusk now and we were still starving. We tried three restaurants but only the third looked open. Rohan ducked into the bathroom to wash and change into better clothes while I locked the bikes up in the lobby. Once complete I lathered up with a thin slice of soap and damped down my hair in the sink. I pulled off my ragbag clothes and replaced them with crumpled trousers and my best shirt. If I squinted I looked almost respectable. The restaurant itself was empty, but the waiter's pomposity filled the space nicely.

'Can we eat?' Rohan asked unsurely when he finally made his way over. His pencil-thin moustache twitched.

'Of course,' he replied through his teeth.

The table was spread with a starched white cloth and laid meticulously with gleaming cutlery. We sat down. A Yamaha keyboard player and a drummer stubbed out their cigarettes and took their positions. Suddenly, the thought struck me that this place could end up eating severely into our budget.

'Do you think we can afford it?' I whispered to Rohan. 'How much money did we change?'

'Not too much. I only changed enough to get us to Odessa.'

We had decided early on in the planning to stash most of our savings away in traveller's cheques and credit card accounts. We figured a wad of cash just meant trouble. It was far safer to keep our savings secure and change as little as we could at any one time.

'Maybe we should leave,' Rohan suggested.

But our escape had already been blocked. The waiter dropped leather-bound menus in front of us and rubbed a handful of fingers through his greased-back hair as if he had narrowly avoided catching fleas. He had lost all hope of a tip.

The duo beside us struck up a number as we studied the menu. Dishes fell over each other, pages long in a hand-written scrawl. I noticed the prices and breathed a sigh of relief. With the help of the dictionary we weeded out sturgeon, numerous caviar dishes and banquet-loads of salads and meats. Being what I have dubbed a 'pescatarian', or a fish-eating vegetarian, I couldn't go wrong with the steamed sturgeon. Rohan picked Ukrainian varenyky, a kind of pasta filled with potatoes. The borsch would be good, with some vegetables on the side. And, of course, a beer.

The waiter had disappeared. We waited, shuffling in our seats. When a flouncy-bloused waitress couldn't ignore us any longer, she strolled over clutching a notebook. 'Da,' she sniffed contemptuously.

'Do you have borsch?' Rohan asked politely in passable Russian.

She rolled an onorous 'nyet' out of her mouth like a lemon.

'Varenyky?'

'Nyet.'

'Fish?'

'You want fish?'

'Yes, please. Sturgeon?'

'Nyet.'

'Other fish?'

'Nyet.'

'Vegetables?' Confusion.

'Potatoes, um, katoshka?'

'Katoshka. Da.'

'Salad?'

'Cucumber.'

The caviar was off and if we had wanted meat she might be able to rustle something up, though it had been bought in the market a couple of days before: there wasn't much call for it, you see, what with having so few customers. The menu obviously had little connection to reality.

'Beer?' I ventured.

'Nyet. Vodka.'

We ended up with a beautifully presented dollop of mashed potato, a sliced tomato and a few curled cucumber pieces pierced with toothpicks. We both sat there and stared at the offering as if it were a plate of sheeps' eyeballs. We knew enough about Russian food not to have expected anything exotic, but we had at least expected to glean some nutrition from it. As it was, we were likely to expend more energy eating these pitiful fork-fulls that we got from them. After more hesitation I scooped up some potato. It was inconceivable that anyone could make something so simple taste like you were eating a cushion, but the cook had performed a miracle. As I chewed relentlessly at the spongy mound of dried-up jelly in my mouth, my tastebuds tried desperately to extract a hint of flavour. I would have killed for some curry powder or a splash of soy sauce, anything to pump some life into it. But all I had was vodka, and that was so rough it sent my throat into revolt.

We left the cucumber, it hardly seemed worth the effort, and upped in a flurry of dirty banknotes and rumbling stomachs. We marched under the leer of the scoffing waiter back into the foyer and began unchaining the bikes. From his position on top of a ladder, a man in overalls who'd been painting the walls when we arrived regarded us quizzically. He carefully replaced the brush in its pot and climbed downwards. He motioned us to remain where we were and scampered through a door at the far end of the lobby, to emerge a few moments later with two plastic cups full to the brim with vodka.

'Stolichnaya vodka,' he said proudly, holding them up for us to inspect. 'Not like the piss they serve in there. Drink. Drink.'

Both Rohan and I stared at him open-mouthed.

'It is a custom to drink vodka after you have eaten,' he said with a chuckle, then leaned forward and said in a whisper, his eyes twinkling: 'It fills the gap left by the meal, don't you think.'

★ ★ ★

Tram lines, processed food factories, and the odd babushka selling her wares on the side of the road escorted us into Odessa—a 'Hero City' and gallant owner of the Order of Lenin and the Gold Star Medal. Our road buckled under the weight of an endless progression of traffic as we entered. Exhaust and chimney smoke choked us. For kilometre after kilometre cars rattled past, spraying us with a slurry of puddled rainwater and oil. It's always a bonus to scramble into a city from its frayed side; that way you get to see what makes it really tick, and see first hand where the mass of people who do all the hard work go about their daily lives. You can write it off as being grim and depressing, and it's true that being walled in with fumes isn't conducive to a good first opinion, but if you look hard you can share in the immeasurable optimism that went into slapping it all together like a soiled jigsaw puzzle. The traffic, though, was monstrous and after a while we hopped up onto a sidewalk rutted with roots and puddles in a bid to save our skins.

From the pedestrians we avoided on our way came the rasp of Russian; in Odessa, the 'City of Humour', people laugh at those who speak Ukrainian in public. The crowds increased as the outskirts rattled into town and nudged up to glorious architecture that could be the envy of even the most sophisticated of cities. The Hotel Grand Moscow, however, had fallen on her luck. Classical Greek statues leant precariously from a plaster façade which shedded itself in lumps. Part of the road in front had been cordoned off—the result of an angel's head toppling off and seriously injuring a pedestrian the week before. Rohan went in to find us a room while I stood outside guarding the bikes. As I waited I looked them over. Muttley had developed a slight buckle to its back wheel, but the spokes seemed to be holding up well. The back light spewed wires from its destruction on the plane to Kiev. Katoshka had a dramatic scrape almost the entire length of its crossbar, from yet another dramatic turn of the handlebars and a collision with a kerb stone, from which Rohan had walked away with little more than shock soon after we first entered town. Rips to their saddles added asthetic balance to the strips of scuffed brown packing tape which still encased sections of their frames, but still almost everyone who passed stopped to admire them. One man even handed me an orange to make up for his conspicious stares.

'You must be thirsty cycling in this weather,' he said, before turning away with a smile that relieved my exhaustion like a tonic.

Our room for the night was thin and long, papered in a meadow of dishevelled blue flowers. A useless refrigerator rusted against a wall beside a black-and-white television. Two single beds were positioned head to base. A plastic toilet in the ensuite bathroom refused to flush. There was cold water for three hours a day. There had been no hot since the Revolution.

We worked on the bicycles that evening in our room. I plastered Rohan's inner tube with yet more patches. She had far more patience for the job, but deferred to my insistence that I knew what I was doing. I didn't think to check for the thorns which had implanted themselves in the tyre. I continued instead by tightening screws that had wriggled themselves free and scraping at a mat of grease, grit and grass from gear cogs with the prongs of a fork. The following morning the tyre was flat again. We agreed to tour the city by foot.

The Odessa opera house was the most important outside Moscow. Mussorgsky, Borodin, Rimsky-Korsakov, Prokofiev and Stravinsky had all performed there, and Tchaikovsky had conducted the Queen of Spades. In the square outside, a clump of peasant women in wrinkled stockings and ill-cut summer dresses trowelled almost lyrically among the bedding plants, while the scales of a solo soprano skipped around them.

Central Odessa was an aristocratic vision, designed by the young Duc de Richelieu, a refugee from the French Revolution. Thanks to Hitler, who had handed the city to the Rumanians in exchange for troops for the eastern front, it largely survived the war. The new administration's public relations had started off badly, though, with 20 000 locals burnt alive in an arsenal, 5000 more hung and an estimated 40 000 Jews murdered too. But the resentment of the local populace wasn't good for business. The Rumanians changed tack—building shops, restaurants, casinos, nightclubs and bodegas and over thirty churches, in an effort to convince the remaining Odessans that they were now the fortunate citizens of the Greater Rumanian Empire. Then they threw themselves into the black market, selling their guns to partisans, who stored them in an arsenal in extensive catacombs tunnelled into the limestone beneath the city, beside a hospital, a bakery and even a sausage factory.

But all that has now gone, on the breeze as it climbs up the Richelieu Steps from the docks below, from where it paces along the blonde-stoned Prymorski Boulevard and into Karl Marx Square and billows out the newspapers in the hands of war heroes sitting on park benches in the shade of an avenue of chestnut trees. Lap dogs with punched-in faces and prancing gaits pull despairingly at their leashes, their owners trickling towards me with shopping bags of lilac nipped from the trees. Dandelion fairies sail through the air. Thuds from the dockyards mingle with the salty odour of the Black Sea.

We start at the top of the steps and work our way down. Outside Red Square and the Kremlin, this is about the only architecture of any significance either of us had heard about in this part of the world before we arrived. Down this very flight a baby had trundled in its pram in one of the most memorable scenes in the history of cinema. At the bottom, the film-maker Eisentein had placed the Ukrainians' beloved Cossacks, who in reality had hacked at their brethren with their sabres. But as we follow this staircase step-by-step to the bottom, I realise it is leaving a feeble impression. At its base, deafened by the roaring trucks on an unsightly road, we turn to look up. The staircase looks bigger than it felt. As I follow it down again my attention is drawn to a cowboy on a motorcycle in a Lucky Strike advert at its base. American imperialism can be just as ominous in the form of its advertising.

Across the road is a modernist passenger port, harbouring bored money-changers and Kashtan shops: counterparts of the 1930s Torgsin stores, which were set up to earn hard cash from foreign tourists. They are stocked with German sausages, French cheeses and Western alcohols. But I am not here on account of my decadence, but to nibble at the very kernel of Soviet history. Into this port the battleship *Potemkin*, the pride of the Black Sea Fleet, docked in 1905 with its Red flag flying and fired salvos at the city and the opera house, while gangs of Cossacks and anti-Semites piled into strikers and massacred Jews. From here, too, Allied ships steamed full-ahead as Odessa fell to the communists; and a quarter of a century later, during the Second World War, thousands of Allied troops, released from captivity by the advancing Soviet forces, embarked for home. During the following decades Odessa's harbour gorged itself on Italian and French cruise ships, and vomited out more than 50 000 Odessan Jews, half the city's Yiddish population—when communism fell.

I looked up. An extensive grin glinted from above an ice-cream. With his curly ginger hair, violently-checked cotton shirt, knee-length shorts and canvas satchel, Richard from Wisconsin couldn't help but stand out in the crowd. Obviously, we did too.

'Hey there. Where you from?' he asked. I told him. 'Wow, you are in some need of a Turkish coffee. Come on. My treat.'

He introduced his girlfriend, a long-haired economics student called Natasha, who held his hand as he led us all towards a fashionable outdoor café, where the waiter brought a tray of Lipton's tea, and thick, black coffee.

For two years Richard had taught prospective Odessan religious teachers the faith they had lost to the communists. 'The young people find it difficult to get the State out of the system,' he said while he stirred in the sugar. 'But it's uncool to be an atheist now. You gotta have some idea about God. Is he everywhere? Is he somewhere? Has he spoken to anyone? For more than seventy years their State was God. "Man is it," they said. Your world view is unique if you believe the Soviet Union will go on longer than any man,' he continued. 'We really need to change people's faith, to change their hearts, and when we change their hearts we change their country.'

'We get a lot of things from Turkey,' Natasha interrupted, tapping me on the arm and raising her coffee cup. 'Russia, or I must say Ukraine…' she corrected herself, '…has completely changed. People go to Turkey, buy some things and we see it here in the markets. We say it is capitalism, but the people think they are extortionists. The old people especially think it is evil to make profit.'

'It's true,' said Richard, caught up in explaining away the contradictions of a nation. 'At least with communism everyone had nothing and everyone could buy the little of what was out there.'

Natasha had been enlightened. Now she had her faith in capitalism. The suffering of the masses was just a natural part of the new order of things.

'You know that it was the people favoured by the State, or who had influence, who lived in these apartments in the city centre during communist times?' she went on. 'The rest of them lived out there…out in the suburbs. Don't you think it is ugly out there?'

'They were in a hurry to build,' I replied, a little feebly. 'In a way you have to forgive them for cutting corners with their architecture.'

'No. They had no imagination.'

'Two million Russians were killed in the First World War alone,' I reminded her. 'They were starving and dying before that. It wasn't all for the bad.'

'Ah, yes. They got those apartments after the collapse,' she continued, throwing me for a moment. 'Now most of the communists have moved to the country, to their dachas, and they rent their city property to those who can afford it.'

'And who is that?' I asked innocently.

Richard smirked above his cup. 'The mafia, of course.' I felt I had intruded on a double act.

'Last month a grenade went off on my street.' He took a sip and waited for my reaction. I gave him my best shot at amazement. 'Everything happens in the street here,' he continued happily. 'Beatings are common. The mafia are unmistakable, especially in the summer. They have a certain fashion. Last year it was Adidas running shoes, Chinese jogging suits and sunglasses, and they always have very short hair and stand beside their Mercedes a lot, surrounded by younger guys. Stuff goes on and you don't know about it, and if you do you really don't want to.'

This stuff wasn't new. Like most port towns, Odessa was steeped in the oily whiff of the underworld. Gangsters had taken what they could since the time of the Tsars, and speculation was the city's blood well before its citizens were granted special favours to prevent them forming ties with the Ottoman Empire. Some even say Stalin worked there, robbing banks to pay the rent for Lenin and other revolutionaries living in exile in English boarding houses and Swiss chalets. But under communism the stand-over techniques spread to the highest levels, becoming officially ingrained in the system. Membership of a particular group, or any position with a touch of power, meant one gave and expected special considerations. Normal people paid bribes. Natasha's mother had recently had a phone installed after waiting for twenty-one years because she had refused to pay a back-hander to the official in charge. Ideas of privilege and living at other people's expense consistently trickled down the classes from above. And it hadn't fallen with communism. Corruption and stand-over tactics were still an everyday part of life, issuing forth from bully-boys and former Soviet apparatchiks. This semi-respectable business class has kept the masses in servitude. Only the ruthless and street-wise make a good living. The Odessans, true to their heritage, had done better than most.

'Yes, we are living in exciting times,' said Richard as he wrote his address on a banknote too worthless to spend. He handed it over with a final cheesy grin, and with common consent we went our separate ways.

✳ ✳ ✳

That afternoon we cycled due west over the Dneister, the chief source of drinking water for Odessa and a river so polluted that in parts it no longer freezes in winter. On its banks stood a nuclear power and heating station, once intended to supply the city with electricity and hot water. Begun in 1981, it was the first of many proposed to supply the energy needs of individual cities. But from the start it had problems. Workers were inexperienced and the plant was sloppily constructed with low quality materials. Even initial Soviet accounts suggested it was unsafe. Fantastically, it was even built on a fault line. But this didn't seem to worry the Ukrainian government, who only decided to mothball it and another outside Kiev, in response to reviews following the Chernobyl disaster. There is now growing pressure to renew the project and get the stations finally on line.

We left the river behind and the country frowned, then threw up hills like a rucked-up bed sheet. Soon after the road began to thrash, trying to shake us off. People attempted to do the same. The further west we travelled the more unwelcoming was our reception. No-one sat beside the road now, preferring instead to watch our passing from the windows. And when we stopped for water, or supplies of chocolate and bread at village shops, there were fewer questions. Invading armies and knocks on the door in the dead of night had taught them the value of keeping to themselves.

In turn we became paranoid too, hiding like partisans in the forests, squeezing Muttley and Katoshka between splintering gaps of plantation firs and waiting until almost nightfall to erect the tent. I kept our fires small and made of tiny twigs, around which we huddled like witches trying to smother the flames with our shadows.

Exercise made us hungry. There were no restaurants in these parts—there was not much call for potatoes and pig when you could eat the same at home. So, in the mornings we demolished bread and jam, and tea if we had enough water. For lunch it was a bowl of soup, and more chunks of bread, baked with caraway seeds and tasting like toothpaste. Or pasta, mine mixed with a tin of sprats, complete with backbones, heads, eggs and guts; and Rohan's with just a trickling of juice from the tin—the jumbled up fish-bits made her gag just looking at them. But it was the evening that we craved for. It was a special time, almost spiritual. Once the tent was up and the bed was made, with the BBC World Service on the radio, we would relish dried beans and re-hydrated mashed potato, or more pasta, with fried onion to make it interesting and curry powder to give it taste. It was bicycle cuisine and we feasted.

7 COSSACK COUNTRY

The road sucked us towards Poland, wiggling around grazes of trees like a worm in a shower of rain; seducing us with banks of seeding grasses and thickets of hazel; all buttoned-up by tiny, bright-coloured villages bracketed on our map with German names, in memory of the Saxon settlers who had lived there well before Stalin had chased them out. From the saddle of my bike the Steppe looked like tilled chocolate, so dark and rich that it was easy to see how the fields around here had once provided more than 20 per cent of the agricultural produce of the whole Soviet Union.

From here eastwards was Cossack territory: the home of the 'robbers', or 'tramps' as the Tartars knew them. Convicts, paupers, runaway serfs, adventurers, political refugees and religious dissenters, they had dribbled into the *dikoye pole*— the 'wild country'—from Russia, Poland and Lithuania in the Middle Ages. They had mixed with the remnants of renegade Tartar bands and formed autonomous communes and village assemblies. They settled along the Dneiper and the Don, gorging on salted pike and carp from the rivers, caught wild horses, women and travellers with nooses tied from the ends of poles, and fired muskets from the hip as they galloped towards the Pacific coast and Siberia. Their pirate ships harried the river settlements and the Black Sea ports, besieged Constantinople and even sailed the North-west Passage. It took Stalin to break them—with death, deportation and collectivisation. It was another sixty years until they had the chance to elect another hetman, or leader, amid firecrackers and vodka, and celebrations of 500 years of history. Sometimes I wished I could have seen them as they were in their day—from a safe distance, the brow of a hill perhaps—as they thundered in a cloud of dust from the bare hooves of their horses.

We are now on a similar latitude to northern France, or northern Nova Scotia. The acacias of the southern plains have given way to maples and birch and the first skinny pines. Meadows are mottled with Friesians. The head-scarves of the women who weed the collectivised fields by hand have shed their Russian flowers and turned Ukrainian white. Horses are common in these lusher lands: sturdy chestnuts pulling carts heaped with grass; their masters lolling behind, clicking their tongues, while glistening foals trot desperately after them on spindly legs. We take rest breaks in fields of flowering clover, rising later every day as the rigours of cycling catch up with us. I have noticed my body is changing, the fat of the easy life tumbling off me like a landslide. Muscles which I barely remember have popped up like dumplings, and at night I feel I am lying on marbles. On these evenings I lie awake imagining my own life out here, fit from the fields with a duck pond of my own. There's something in the broadness of the Steppe now that—unlike our experiences before in the drier country further south—makes the imagination expand, its sameness forcing one's mind to roam like the Cossacks. One focuses on landmarks too. Today Rohan's pregnancy is the biggest cairn on the horizon.

The only thing I've had to do with children was with the twelve-year-old boy still inside me, who had waded through atlases late at night and closed his eyes and wished so hard to open them again and be on a camel crossing the Sahara; or drifting down the Amazon; or passing through the Alps by train; and whom I still reward on my travels now in later life by opening up my eyes for him as a treat and willing him to guess where we are now... But with other children I feel awkward. My culture has managed to shield me from them as it has largely done from the old. But now all that was about to change. It scared me so much that as soon as I had the thought I tried with all my might to snuff it out again. The reality of cycling great distances is that you spend hours and hours in silent thought. Perhaps it was the continual turning over of my mind that caused it to twist and accommodate the unthinkable, to become an almost physical sensation: my mind wrapping around itself and turning inside out. I began to shudder at the significance of what I—we—had done. A child. My child. I shook my head in disbelief.

Then Rohan's father rushed into my head. I remembered a story of when he had worked as a paediatrician in the 1960s, right in the heart of the thalidomide scare. It was a time when the first question a doctor asked, when he heard of a birth of a child, was not whether it was a boy or a girl, but whether it was normal. At Rohan's eldest sister's birth, her father rushed into the maternity ward and desperately held the newborn up to the light in order to see if its fingers and toes were all there. He resigned soon afterwards, too disconcerted by the experience to continue in medicine. I mulled over that image of him, me, and that baby, but my contemplations always led me to the same conclusion: deformed or not, my instincts said I wanted it.

✲ ✲ ✲

Bogdan Khmelnitsky lunged at us in the town bearing his name, skewing sideways on his sinewy bronze mount, his mace raised to strike. Unlike the dukes and generals who sit uncomfortably on stunted carthorses in our Western cities, this greatest of Ukrainian heroes is caught in roaring action, his steed galloping furiously towards battle. But like many a 'hero', he has been misjudged by his people. The son of a wealthy Cossack in occupied lands, Khmelnitsky supplemented his Christian schooling with a warrior's apprenticeship, learning to take the sacrament and slice a man in two at striking pace. Life was relatively quiet until he reached middle age. But when a petty argument with a Polish neighbour ended in the murder of his only son and the kidnap of his mistress, and with no redress in Warsaw for a mere Cossack, Khmelnitsky fled eastwards to join his brethren on the Dneiper and the Don, then southwards to meet with the Tartars. A charismatic man, he convinced them to attack their Polish landlords. Victories mounted. Ukrainian serfs—seeing the meagre surplus from their plots mopped up like gravy by the bread of the gentry—surged westwards, burning estates as they went. From Poland and Lithuania the peasants marched, massacring overseers, shop owners and tax collectors—mostly Jews—as they went.

But memory is short and history easily tampered with. In reality, this folk hero, held to be the leader of the insurrection, sold out the peasants and sent in his fellow Cossacks to quell the unrest and slaughter thousands. The Polish even offered Khmelnitsky an independent Ukraine, but he refused and chose to swear allegiance to the Tsar of Russia instead. Eventually, further war saw Ukraine split in half between its powerful neighbours. The serfs would have to bide their time for freedom.

Beneath that frozen blood-curdle, Rohan nursed her ailing bike, fruitlessly trying to pump air into her tyre. 'It's never going to work,' I heard her curse, as she whipped the useless pump in anger against her thigh. Nearby, a stranger fumbled for a cigarette in the pocket of his creased blue railway-issue shirt. He lit up and flicked the match onto the ground. Soon, his baggy red running-suit bottoms and checked slippers appeared between the wheel spokes. I straightened up from my crouch to meet him.

'Give it to me,' he mumbled, pinching the cigarette tightly into the corner of his mouth. His eyebrows were so heavy he could hardly carry them.

'It's broken,' I offered. 'We need a foot pump...'

'Please, I try.' He took the pump and screwed it awkwardly onto the valve. The last of the air hissed out. He scratched his head and took another puff of his cigarette before beginning his attack again. After a while he raised himself up. 'This...' he shook his head at the pump, '...no good.' Talk about stating the frigging obvious.

With this he twisted his cigarette butt beneath his boot and set off across the square. I watched him go, his slippers padding along on the concrete and the hem of his shirt flapping behind him. He approached a taxi driver standing beside his vehicle with his elbow resting on its roof. A few words were exchanged, then both Ivan and the driver braced themselves against a door frame. Together they pushed the taxi up over the kerb and onto the paving stones of the square itself, rolling it slowly towards us.

'Why didn't he just drive across to us?' I asked Ivan when at last the taxi was parked at our feet.

'Petrol...' he replied breathlessly, before lighting up another cigarette. 'Petrol is very expensive.'

The ritual of meeting and greeting started again. We told them our plans and they whistled appreciatively, discussed the merits of our bikes and offered to buy them. In turn, I underestimated their worth. They sucked in their breath. A pat on the shoulder. It is time for a vodka. But this time there is none to be had. Curses.

A foot pump was extracted from the boot instead, and a shoe rested on the foot grip. Within seconds the inner tube was straining at its rubber sheath, and when he was quite content the cabby jammed his shoulder into the door frame and with hearty refusals of help pushed off across the square again.

I felt deeply indebted. Not once had someone refused to assist us. Nobody had been in too much of a hurry. Perhaps it is simply an expression of that universal desire to help the traveller, to step out of the routine for a moment and join us on our journey. Or that feeling we sometimes have when we encounter someone who is obviously different: a foreigner perhaps, whom we make a special effort to befriend, not because we want them as an accessory to show off to our friends—or through some feeling of guilt we might have buried deep inside us as we rail against the injustices of others—but simply because they are a stranger, and we are curious and protective in the same measure. But it was more, even, than that. We were experiencing a culture focused on community, something we in the West have largely traded-in for a big screen TV, or a gun, or a harsh word to defend ourselves with in our isolation. It saddened me to think that way, but there was nothing I could do but go back to my own country and make a special effort to open my own home.

Ivan smiled broadly. 'Good. Now can you buy me a beer at the kiosk?'

'But it's very early,' I replied, tapping the face of my watch.

'Of course. But it is night time for me. I will have a beer then go home to sleep.'

Ivan was a night porter on the train line between the Belarus border and Simferopol, but he lived here in Khmelnitsky. On board he collected passenger tickets, handed out sheets and blankets, made tea, and spent the long dark nights helping passengers on and off at stations he had never seen beyond.

'I live there, with my mother and father and my grand-mother,' he said, pointing towards a four-storey block shouldering its way over the tarred roof of the nearby kiosk. 'She is eighty-five. Did I ask you for a beer? Sorry. I need some sleep.' He led us over to the kiosk and, foaming beer in his hand, plonked himself down in a plastic chair. 'Your bicycle. Tell me how much it cost again?'

'Two-hundred-and-fifty American dollars.'

'Oh,' he exclaimed, slapping his hands to his forehead. 'I must work for more than six months for money like that.' He leant towards me, and all of a sudden a sorrowful expression engulfed his face. 'I want to come with you. Take me with you. I want to travel,' he pleaded, before breaking off to gulp at his beer and gasp for air. 'Men...are bad. Women...here...are bad.' Scorching tears welled up in his eyes as he reached over to put his hand on my arm. 'Listen...' he wiped his eyes with his sleeve. 'I come on your bike. Now. I sit on the back.'

And as he spoke his eyes glazed over and I was suddenly wrapped up in his years of being in the same spot, on a carriage forever moving while he is going nowhere, from which the platforms come and go and all he can do is imagine what's out there, behind the façade of the railway buildings. And I am flying with him now across the expanse of Steppe. It is dark out there, with smoke peeling from a thousand cottage fireplaces, with the candle light buttering up the windows, and the train whistle screeching in the wilds, spooking the horses caught in the steady moonlight. Then, as suddenly as we were away, we rush back again—like the wind—and I hear his voice clearer than any other.

'Just once. I want to leave a place and never come back.'

I was powerless to help him, of course, and in the end he was as resigned to his staying as we were to our moving on. 'Look…things will get better,' I heard myself blather out as I rose from my chair. 'I promise you. Maybe in ten years or so you'll be like us.'

He said nothing, but smiled wryly and held out his hand, gripping mine firmly. Then he jolted into an overtired laugh. Like many Russians he was violent, but fleeting, in his emotions. 'I'm tired,' he repeated, wiping his brow. 'I have not eaten. Do you know varenyky? Where else can you find such wonderful food?'

'Nowhere else,' I said.

'Yes. Nowhere else. We have the best food. That is one thing.'

I took one last glance at Bogdan on his plinth before we cycled away, and wondered for a moment how he will fare in place of Lenin. Then I watched as Ivan loped home to his tiny apartment, where a plate of last night's dinner sat drying on the table, and where his bed was fresh from the smell of his mother.

* * *

The trees evaporated like puddles in the sun. Rohan was flaked out beside me; the remains of lunch, plastic plates, knives and forks, the pans, the packets and the burner were scattered in the grass. The air held its breath. A tremendous explosion, deafeningly loud, low-pitched and tailed by a horrendous rumbling, ripped through the summer heat. At once we were both on our feet and the sky was alive with birds and my heart was thumping wildly in my chest. Somewhere to the north of us was the town of Neteshin, the home of the Khmelnitsky nuclear power plant. To the north of that was Rovno Nuclear Power Station. I tried not to think of the possibilities, but I couldn't help it. It was like a fever. I ran out onto the road and looked up. The sky was a vivid blue. There was not a cloud in sight.

'What do you think it was?' Rohan shouted, panic in her voice. 'It's a power station, isn't it?'

I didn't answer, but paced back nervously to our belongings and quickly turned on the radio. I didn't know what I expected to hear: a siren perhaps, a warning voice telling us to run. Later, I would mull over my feelings incessantly: so soon after the explosion it would be madness to believe there would be a report on the radio. But how long would I have had to wait before I knew enough to save myself, my partner and my unborn child? Days? Weeks? Years?

Come on! Come on! Where is it? Why isn't there anything? Work, damn it… All I got was static where the stations should have been. My body was charged with fear, my mind as sharp as a sliver of glass. It had to be a power plant. There was no other explanation. The sky was clear, there was no traffic and all around us nothing but fields. Any moment we would feel the shock wave. We would die here beside the road, or end up in a pitiful line of refugees winding our way through the countryside…

'It could have been a truck,' Rohan said quickly.

'It was too loud for a truck.'

'Mining perhaps?'

'There are no mines marked on the map.'

A BBC World Service announcer broke through the crackle on the radio at last. I heard the word 'Russia', before Rohan snatched it up and placed it to her ear.

'What did he say?' I asked frantically, my hands grasping for an invisible volume knob in front of me. It was after an age that she turned to face me, my startled eyes reflected in hers like a rabbit on the road.

'He said… '

'What?'

'…there's been…'

'WHAT?'

'A devaluation.'

'What?'

'A devaluation in the Russian rouble.'

'Ah.'

It was then that the wind hit us, a violent gust that whipped up the trees to a ferment, sending a flurry of yellow leaves around us like a snowstorm and me yelping and running onto the road again. A large mass as black as caviar, billowing like squid ink, was rushing through the sky towards us. Another explosion ripped through the air, followed a heart-beat later by a vicious slice of lightning. Rain began pummelling the road.

'It's a storm!' I shouted. 'A bloody storm.'

I ran to my bicycle, relief flooding through me, wrenching at my raincoat, while Rohan burst out in nervous laughter. By the side of the road not far ahead was a white concrete bus shelter. We would be better off seeing the storm out there instead of here in the open. We repacked hurriedly and spun out onto the road, with the cloud almost on us and the rain chewing up the bitumen ahead. I pushed off then stopped dead, grasped my knees against my front wheel, pulling the handlebars back in line with the frame from where my sudden turn had dislodged them. I pedalled off again as fast as I could, hitting the rain head-on moments before I reached the bus shelter. Rohan swung in on my tail. The road puckered maddeningly behind us, the gale lashing the rain horizontally. I plonked myself down on a slatted bench and Rohan's hand reached out for mine.

Our fear about a nuclear explosion was not just paranoia. Khmelnitsky Power Station was a disaster. By the time the first reactor came on-line in August 1988, 500 specialists had been sacked, accused of mismanagement and embezzlement. Even the deputy chief of the plant's construction department had been charged with stealing materials. A lack of both spare parts and funds has meant repairs rather than replacement of faulty or old equipment is common. More worrying still, three more reactors are due to come on-line.

Not much further north, in the small town of Kuznetovsk, was Rovno Nuclear Power Station. Many of the engineers who built Chernobyl were transferred there, after most of them were ordered to dry out in the Russian equivalent of the Betty Ford Clinic. In the first five years of operation alone, there had been 117 potentially dangerous incidents at Rovno, including two considered serious on the International Nuclear Event Scale. Control rods, which are supposed to stop the nuclear reaction, often become stuck in the reactor's core. Hydrogen leaks and short circuits which can lead to fires are also common. The situation got so bad that the Russians finally insisted on installing computers to aid plant operations, the first time they had been used at a nuclear power plant in the former Soviet Union. But the scariest thing of all is that no nuclear power plant in Ukraine, or elsewhere in the former Soviet Union for that matter, has an adequate containment shield to prevent irradiated material escaping should a major accident occur. My shivering wasn't entirely to do with my rain-soaked clothes.

By now, the earth was beaten to soup, and the air sticky with a heady odour of grass, and dust turned to mud. Thunder cracked deafeningly, vibrating through my body and shuddering the thick walls of the bus shelter, until I began to fear that after escaping a nuclear blast we were going to be buried in rubble.

SCREEEAACCHH!!! THUD! A white Lada skidded through the mud at us and slammed into the kerb. A door opened and a woman emerged. She began frantically pulling at a knotted rope, which held in place several large, sodden card-board boxes on the roof. A box in her arms, she scurried towards our shelter, then dropped her cargo on the bench beside us before retracing her steps. We followed her into the deluge, helping her ferry the boxes in one by one and piling them up to the bus shelter roof. At last, when all were inside, she peeled away a corner of a soggy parcel, checking the contents.

'What a storm!' Vera puffed. 'I thought it was the power station.'

'So did we!' we both exclaimed together.

'Lucky for us it wasn't.' I heard myself laughing almost hysterically.

'What's inside the boxes?' Rohan asked, more calmly than I thought she was.

'Cigarettes. I'm taking them across the border into Belarus. They are Ukrainian cigarettes. They cost more in Belarus than here.' She would mark them up, sell them to her contacts and return home to Khmelnitsky.

'Do you make much money from them?'

'Enough to eat and buy clothes. But I could make more if I didn't have to pay the border guards.'

There were worse things smuggled over the borders. Nuclear material was slipping across into western Europe in the briefcases and cars of former KGB officers, mafia and international racketeers. Strontium-90 from Russia has been found in a Frankfurt railway station locker; weapons-grade uranium has been seized by police in Munich; scores of suitcases containing miniature fully functioning nuclear devices unaccounted for…

As quickly as it had come the rain abated, leaving the road steaming. I helped Vera load the boxes back onto the roof, while Rohan checked for rain damage among the contents of our panniers. When we had finished Vera wrote her address on a limp piece of paper.

'You must stay with me in my home, I insist,' she said and shook us both warmly by the hands. 'When you come back of course.'

If we were passing by again we would, I said. She looked into my eyes and handed me a packet of cigarettes for our troubles.

'Stay healthy,' she laughed and vanished into the distance, a spray of water fuzzing up behind her.

8 MISHA AND THE MAFIA

Ginger hair burst from Misha's overalls and eddied around his chest and arms. His feathery eyebrows looked like shaggy red caterpillars about to crawl across his brow and disappear behind his ears. He agitated the chickens around his feet as he straightened up, while in the pen beside him a large, muddy sow continued ducking in and out of a bucket of potato peelings as her piglets burgled between her trotters.

Taking our water bottles from our outstretched arms, Misha strode towards a hand pump. He unscrewed the bottle tops carefully and plunged each container in turn into a chipped enamel tub already filled with water. When they had finished blubbering he waded towards us again and handed them back, nodding towards our bicycles.

'Polish?' Anything with plastic reflectors and a shiny bell had to be from across the border.

A woman dressed in a flowery dress and a stained apron emerged from the shack to inspect what the road had blown in. Her thick dark hair was piled in a bun, a crooked elbow supported a clinging young boy. She grinned when she saw us, her cheeks plumping out, her eyes narrowing to almonds. 'Borsch,' she insisted. 'Misha bring out the table and get them a drink.'

We propped our bicycles against the fence and were ushered through the gate with the sweep of a scrubby arm. By the time we had removed our helmets and gloves a small wooden table and chairs were set out in the yard. Misha plonked down a large jar of fruit juice and three glasses.

'You must have some apple juice. We make it here. The best apple juice in the Ukraine,' he said warmly, pouring the cloudy liquid into a glass and pushing it towards me. I took a sip. My mouth lit up. I took a gulp and another, my thirst carrying me on to the dregs.

'Good?' Misha asked, and filled my glass again.

'Beautiful. The best apple juice.'

'I told you so. They are from my trees.'

We had seen some of them flanking the dirt track we had cycled up from the main road. Soon after we had come to a halt beside a startling sculpture of a nun supporting a dying man around the chest. Beside the couple were three mons-trous cuboid heads carved from huge slabs of stone. It seemed such a formidable monument for such a tranquil place.

'It's about the men,' Misha explained. 'They took all of them over 16. Forty-two men. All those in my family killed except my father. He was too young. They are evil people, all of them, brutal, like animals.'

'The Germans?'

'The Germans, no. Some of them are stupid people maybe, you know in Russian they are called nemets. It has two meanings, the first is Germans and the second stupid.' His chuckling sent his eyebrows into contortions. 'But most Germans are like us: workers. Workers are honest people, but they always let themselves get into trouble. Nazis are different. They said we were partisans with guns, but we were just peasants with a few cabbages.'

His wife appeared as if on cue with a plate loaded up with black bread and bowls of borsch beaded with grease. She placed them in front of us and gently stirred the murky water in each. I noticed small slivers of potato and greenery and specks of bacon as I took a taste from a metal soup-spoon.

'Beautiful,' I declared and took a mouthful of bread.

'Have more apple juice. I told you it was the best,' Misha retorted, watching us intently as we ate and drank, nodding encouragement. I protested gently as he tried to fill our bowls once more. He clucked sadly, shaking his head. 'Please,' he insisted. 'It's rare we have visitors.'

An old man had appeared at the fence. Misha greeted him

with a call for vodka. The old man scurried away, to return a while later with a bottle clasped between his fingers. Glasses were raised and chinked. 'Nostravia,' I toasted in Russian. Misha shook his head disapprovingly and announced the equivalent in Ukrainian. Our glasses clashed again.

Two more villagers, gaunt and dressed in sepia in my memory now, approached our little gathering with calloused hands reached out in greeting. More glasses were brought and more salutes made, and all except Rohan (who rolled a hand over her belly to emphasise her pregnancy) knocked the foul warm liquid back with barely a grimace.

The word that there were strangers in the village had spread rapidly. Yet another man arrived, carrying a sack-cloth bag. He opened it carefully with a gummy grin. I peered inside and saw a pile of fresh chicken eggs. He beckoned for me to take them.

'Thank you, but no, we can't. They will break,' I said tentatively as more vodka was dispensed.

The neighbour took a sad look at his offering and shuffled out of the yard. I realised I had probably offended him, but my attention was quickly drawn to the glass held up before my nose. We drank again to our health and toasted in turn Ukraine, America, Australia, England and France—allies in war.

By now a host of villagers had turned up, several carrying small sacks of potatoes, one with armfuls of onions, and another with a bag of walnuts. They placed their loads on the ground beside our bicycles and, after much ringing of our bells and debate about the gear systems and tyres, began to press their offerings into gaps in our panniers. Despite my remonstrations, when all the nooks and crannies were full they resorted to tying their sacks to the bicycle frames like Christmas stockings. We thanked them profusely, all the while wondering how on earth we would be able to ride with such weight, while also already planning the feasts we'd be having in the days ahead. It was then that I felt a tap on my shoulder. It was the egg-man again. He held out the sack. I took it from him—it felt warm. I placed my hand inside and grasped an egg in my fist. As incredible as it seems, he had actually taken them home and boiled them for us. They wouldn't break now, he spluttered through a toothless smile.

With those faces beaming openly around me I couldn't help but be struck by the thought of the brutality that had occurred here. How the hell could they have murdered people like this? These wonderful people—poor people—who were giving us the very food from their pots with such an unaffected generosity. It wouldn't have surprised me if they had greeted the invading Germans in the same way! All we had to give them in exchange for their hospitality was a few pens. Rohan handed some out to Misha's wife. She put them to her bosom. 'They would be good for the school,' she clucked.

It was explained that two hundred children from all over the area attended the village classrooms. Some walked for hours each day to get there, while others hitch-hiked.

'It is sad about the bad children,' Misha announced. He absentmindedly tried to catch a fly with his hand. 'Chernobyl,' he hissed.

The very word sent a shudder down my spine. Like Bhopal, Hiroshima, and Auschwitz, this once innocuous name sounded desperately ugly. But I was confused. I was sure the fallout had not fallen around here. A map I had eventually acquired from an environmental organisation in Germany had shown an ugly stain where the main contamination had occurred. It had stopped more than 140 kilometres to the east. We had purposely skirted it, aware that on bicycles the risk would be too great.

'There are about twenty of them,' Misha continued and he made out the Mongol features of a Down's Syndrome child. Those around us nodded, their babble now silenced. 'Before, children like that were rare, maybe one, maybe none.'

If what he said were true then 10 per cent of the area's children had been genetically affected by Chernobyl. It also meant that our empty bowls and glasses had more than likely contained contaminated food and drink. I froze. As if to confirm my fears Misha pointed above my head to the overhanging branches of a cherry tree. 'You see the fruits?'

I looked carefully, and noticed odd clumps of small, mis-shapen green cherries among the leaves. For a moment Misha was silent, as if purposely building up the tension. 'This is the first time in more than ten years, since Chernobyl, that this tree has produced cherries,' he said at last.

I felt like vomiting.

★ ★ ★

We cycled out into the country again with the road swimming beneath me and the heavy pats of friendship still tingling on my back. My head was light with vodka, but even that couldn't stop me brooding. I could tell Rohan was shaken too. We pedalled hard and fast, as if every yard of road pushed the contamination a little further away from us. We hit a downward slope, the huge weights beneath us dragging us at speed. I kept my hands well away from the brakes for the very first time. I whipped around a bend, over-ran the central line and hit the flat again. Only after half-an-hour of heavy graft did my fear begin to seep away, leaving me with the first throbs of hangover.

By now it was late. Realising we couldn't cycle all night, we began to look for a camping spot away from the prying eyes of villagers and motorists. I scanned the fields on either side of the road for likely-looking clumps of trees. Finally, I spotted a cluster on the brow of a hill across a swampy pasture. A turn-off angled us onto a bridle path, where chalk plumed from beneath our tyres. We cycled past a pond surrounded with bull rushes and up a rise, ledged here and there with grassy patches and foresters' camp fires. At the top of the slope the path swung sharply and drew us over corrugated tractor tracks and into a shadowy hornbeam forest. Rohan thought it a spooky place.

'The trees are spaced a long way apart,' she noted nervously. 'Anyone could see us in there.'

'Anyone' meant the axeman. 'Maybe we should get as far

into the woods as we can and see how visible we are once we are in there,' I said.

Rather reluctantly, Rohan followed me down into a ditch of straggly grass and up a crumbling bank on the other side. We pushed our way in among the trees, the tyres crunching over fallen sticks and small branches. After a while, I turned to look towards the path. It had disappeared.

'This should do,' I said at last when we had come across a flat enough spot. I rested Muttley against a tree, but its heaviness carried it sprawling around the trunk, sliding with a twisted neck onto the mulchy floor.

Rohan looked around nervously. 'It really is spooky in here.'

'It's only a forest,' I reassured her. 'It's only in fairy tales that the big bad wolf gets you.' I began clearing away the larger sticks from our camp spot. Suddenly, I saw something move among the fallen leaves in front of me.

'What's wrong?' Rohan whispered hoarsely.

'The ground just moved,' I gulped.

'What?'

It happened again. This time patches of leaves seemed to move all around us. 'What ...?' I fell to the ground and buried my hand into the damp leaves and felt something cold and deathlike. I jerked back, with a toad squirming between my fingers. For a second or two a pair of yellow slanted eyes caught my own, before a kick of its powerful legs sent it flying at my face and thudding into my nose. The monster tumbled to the ground again, sending my heart racing and the whole floor shuffling. I jumped back and shook my head. There were toads and frogs everywhere—climbing over our luggage, burrowing head-first into the leaf litter and hopping ungraciously this way and that. Rohan began to giggle.

'Well, I guess this proves it's a healthy forest,' I said, though I was still unsure.

We prodded away as many animals as we could and raked up the leaves around us to flush out more. We erected the tent together and while Rohan zipped up the sleeping bags inside I walked off in the direction of the path, the moss softening the crack of twigs beneath my boots. After a while I turned around. There was no sign of the tent; the trees had broken it up like tiger stripes. I drank in the cool, earthy dampness of the evening air. For a moment I was truly a speck upon the earth, in some forest in Ukraine where no-one I knew could even imagine. I closed my eyes and listened.

There is quietness. A thick, dense swaddling silence. Like snow. It crosses my mind that I am probably standing in the very same place as a peasant now dead for hundreds of years had done. We meditate on the silence together. I open my eyes. An owl flutters in the dark foliage above. Dusk has fallen and I slap the side of my face, starting myself. I slap again, conscious then that I am being repeatedly bitten. I start running, stumbling through the brindled greyness towards the direction of the tent, to find Rohan struggling desperately to get our things inside and squealing something about mosquitoes: millions of them.

★ ★ ★

Morning broke with the BBC World Service. The last of Ukraine's 1600 strategic nuclear warheads had been removed to Russia, it was announced. The world's third biggest nuclear power had voluntarily disarmed itself. Unfortunately, some warheads had gone missing.

Raindrops pattered on the tent's flysheet. I turned off the radio with the end of the news, and yawned. We had both slept badly. Renegade mosquitoes had harried us throughout the night and frogs had headbutted the tent with irregular, disquieting thuds. We were both glad to wait out the downpour in the comfort of our sleeping bags.

It was early afternoon by the time we crawled out. It was bleak and chilly. I laid out two plastic bags for seats while Rohan boiled up some tea. We ate the last of our muesli from Germany, sprinkled with the end of our dried milk. When we had finished we piled our gifts from the previous day at the base of a tree trunk. We strapped on our panniers and bags, pulled on our gloves and helmets and gave our bicycles the once over. Finally, we had to face the dilemma of what to do with all that food. It was obvious we couldn't take it with us, it was far too heavy. And we couldn't take the risk of eating it. Even if the reports were right and 90 per cent of the radiation from Chernobyl had leached into the ground, that was exactly where potatoes and onions came from. Chickens were habitual muck scrapers and walnut trees drew their nutrients from below the surface too.

'We could give them to someone or cycle for a while and leave them beside the road for someone to claim,' I suggested.

'But it would be pretty bad if the villagers found out about it,' Rohan concluded. I certainly didn't want to offend them. No, there was only one option. We left out the eggs for the pine martens and planted the walnuts, potatoes and onions and willed them to grow. Even so, as we walked away from our offerings I felt a wave of shame as I remembered their faces as they packed us up with all they had.

✶ ✶ ✶

The hills gave way to flatter lands where a fearsome heat melted the road to chewing gum. We progressed with an audible slush, leaving tyre tracks behind and picking up tar which clogged up our wheels and brake pads like black treacle as we went. There were few trees, just occasional skeletons buckling under enormous crows' nests. Despite the conditions we dared not stop, even for rests, for when we did a swarm of tiny flies would dive upon us, some trying to hold us down with their pincers, while others would aim for our eyes, or fly up our noses to lay their eggs.

As I cycled I read the map. It gave us a choice. We could continue on this yellow link road or take a white secondary one. A junction appeared ahead of us.

'Which way?' Rohan called from behind.

I decided on the yellow road. We cycled wearily onwards, the kilometres slowly ticking away. Then, more than an hour after I had made my decision, the road disintegrated into ruts and white dust. It was my turn to find the going hard.

My water was nearly finished and I had resorted to wetting my lips with a drop now and then to stop them cracking. I fell behind. Finally I called out to stop.

We sat scrunched up in silence in a freckle of shade under the only tree for kilometres. I poured the remnants of my water into a pot, added some pasta and watched it come slowly to the boil. I was desperately tired.

'I think we must be on the wrong road,' I said quietly at last.

'What do you mean?' Rohan snapped.

'What I said.'

'You mean you've taken us the wrong way.'

'Well, I was following the map...'

Silence. The anger grew inside of me. 'Look. I've been guiding us since the start. I haven't made a mistake yet.' More silence. This time calculated for full effect. 'Apologise!' The demand escaped from between clenched teeth.

'Why? You'd blame me if I'd made the mistake!' she bawled back.

I stood up, a feverish rage boiling inside of me and I did the only thing I could think of doing—I slammed my boot into the primus, sending pasta marinara flying across the road. Rohan glared at me.

'You stupid idiot,' she yelled and wrenched herself from the ground and stormed off towards her bike. 'I'm going!'

'Where?'

'To Poland!'

'Well, I'm going back to the junction to take the other road.'

'It's 15 kilometres away, idiot.'

'Don't call me an idiot!'

'Why? What are you going to do. Kick *me*?'

I gathered up the cooking equipment, wiping pasta off with clumps of grass, and replaced it piece by piece in my panniers. By the time I had finished Rohan was already far ahead.

'I'll see you back in Berlin, stupid,' I yelled, and swung my bike around.

'Don't bet on it,' the reply floated back.

I set off, retracing my route, full of self-righteousness. How dare she criticise my map reading. It was a simple mistake, that was all. She would have messed it up long ago. I looked in my mirror. Rohan had disappeared. I cycled on further, then stopped, dismounted and lay Muttley down on the road. I would wait here until she cycled back to apologise. The minutes passed. There was still no sign of her. Another minute. I pulled Muttley up and mounted again. I couldn't just let her cycle off alone. 'Damn it!' I took off after her as quickly as I could, resting my weight on the pedals rather than on the seat to soften the jolts.

I passed the place where we had split up. A gluttonous mess of pasta was being set on by ants. I suppressed a bubble of guilt ruthlessly. Finally, I saw her up ahead on a bitumen road. I couldn't believe it. It was the right one after all. I bumped over the border between dust and smooth tar and set off after her at an exhaustive sprint. I finally caught up and pulled into line behind. We were both too stubborn to back down.

We hit a village just up the road, still in silence. My mouth was bone dry. At the first house Rohan dismounted and collected up our water bottles.

'Here, take the map too,' I said, handing it over. 'From now on you are in charge.'

'OK,' she said simply, and tucked it under her arm and set off down a dirt path towards a shack. She was back in an instant, clutching the water bottles and map to her chest. Behind her bundled a turkey—an ugly brute, black and mean, ogling furiously, flapping its wings and fanning out its tail, while its long, red wattle writhed like an epileptic worm from the tip of its beak. An old woman cackled. The turkey stopped and glared menacingly through beady eyes. Rohan looked at me, and I at her. We both burst into laughter.

✳ ✳ ✳

The following day we reached the town of Kremenets. At the bottom of a hill we pulled into a garage forecourt. The two petrol pumps stood idle, but the one for water had a small queue in front of it. I stood in line to fill our bottles. Rohan found a couple of loaves of bread in a nearby store.

We continued on into the town, past a few well-constructed brick houses and a domed Jesuit cathedral, cut in slices, as all photogenic Ukrainian buildings are, by telephone cables.

If there was ever a cursed land it was here. In Kremenets itself, the Nazis had killed around 300 people and burned their homes to the ground. Around 35 kilometres to our north was Dubno, where hundreds of Jews were clubbed to death; and between Kremenets and Rovno, some 70 kilometres to the north, were German prisoner-of-war camps where as many as 80,000 Russians died of starvation—an amount easily overlooked when compared to the other three million Soviet POWs who never made it home. But I was curious that day not for that war, but for another—for Kremenets was home to the Cossack cemetery. Prickling the top of a hill, and glaring white and lichen-spotted in the bright morning sun, were a hundred knee-high crosses. Walking between them we tried to pick out the fading inscriptions, but neither of us understood ancient Slavonic. Beneath each memorial was the body of a Cossack horse-man, killed while forcing back the Poles in Khmelnitsky's war of 1646. I was in a maudlin mood as I sat there in the grass, amid the wildflowers, and looked across the mass of graves and over the ridge towards a monastery bulging from another hilltop. I wondered, as I often do when I see the graves or signs of the dead: was it really worth dying for? With each person's death potential children were never born. It was the biggest price to pay for the generations that were never given a chance to live...

✳ ✳ ✳

The last city in Ukraine refused to get any nearer. The sign to Kovil taunted us with another 20 kilometres, but the next, 10 kilometres further on, told us we had another 20 to go. I had heard it was meant to confuse invaders, but in reality it had come about through inefficiency. It went something like this:

two men set out from two major cities, each with a measuring wheel. They moved towards each other gradually, stopping here and there for a chat, a rest break and perhaps a tot or two of vodka. As each kilometre passed they would erect a marker post—some of which would later be turned into signs. When the two measure-men met up half way they added up the kilometres they had measured. If the figures didn't make sense they compromised. They never thought of the consequences for the poor cyclist. Whereas a car driver can shrug his shoulders at the discovery of 15 or 20 extra kilometres and just put his foot down, it can send a cyclist into tears.

We slogged up yet another hill, and rounded the remains of an abandoned mud-brick hut embellished with weeds, its door hanging off its hinges. The road deteriorated. Each revolution of the chain wheel brought knee tweaks and back throbs. There was a hole where my stomach should have been. Rohan looked pale and distressed. I began to despair of ever finding a suitable camp spot. A lack of trees was forcing us on, Kovil was getting closer, and so was late evening. I checked my odometer. We had been on the road for more than twelve hours and had covered 120 kilometres, mostly over hilly country. We desperately needed to stop this madness. My eyes flickered across our desolate surroundings. Far in the distance I could just make out a blob of greenery. We levered our feet back onto the pedals and pushed off. The ride seemed interminable, and when at last a stretch of shaggy pines gambolled up to our side, we swung weakly onto a dirt pathway, almost tumbled down a steep slope and emerged in an earth clearing like pilgrims reaching their chapel. My legs felt like butcher's meat, and I almost fell off my bike as I came to a halt. I tried to walk, but could only manage a waddle. My whole body was numb with fatigue.

It soon became obvious, though, that this was no place to set a tent. Detritus was everywhere. A broken toilet bowl gaped from the side of a bush, and someone had tossed away a soiled mattress, its coils pushing out its stuffing in clumps. Shredded plastic bags, empty cigarette packs and old food packets guided us towards a slippery quagmire where an awful stench drove us back again with our hands gripping our noses. We had stumbled on the city tip, and there was nothing much else to do but coax ourselves onwards towards its benefactor.

By the time we reached the outskirts of Kovil I was abandoning things by the roadside. The first to go was a collection of Chekhov's short stories, followed by a water bottle which had split so badly that it completely soaked my panniers when it was filled and left a line of drips like bread crumbs along the road.

Soon, the streets were full of sparklingly clean pedestrians with well-brushed hair and pressed clothes. They looked wide-eyed at the baggy-eyed, mournful cyclists who passed them slouching over their handlebars. We stopped a gleaming specimen for directions to a hotel. She shook her head and walked away without a word. We were luckier on our next attempt. A middle-aged man pointed on down the road. 'But hotels are expensive,' he said looking us up and down.

We pedalled wearily on, past well-presented office buildings, rows of stores and sturdy, nameless edifices for local officials. A signpost directed us to the hotel, a large concrete structure up a flight of shallow steps.

'I'll go,' Rohan volunteered.

It was for the best. Her Russian was now so good that she found little problem in simple conversations. Mine on the other hand was still restricted to a few badly pronounced phrases. We parked the bicycles against a concrete bollard and I sat down on a step to await news of her negotiations. Two young men in dark sunglasses and smart suits stood nearby, glancing occasionally across at me. A tramp stumbled up the steps, dressed in an old winter overcoat, stained army trousers and laceless brown shoes almost falling off his feet. Bloodshot eyes stared at me from between rat-tailed ginger hair and a matching beard.

'Gimme some money,' he grizzled, motioning to his mouth with a grubby hand. The stench of dirt and vodka was overpowering.

'I have no money,' I said truthfully. As Rohan had slipped into doing the shopping the same way I had done into the cooking, it was her that carried the kupons.

He came closer, his stench forcing my hands to turn out my pockets to show him I wasn't lying. But as it turned out I did have something—a brown note which I had no idea of the value of. I looked at it more carefully. It had the figure 2000 on one side. I decided to give it to him. We were on a tight budget, but as I couldn't remember how the money got in my pocket in the first place, then Rohan probably didn't know it existed. I handed it over. He grasped it in an unsteady hand, turned it around and inspected it more closely. It was a perfect opportunity to make a break. I walked across to the hotel's glass entrance door and stared inside.

Rohan was talking to a thick-set man in a suit. He flashed gold rings as he gesticulated. I opened the door and in a break in their conversation called out to her. 'What's he saying?'

'It's really expensive. They want to charge us foreigner price again.'

'Have you told him we are on bicycles?'

'He knows.'

The man beckoned me over. I turned around in time to spot the tramp coming towards me. I slipped inside and approached the desk. The man was demanding an enormous sum for the room. Rohan offered him a tenth of the price. He laughed, glinting gold incisors.

'It is impossible. You are foreigners. The management says no.'

'Are you the manager?' Rohan asked. The cashier behind him slowly shook her head in silent reply.

But in effect he was. He was a self-employed overlord. A peacemaker in a way. His business, with the help of his associates, was to make sure others like him didn't threaten to blow the place up and cut up its real owners—the faceless party apparatchiks. But despite his position, he obviously failed to intimidate the panhandler, who had now taken to waving the note I had given him in front of the overlord's face, mumbling in Ukrainian, with saliva spilling out the corners of his mouth. His victim growled dismissively and clicked his fingers, and a burly youth appeared to escort the unwanted guest back to the streets. The overlord turned to us again and huffed.

'OK. You can stay for your price.'

Rohan later informed me that I had handed the tramp the equivalent of less than one US cent. In turn the overlord had taken pity on us. We were obviously poorer than any Ukrainian he knew.

✷ ✷ ✷

Towards the border the road grew smoother, like a soft black sweater. Crisply-painted road markings appeared. Ukrainian Ladas, and others with the red-and-white number plates of Belarus, coasted along without the usual rattle. But it was all typical post-Soviet gloss. This road existed to show visitors they had entered Ukraine, the land of good roads, and to remind those leaving that the roads were worse on the other side.

An articulated truck was up ahead, pulling through a boom gate. When it passed us I saw it was German. It was soon followed by another. A British one, with a black driver bare and muscly to the waist. I waved furiously, elated that one of my countrymen was here in Ukraine. He was probably on his way to Kiev to dump his load of Mars bars and McVities biscuits. He waved back unsurely to the scruffy mad Russian, or German, or whatever he was, on the bike followed by, yep, a woman. Funny what you see on the road when you're far away from home.

I approached the border guards expecting trouble. There was a queue of cars waiting to go through. For a moment we hung back, unsure of what to do. I unclipped my helmet and strapped it to the handlebars. A guard spotted us and waved us forward and through a gap at the side of the lowered boom. He flicked through our passports until he found our visas. He pointed at the Belarus exit date. We had four days, he warned.

'Was that it?' Rohan whispered as we pedalled slowly towards another gate on the far side of a concrete pull-in area. Obviously it wasn't.

'Halt!' A customs' officer marched over. 'Where are you coming from and where are you going?'

'From Sevastopol to Murmansk.'

His grimace hung uncertainly for a second, then relaxed into a huge smile. He slapped me on the back and handed back our passports.

'No problem!' he declared in English.

And we were through.

9 COME HOME LITTLE RUSSIA

Three chalky-haired children met us over the border. Faded shorts and T-shirts half-cloaked their flimsy bodies and the remains of shoes gaped across their dirty feet. Accents rolled like the hills of Sweden as they strung our bells and knuckled excitedly on our helmets.

I was not expecting much from Belarus: the land of the white-haired Russians. The image in my mind of that country was of a bleak, washed-out flatness: an achromatic place dowsed in fallout. On the map it looked wet: frilly with swamps and marshes. As for the Belarussians, they reminded me of a friend from my schooldays who seemed to run from one disaster to another. Wherever she went she was hit with family crises, inadvertent deaths, muggings and illness—and she always managed to wind up in avalanches, earthquakes and revolutions. Like her, these people became known for their silent endurance. They certainly had had a lot of practice at it. For a thousand years these Slavic migrants into Baltic lands had found themselves caught in unceasing squabbles over territory, power and ideals. Crusading knights had clomped through in search of booty some 140 times in little more than a century, the Tartars 75 times in just a little less. A Russian invasion in 1664 destroyed all its libraries and most of its cities. Half the population perished. Thirty years later the Grand Duchy of Lithuania outlawed the language of the peasants in favour of gentile Polish, replacing the Latin alphabet with the Cyrillic into the bargain. By the end of the 18th century the Russians had reconquered and were busy destroying any sense of distinct nationality in its downtrodden minion. Then came

the First World War, and a fifth of Belarus' population suc-
cumbed, while hundreds of thousands more vanished in the
Revolution and the purges, when mushrooms fit for the table
flourished like never before on the pits of sand heaving with
the still-twitching bodies. The forests were soon alive again—
with hundreds of concentration camps, equipped with
mobile gas exterminators and open-air furnaces. In the part
of Belarus we were cycling through, the Nazis had erased 186
villages; flattened crops with specially designed rollers;
slaughtered livestock; demolished three-quarters of the
housing and sent a quarter of the population to their graves.

After the war, Belarus became a perfect example of a policy
aimed at making the Soviet states fully dependent on each
other. The country churned out massive amounts of synthetic
fibre, mineral fertilisers, plastics, car and truck tyres,
tractors, and electronics. It was the Soviet Union's most
important dairy farming and livestock producer, each year
fattening millions of cattle and pigs for export. In return it
received completed parts and raw materials from other
states—and power. Ninety per cent of its oil and 95 per cent
of its coal was imported. A quarter of its electricity came
from the nuclear power stations at Ignalina in Lithuania,
from another in Smolensk and from Chernobyl itself—the
plumes of radiation from the latter affecting Belarus more
heavily than anywhere else. Eighty per cent of the fallout
landed on its territory: approximately the equivalent of
ninety nuclear bombs of the size dropped on Hiroshima.
Forty per cent of the forests and one fifth of the country's
most productive agricultural land were badly contaminated.
Tens of thousands were to die as a direct result within a
decade. Thousands have been born with birth defects or
genetic mutations, and countless more have developed
serious illnesses and psychiatric problems.

There are no nuclear weapons remaining in Belarus. The
last of its eighty-one warheads were removed five months
after our visit. There are no nuclear power plants either. But,
incredibly—despite the damage and trauma caused by

Chernobyl; the collapse of heavy industry; the resulting fall in energy demand; the inefficient use of imported power and the practical alternatives available for power generation—the government, driven by an obsession for advanced technology, is committed to building at least one nuclear power station before the year 2010.

★ ★ ★

The bucket clanked violently downwards. I heard a dull splash. The young girl, the effects of Down's Syndrome frozen in the blank stare she held us in, pulled up the bucket again and filled our two bottles. When both were full she spotted something. She thrust her earth-blackened hand into the bucket and fished out a fist-sized lump of pig gristle, tossed aside from a previous dinner. We poured the water away around the corner, but for days whenever we drank we tasted grease on our lips.

The moon hid under blankets of cloud that night. Rain tapped at our tent inside a thicket of silver birch. The next morning was wet too. I only emerged once, following perhaps the first truly original sentence I have ever spoken: 'I want some sprats,' I announced, before delving into my panniers for the very last tin. Rohan meanwhile was intent on her fast, finding the thought of fish guts and brains too revolting to stomach.

The temperature plunged with the rain. We were damp and tired and the relentless days on the bikes were taking their toll. I snuggled deeper into my sleeping bag. Rohan slapped a mosquito off her arm. I fell asleep. It was past noon when I woke again, and rolled over into a puddle.

'I think we'll be in Vilnius in another five days,' Rohan announced, the map spread out roughly in front of her, the lands east of Moscow concertinaed over my prostrate body. 'If we actually get any cycling done, that is.'

The Baltic States meant civilisation. I couldn't wait. I nudged up closer to her, crunching up the thousands of kilometres in a crinkle of degree lines and time zones. 'Where are we now?' I asked sleepily.

She struggled noisily with the folds, tucking in the useless parts, and traced our route to the Arctic. The distance still to go was enormous. Despite what we'd already done, the journey ahead was so long it was difficult to fully contemplate.

'Maybe it's not worth pushing ourselves so hard,' I suggested casually, the image of a few days in a sleeping bag floating warmly through my mind.

'We should rest in Vilnius for a few days and see how we feel,' she replied.

It only occurred to me much later that a change had taken place. Rohan had become just as driven to complete the ride as I was; at times, like this one, with much greater enthusiasm.

The rain refused to ease. Our agitation increased with the hours. In the end we could wait no more and threw everything into our panniers, pulled down the tent and set off again with the wind on our tails towards a flyover bumbling with matchbox cars. It spat us into the city of Kobryn.

It was a city of prefabricated concrete blocks with a thorny hide of television aerials. It looked unfinished and patched, as if all the architects had been shot and the job left to the work experience kid. Paving stones glistened with broken glass. Hard-featured men lingered in clouds of cigarette smoke. Trousers were far too short, jackets too baggy or too tight. Jogging suit bottoms and sunglasses predominated. If we hadn't needed to stock up on food we would have passed right through. But Rohan had spotted a busy market place just off a side road. She led me towards a plank bench in an adjacent patch of grass, where tree stumps and rusting metal bars made up a playground. There were no children.

The main part of the market was contained in a shed, but was rimmed outside by rows of private stalls. I entered the main building and sidled past a row of four check-out women. Despite the obvious poverty outside, this was the largest state-run food hall I had seen so far, with chickens, dried fish, and hunks of fatty fresh meat. Frumpy women in shapeless skirts and coats too heavy for the weather shuffled around, deliberating over every rouble. Outside, a man had ten ripe tomatoes for sale, together with a few packets of Italian spaghetti. A woman from the country had jars of milk and another a tray of smoked fish half covered in newspaper to keep off the flies and the sun. Wiry hounds sniffed for scraps of food. One lay dead in a gutter, its entrails being tugged at by a crow.

Rohan returned with tomatoes, potatoes, chocolate bars, bread and onions.

'Guess what happened with the potatoes?' she prompted brightly.

'What?'

'Well, I asked for five and she thought I meant five kilos. When I explained I only wanted five potatoes, she shrugged her shoulders and handed them over to me and refused to take money.'

I shrugged my shoulders too. I was getting used to it.

★ ★ ★

A rutted mass of mud and dust dunes shlewed me sideways and jammed me to a halt up to my spokes. For more than five hours the miserable yellow sod had made my life hell—five hours and just 35 kilometres. According to that other scoundrel—the map—the ragged fringe of trees on our left was the far eastern edge of the great Belavezhskaya Nature Reserve, the largest ancient lowland forest in Europe. Somewhere within the impenetrable saplings were the remnants of herds of European bison. At one stage I even pointed one out, but it turned out to be just the buttocks of an elk. Like the Belarussians, the bison were used to hiding. Catherine the Great liked them smoked, delivered in boxes from the last Polish king. Trigger-happy Tsars took pot shots at them with hunting rifles, while Austrian Archduke Franz Ferdinand preferred a machine gun. They were finally wiped out with the help of Bavarian loggers, who spent the quiet times of the First World War obliterating bison and elk with heavy artillery. Having been reintroduced from fragmented groups in southern Poland and European zoos, the bison went on to find its unlikely saviour from the Blitzkrieg and the SS flame-throwers to be no less than Hermann Göring, who recognised them as the fabled animals of his Teutonic ancestry. Forty years of communism later they were well fed at least, with the tastiest grasses to be found along the 12 metre strip of cleared land that split the forest in half between Belarus and Poland.

The forest ended for us without a sniff of the brutes. The fields and swamps that headed in as replacements offered little more than side-swipes of wind. We tucked ourselves in and slogged against the pedals. The wind switched tactics, swinging around to batter us from the other side. Heavy clouds swaggered overhead. It was cold and it drizzled on purpose. But the village of Vjal seemed to charm even the elements.

Just past the duck pond the wind caught its breath and the rain dried up. Shacks appeared painted in fairground colours, some lengthened into barns crammed with winter firewood, and all angling themselves at 30° to the slick new bitumen road. Smoke from kitchen hearths wisped from chimney stacks and settled for a moment around lichened roofs. Play School windows bloomed with bright red geraniums, and gardens and alleyways waddled with ducks. Outside almost every gateway sat an old woman, watching the world pass by. In the middle of the road we came across a turkey, standing its ground and scraping its outstretched wings aggressively against the oily gravel. I swung around it, half expecting the beast to start chasing me through the village, snapping at my wheels. Instead it simply turned its blubbery head and stared after me furiously. I stopped and pulled out my camera from my handlebar bag. As I wound on the film I saw the face of a woman in a window. Our eyes met. Flustered, I didn't even take a turkey shot, and took off again with Rohan close on my tail. Later, I would remember that woman in the window and would wonder why I had been so bashful. I find that often when I travel I just carry on when I really should have stopped. It would have been best to stare at this stranger's face, to look her over and inspect the textile of her clothes, to walk into her house, to pat her dog. But instead, as she looked at me, I just lowered my gaze, and moved on, past her chickens pecking at weeds in the dust, and out of a world I could have shared for a while. And I tell myself I will be braver next time; but for now it's too late, the moment is lost and my memory of her is doomed to fade away into nothing, when it could have been so much more intense.

The bitumen ran out with the last of the houses. Down the track we stopped a woman in a red head-scarf and rubber boots for more water. She pointed towards a well. A chain was wound round a wooden haft. We were to do it ourselves. Taking a handle each we unhitched the bucket from its nail and it tumbled down the hole. With a fearful jerk the handle was ripped from our fingers and Rohan was almost pulled in head first, only saving herself with a wild, last-second grab at my arm. The handle whipped around as the bucket plummeted downwards with a series of crashes and a rattling of chain. With a final clatter and a splash it hit the water. Shaken, Rohan left it up to me to pull it up and fill the bottles.

We picked up speed as the sun came out, and flashed along with only the heavy blue trucks of communal farms, loaded up with shivering pigs, for company. We propelled our way past tractors and their crews at work in the fields, a horse pulling a till, and a man sweeping the verge with his scythe. The Polish border was a hair's breadth away, and we both felt safer knowing it. It felt like the doorstop to the comforts of home.

We rested in a field of tiny purple pansies at lunchtime and soon became the centre of attention for a group of peasants under a nearby tree, who interspersed their stares and whispers with bites from hunks of bread and swigs from a vodka bottle. Others followed our progress as we rode onwards, and I wondered what they were thinking as they watched us go, with me feeling like I was at the centre of the universe, while all around me were just fleeting moments, come and gone again forever.

Later, we chewed on bars of chocolate in a clearing of straggly heather, as forty Russian soldiers met their deaths trying to storm a rebel base in Chechnya.

★ ★ ★

A line of cherooted factories huffed smoke down in the valley, where the once-Polish city of Grodno cowered like a concrete white rabbit. On the lookout for a hotel, I pulled over at a roundabout to ask directions from four middle-aged men in cheap polyester shirts. One, with lanky black hair, offered me a cigarette. I accepted it to be polite. He cupped a flame between worker's hands.

'You look for hotel?' he drawled thickly. 'Where you from? Warsaw?'

They listened to our improbable story, shook their heads in unison and launched into animated conversation. Lanky hair offered to take us back to his place where we could make a phone call to a hotel somewhere. But he suddenly remembered he had an appointment with his children. It was the only day of the week that his ex-wife allowed him. He wrote directions on the back of a cigarette packet instead and we headed off to the Hotel Belarussia.

We skirted the city on a road fogged with traffic. Three kilometres passed on my odometer, followed by two more, yet the turning we wanted refused to appear. Finally I pulled over, convinced we were lost. Then a horn sounded behind us. At first I ignored it, but then it parped again and an orange car drew up beside us. The driver wound down the window and stuck out his head. I recognised the hair. He had left his friends, picked up his kids and had come after us to make sure we'd find our way.

'Follow me,' he called out. 'I'll take you there.'

The road narrowed and swept to the right. We pedalled harder trying to keep up, missing as many pot holes as we could, crunching through others. A patient queue of cars waddled behind us, but our guide refused to let them pass. After ten minutes of catch-up he stopped. A hotel sign hung from a wall with its letters rubbing off. With a wave of his hand and a cheery smile our guide took off in a cloud of acrid black exhaust.

The cavernous hotel lobby was suspiciously lined with painted women in mini-skirts and pancake make-up. There were no rooms, we were told, though there were lots of keys hanging up behind the desk. I pointed at them. Shoulders shrugged. Rohan took out her purse. The wobble of a head showed a free room was remembered. We could have it, but only if we changed dollars into roubles with her. She had kids to feed after all. Did we think she was sitting behind this desk for the fun of it? She checked the lobby, before pulling out a tin crammed with notes. We reluctantly agreed to hand over some dollars in exchange. She gave us a bad rate, but we expected little better.

★ ★ ★

A contrived referendum had replaced Belarus' victory banner—a bandage with a stripe of blood across its centre which represented a medieval battle against German knights—with the old flag of the Byelorussian Soviet Socialist Republic. Gone with it too was the traditional symbol of Belarus, the Pahonia—a medieval knight on horseback representing a mixture of St George (the Greek-Byzantine sufferer and conqueror and the patron of farming), and the pagan god Iaryla (who symbolised life over death). The Nazi regime had allowed their usage during the occupation. They were re-adopted after independence from Russia. Now they had been condemned by the former collective farm director and virtual dictator, President Aleksandre Lukashenko. The link to Nazi sympathisers and collaborators was too hard to swallow. Lukashenko wanted union with Russia and a recreation of the Soviet Union. Above all else he wanted to be the leader of a Union of Slavic Republics. He had re-established strict ideological censorship. Newspaper bank accounts had been frozen, independent radio stations closed, journalists routinely beaten, opponents tortured and jailed. Belarussian was abandoned and Russian became the official state language, yet again.

Nikolai, the hotel doorman, was in his early twenties. To my eye, his youthful exuberance and flashy waistcoat were sure signs of a budding capitalist. But in Belarus, with its massive unemployment and malnutrition, it became obvious that having a job was a sure sign you showed unquestionable allegiance to the President.

'I am a child of the Great October Socialist Revolution,' he professed grandly when I asked him what he thought about recent street demonstrations in the capital, Minsk. 'Lukashenko must crush the dissidents. We must become closer again with Russia. We must work. We must build. We want peace and friendship with the West. We need peace. But NATO wants to destroy Belarus. We are encircled by enemies.' Any country that was once part of the Soviet Union and which joined NATO was making a grave mistake, he said. Had I seen the celebration in Lenin Square that afternoon? We had arrived too late, I told him.'There were people from all over the Soviet Union, from Uzbekistan, from Siberia, from Korea. It was a cultural procession. You see, we are together. We are strong.' His outstretched hand grabbed the Baltic States, Poland, Bulgaria and all the rest and he crushed them in his fist. 'We are ready,' he said before politely asking for a foreign coin to add to his collection.

'But what about me?' I asked. 'I'm from the west. Looking at me now, would you be happy to kill me?'

He brushed his hands down the front of his waistcoat and thought for a second.

'Tourists,' he affirmed finally, 'are good for business.' He had jumped into an ideological bunker. I knew there would be no point in trying to prise him out. It was easier just to ask for the address of a good restaurant. 'There is one in the hotel, but the food is bad,' he warned, before pointing across the square. Over there was a better bet.

It was dusk and raining. Pedestrians scurried towards the overhangs of the vodka booths. Pigeons cuddled up limply in the eaves. We pelted across the square and dribbled into the restaurant. There were few customers and only one waitress.

She was dressed in a tight black skirt and frilly white top. A stage had been set for the band. My spirits dropped. I had learnt to expect the worst from places that looked like they offered the best.

'Please. Can I help you?' the waitress asked optimistically.

'What do you have?'

'Potatoes.'

'Potatoes?'

'Da.'

'Do you have a salad?'

'Yes. Meat salad.'

'Can you take the meat off?'

'Nyet. It is not possible.'

'OK. We'll have two of those, and we'll take the meat off ourselves.'

'But then there will be nothing left.'

'Bring whatever you have,' Rohan said solemnly in her perfect tourist-phrasebook Russian.

It was a draining wait for a minute-flat meal of mashed potato and a piece of sturgeon, wrapped in a macintosh of gristle. We both struggled to skewer a piece on a fork. It tasted like rubber and, as an afterthought, gave off a faint whiff of silage. The waitress fixed her eyes on the remains as she returned to take away our plates. She shrugged. For our part, it was a relief to get rid of them.

We sat in silence, storing away vodka in sips, the way we both preferred. The waitress intercepted us just as we were about to leave. She had a tot more of vodka for each of us. A gentleman, sitting at the table behind, had bought them for us, she motioned. She had never seem him before, but it was not her job to refuse to offer drinks to foreigners, especially when the man had been so insistent.

I turned around. The door out the back was still slightly swinging to show where he had just left. Rohan asked what he had looked like. A big man, she said. With a Moscow accent. She'd spotted a tattoo on his arm. An anchor. She wouldn't be surprised if he was a sailor, though it was strange to see one so far from the sea. Still, these were strange times.

Outside, the rain had calmed to a drizzle and the sky bulged uneasily with the weight of the clouds. The kiosks were closed and the crowd which had been milling about beneath their eaves had gone. I lit up a cigarette. A car swung around a curve. Its headlamps picked out a large, warty cone the colour of marzipan on a scuffed patch of grass. As we got nearer we saw it was held together with unfeasibly large rivets, like a festive orange punctured with cloves. It was a Sputnik. It had been to space and ended up in Grodno—a town where they could barely assemble a Russian salad. It wasn't comical, it was a national scandal.

★ ★ ★

We nudged closer to the border next morning, past cows in fields of puffy dandelions and storks sitting atop telegraph poles on bundles of chicks. We had been in Belarus for just four days, and whereas Ukraine had stamped a memory of golden hues in our minds, Belarus and its constant rain would leave behind an Irish green.

Just short of the checkpoint we ate breakfast wrapped up in our waterproof ponchos on a carpet of strawberry flowers. Behind us, lily of the valley, like miniature china milk jugs, salted the bases of tall Scotch pines. On the other side of the border, I couldn't believe my eyes. The sideburns and sequins were unmistakable. Elvis, in white satin suit and a thin red tie, was behind the wheel of a Lithuanian-registered Skoda.

10 THE RENEGADE

The old woman thrust her trowel into her allotment, scraping metal on rock as she twisted it deeper. The Russians could get their own water.

'Oo vas yest vadar?' Rohan bleated for a second time. But the language of the invader could expect no favours. 'How am I supposed to know what's Lithuanian for water?' Rohan skulked as we closed in on a thick-set form purging specks of soil from her forehead with a rag. From behind double-glazed windows two young children eyed us inquisitively. The scene reminded me of hobby farmers in suburbia. Their attitude made me feel like a beggar.

We tramped towards the next in a row of pan-faced brick houses. Another woman eyed us suspiciously from above a spade.

'Vadar?' Rohan tried again. 'Ya nyet Ruski!' But even the news that we weren't Russian failed to raise an interest; the woman simply took our water bottles grudgingly and slouched through a doorway.

'Why's she taking so long?' I whispered after a while. 'Why did she go inside?'

'I don't know. Maybe the well is behind the house and she's gone out through a back door.' It didn't strike us until later that she had filled our bottles from an indoor tap...in a real kitchen. We were suffering from culture shock.

The roads didn't make things easier. Ludicrously smooth things, they were folded down the middle with crisp white paint and ironed on either side by Mercedes, Opels and BMWs. I half expected to be ambushed by a gang of road workers around every corner, laughing hysterically at their own joke, a track full of potholes behind them. Signs threw me too. For weeks I had been stuttering over Cyrillic. Now I found myself translating the letters of the Roman alphabet into their Russian equivalent like a travelling dyslexic.

★ ★ ★

Slugs veined our tent that night as we camped in a double-breasted forest: a sacred, pagan place, where priests once felled holy oak trees with holy axes and kept them alight for eternity. In this sparsely populated region, forests were castles. Within them, tribal Balts wrung beer from wild hops and lubricated the dark ages with mead from their honey. They wove mats, dishes, shoes and shelters from the trees, swigged birch and lime sap from stag horns and lit lamps with the resin from pines. Food was mushrooms, game and berries, while bear, elk, lynx, beaver, sable and mink were plundered of their skins to be exchanged for iron and salt from abroad.

Old Lithuania had extended from the Black Sea to the Baltic, but it was politically, culturally and linguistically marginalised—a wart on the Polish backside. In 1795, it was cauterised by the Russians.

But history means little to a traveller in the rain. Tyres tacked to the road surface and high winds billowed us back into the lower gears. Cars hugged the road, edging past closer than we were used too. The downpour that had brought us sopping from Belarus intensified.

A hard hour later a slither of trees appeared on the horizon. I squeezed out the last of my energy to make it there. It could be good cover for lunch. Reaching the first of the trees I stumbled down into a ditch and up again into the clotted interior of dripping firs. I removed a branch from between Muttley's spokes. My breath steamed. Heavy drops landed on my head and ran down my legs in rivulets. It was wetter in here than outside.

'There's a shelter just off to the right,' Rohan shouted from the road.

I trudged out of the trees, mounted up again and followed

her finger to a wooden umbrella in a pull-in. I mopped my fringe from my eyes with a glove and bumbled onwards. Once there the bikes were left to slither down our legs and onto the ground, and stringy messes of hair were pushed back into plastic hoods.

'Do you think you could get a fire going?' Rohan pleaded.

I mustered my strength and began searching through my panniers. We had used the last of the fire-lighter cubes we had picked up by chance in a village shop the day before. Our bread was sprayed with mud and had disintegrated into soggy clumps. We had a small packet of dehydrated rice and the last tin of sprats. Vilnius, and with it a good meal and dry clothes, was more than 50 kilometres away.

I dug a small pit with a screwdriver to shelter the flames from the wind, while Rohan searched for twigs. Pages torn from Gogol's *Diary of a Madman* made perfect tinder, and seemed apt. But the wood was wet, and the best I could get out of it was a trail of smoke.

Meanwhile, Rohan had poured the rice and its sachet of curry flavouring into cold water and put it aside hoping it would soften. After an hour I gave up with the fire. Rohan refused to touch the sprats—while I merely refused to look them in the eye. Eventually, weary, hungry and cold, we took off again with bulges of crunchy rice in our cheeks.

✸ ✸ ✸

Vilnius was like an old boot, entrenching its heel in the hill named after its founder, Lithuanian grand duke Gediminas, who had followed a dream to build a city as powerful as 'the howl of a hundred wolves'. In recent times, though, the citizens of Vilnius had been living more like sheep, fattened up on Slavic dumplings and beetroot soup. In the end they couldn't stomach it any longer. They realised the essence of power was either a bigger weapon or a state of mind. They took the power into their own hands. Even the communists couldn't annihilate a whole country.

The determination to rid the city of its inheritance was frantic. Property was privatised almost immediately. Catholics reclaimed the Soviet museums of atheism and scientific thought for places of worship. State-owned canteens, where you could only get a meal if you had connections to get past the doorman, metamorphosed into slick restaurants serving international cuisine. Paint was splashed around. Roubles were exchanged. Lenins were hidden away. The Russians were gradually being ushered out.

Rohan loved it. For the first time in weeks she felt truly safe. Like always in our travels, we headed for the old part of town, with the crooked streets on the map. Once out of our cycling gear and with our bikes locked away in a cheap hotel room, we took to the open and were immediately hit by the lack of second glances we received. We wallowed in our anonymity, more buoyant than we'd been for days, and wandered like ghosts through medieval streets dangling with trolley buses and flanked by portly residences, Baroque churches melting like chocolate, stucco apostles and crumbling Jewish ghettos.

Half the residents of Vilnius used to be Jews. The SS, under Karl Jäger, had done away with virtually all of them. After his eventual arrest at the end of the war, Jäger stated: 'I was always a person with a heightened sense of duty...' But for me, one story seemed to personalise the gratuitous slaughter more than those which tripped on their numbers like shoelaces. It involved a Lithuanian, a young man, who rolled up his sleeves and set to work on a line of communists. One after another he calmly beat his victims over the head with a crowbar, while women and children clapped in appreciation of the show. After he had killed fifty people he put his crowbar aside, picked up an accordion and stood on the corpses and played the Lithuanian national anthem. It was a grim fact which made me second guess the intentions of any Lithuanian I shook hands with.

★ ★ ★

We had lunch in a pizza restaurant with money gleaned from the country's first automatic teller. Through the window women bulged out of stylish dresses, their amber jewellery like drops of lager against their creamy skin. Tall, Viking males traversed the cobbled city unladen with the polyester and shapeless cotton we'd become used to. They were obviously different people to any we had seen before. Adoption couldn't wipe that out. I was amazed that anyone had fooled themselves into thinking it might.

On Gedimino Prospectus we found a café and celebrated my birthday with a dinner of pan-fried salmon steaks and chips, apple pie and dark Lithuanian beer. We wanted to gorge, to re-fuel for a few days, while we applied for a visa for Russia. At the end of the meal we left the waitress a small tip.

'But you have paid me too much,' she cried with a look of concern.

'It's a tip.'

'For what?'

'For your good service.'

'Oh,' she said, still unsure. Things never used to be like this.

Over Lithuanian potato dumplings the following day we met Ausra, a journalism student. She wanted to practise her English. She ordered a coffee, which she didn't drink, her gold-banded fingers playing with the cup handle as she talked instead.

'I would have sat over there,' she said, motioning to a large table occupied by two heavily-built men chatting animatedly in hushed voices. 'They have spare chairs, but...' she lowered her voice to a whisper, 'it's a mafia table.'

I thought of the beatings I'd heard about in Odessa and the stand-over tactics in Belarussian hotels.

'Foreigners have a bad impression of us,' she responded bleakly to our silence. 'Let us not talk about the bad impressions.' She smoothed her smart suit trousers with her gaunt, white fingers. 'You see, a lot of Lithuanians went abroad after independence. They stole things, they cheated, they saw a better level of living. Now foreigners don't trust Lithuanians. But that point of view is changing. I will not talk about the mafia.'

But however much she tried to avoid it the subject refused to lie down. We talked about living standards, how nobody wanted the public servants who worked under the Soviet system any more, about the Ukrainians and Belarussians who sold oil and butter in the markets from their suitcases, and the threat of another Russian invasion. But each topic tailed off with the men in running shoes and jogging suits.

'The government has lost its strength to fight. How can you fight yourself?' she announced, finally giving in. 'There are too many connections. The police don't have any strength any more. There was a special group formed to fight the mafia after independence, but in reality it's already been destroyed and the heads of the group have lost their jobs. It was arranged. It is finished. Now the mafia are fighting among themselves. Vilnius gangs against Kaunus gangs. There are a lot of mysterious things. The government is too corrupt to catch the big power on the street.'

She pulled out an old copy of the *Baltic Times*, written in English, from her black leather bag and flicked to an article. 'On May 15, border police at the Dieveniskes border crossing near Belarus stopped a bus, en route from Romania, that was allegedly attempting to smuggle over three tonnes of wine and cognac,' she read. 'But you see, they didn't have the right connections. Only journalists have the power to talk about it, even though they are afraid.'

As for the Russians, she refused to believe the threats from the extremists, like the Russian presidential candidate Vladimir Zhirinovsky, who warned he would 'liquidate' the Baltic peoples by lining up radioactive material along the borders and wafting it across with great fans. They no longer had the power to invade, she concluded. The mafia had too much to lose. They would stop any attempt to damage their business interests.

Later, she took us to a cycle shop where we finally found a new pump to replace our faulty one. It was a weight off my mind, but I still couldn't help thinking it might be the end of an era; flat tyres were a great entrée into a culture.

The next morning we cycled to the Russian embassy. A huddle of Lithuanians waited outside the gates.

'Tourist?' a guard asked.

'Yes,' I replied through the bars.

We jumped the queue. Within ten minutes we had our visas, for a fraction of the cost we'd have had to pay in Berlin, and without the obligation of stating where we would be spending each night. We picked up a bottle of vodka on the way back to our room to celebrate. We were going to Russia.

That evening we met Ausra again at a bar near the university, where instead of babushkas with hair on their chins we were served by trendy young Balts. We were uncool: we drank beers instead of cocktails. But at least, like almost everyone else under those disco lights, we spoke English. That represented progress, perhaps more than anything.

As I watched Ausra sipping at her daiquiri I couldn't help but marvel at the pace of change. It seemed unbelievable that just five years before this place was as undeveloped as Belarus or Ukraine. I felt a twinge of excitement. There was a virginal feeling to this city which was intoxicating. It had never been so alive, so forward looking. The destruction of the ghettos, the wars—they were things of the past. The young people were looking at now, and the future.

'Young people are getting more and more possibilities to work at their lives, to create something,' Ausra said between nibbles at a strawberry from the bottom of her glass. 'There are a lot of possibilities. I am part of the middle generation. I have got a Soviet view and the new way of thinking too. In Soviet times you couldn't act the way you wanted, there were always certain frameworks. I don't think it was that cruel, not like everyone was getting strangled if they didn't have the right opinion, but they wouldn't let us ask questions about what was outside.'

She replaced her glass on the bar. I asked her if she knew anything about Ignalina, the nuclear power station somewhere to the north.

'I think everyone is used to it,' she said dismissively. 'It was built in the Soviet time and people didn't know what danger was waiting for them. Our people thought it was OK. We would get a lot of power, lots of electricity...' she pumped her fist forcefully in emphasis. 'Now all the newspapers and the TV are talking about it, but the people are still not scared— you can be used to it, anything can happen...' She trailed off. 'I don't know. I'm not afraid of it too much. Do you want another drink?'

'Vodka,' I said, just for the hell of it.

★ ★ ★

A hideously-faced water beetle hauled itself out of a pond and onto a stump of reed. It tore at its dry outer skin, letting it fall like an autumn leaf into the water beneath. Around it the fields rippled with the purple berries of deadly nightshade. Ignalina got closer. I was determined to get a closer look.

We passed Ilgis Lake. In its place, legend has it, there once stood a small castle, in which a happy young couple, Ignas and Alina, once lived. Why the gods got angry with them has been forgotten with time, but we know the castle vanished into thin air and in its place the lake appeared. When people began to settle in the surrounding forest they named the settlement Ignalina—'the town of Ignas and Alina'. I hoped under my breath that the gods would see fit to keep their tempers.

We rode into town towards two sooty chimneys and a set of locked gates with an illegible sign scrawled on a plank of wood barring our entrance.

'Do you think this is it?' Rohan asked unsurely. We spotted a woman in a raincoat struggling homewards to a tatty three-storey block with a rusting car battery.

'Excuse me,' I asked. 'G'dye atomic energy station.'

She looked at me blankly.

'Atomic, um, nuclear. Ignalina.'

Nothing. Rohan flicked open her front handlebar bag and pulled out a pen and paper. The woman watched her intently as she drew an atomic energy sign.

'G'dye atomic energy. Ignalina?'

'Ignalinos Atomine Elektrine?'

'Da, da.'

Her face creased into a smile. Over there, she gestured with upward swings of her head. Northwards. A long way. Fifty kilometres! It had never once crossed my mind that Ignalina power station would be anywhere else but in Ignalina. There was little else to do but head back to the lake and camp.

I made a big fire that night, to keep away the wolves which howled in the forest. After dinner I brought out the map again.

'It's only about 20 kilometres out of our way,' I said quietly.

'What? Twenty there and 20 back—that's half a day. What do you think you're going to see? They're not going to let you in. You're just going to see a couple of chimneys.'

'Well, you don't have to come,' I said, avoiding her eyes.

'I still have to wait for you.'

I shrugged my shoulders, again.

'What's your fascination with nuclear power stations anyway? It's like some sort of obsession. Can't you just enjoy the ride?'

It wasn't as if I hadn't questioned my motives myself. When I'd first come across that sweep of power stations in the atlas all those months ago in Berlin, I'd seen them as little more than convenient markers along an interesting route from south to north. But along the way they had taken on a far deeper significance. In my mind they had become like Trojan horses. The upshot was, those who had opened the gates still refused to recognise them as such. I knew I could do little to warn them of their likely fate, but with the morbid voyeurism which turns some people to watching motor racing on the off-chance of seeing a fatal crash, I simply wanted to see what was likely to do them all in for myself.

✻ ✻ ✻

It was the children which really disturbed me. On the long approach road to the reactors they cycled around us on tiny bicycles in their dozens. Research carried out around French nuclear power stations has shown leukemia is more common among young children there than in other areas; while genetic mutations as gruesome as Cyclops Syndrome, where children are born with only one eye, have occured around British reactors. I had no reason to suspect Ignalina was any different.

'How could they be so stupid?' Rohan said angrily. 'If I had children I would be as far away from here as possible.' The irony of her own situation escaped neither of us, and we rode on in silence.

A while later we passed two old fire engines and a rescue van garaged in a concrete bunker. Two modern buses crammed with workers slipped past us on our left. The men inside looked tired and unshaven and as dark as coal miners. A little further on, enormous silver water pipes sprang up from a ditch and began tagging along beside us, until a junction of pylons cleared a swath of trees on either side of the road. 'IGNALINOS ATOMINE ELEKTRINE', a sign read at a turn off. I gulped and turned my handlebars warily in the direction it was pointing.

I remember the tick of our wheels and the purr of our tyres. The twittering of bird song. The sun, warm on my scalp and baking through the blackness of my jeans. Then a moment later two huge sets of three white-and-red chimneys, bent over and tied at their necks, burst around a curve in the road, plummeting downwards to a seventies-style brick and glass building. There were no guards or checkpoints, despite threats from mobsters and extortionists to bomb it, and at least 270 kilograms of uranium and strontium having somehow found its way into the hands of the local mafia.

We cycled to the front door. A rusting entry gate to a reactor was chained shut with metal poles and barbed wire. A wood pigeon cooed. The air hummed gently. We both snuck out our cameras like spies, took a snap each and fumbled them back into our bags again. Then Rohan took another with me striking a pose. It was all so surreal. 'This is me, on a hugely-laden bicycle outside one of the most dangerous nuclear power stations in the world.'

Ignalina's two oversized Chernobyl-type reactors produce around 80 per cent of Lithuania's electricity. As usual, corruption, theft and drunkenness contributed to its poor construction. It was also built between two moving tectonic plates (the area experienced an earthquake in the 1920s). Swedish experts have found hundreds of serious faults and were described after a visit as being 'in a state of mild shock'. Reactor number one will probably be shut down no later than 2004, and reactor number two before 2010. There are plans to build a new reactor, along Western lines, in their place.

I shook my head as Rohan clicked off another, then turned it sideways to give her my best Napoleon. Suddenly, I noticed a figure behind the glass pointing at us.

'Let's get out of here,' I said quickly.

Rohan stuffed her camera away. We cycled back the way we had come as casually as we could manage. At the sign post that had led us in, we met a woman cycling towards the station with her eight-year-old daughter standing on the back rack, her hands wrapped for safety around her mother's neck. She was a Belarussian from Gomel—a town so saturated in radiation from Chernobyl it has earned the nickname 'nuclear city'. The family had come here three years before. They lived in the nearby workers' town of Visiginas; her husband was a well-paid engineer at the plant. She liked it here, she told me. They lived comfortably. Everything was written in Russian. It didn't feel like she was in Lithuania at all. And her child? She didn't worry. Why should she? The plant took precautions.

We sped away quickly, each kilometre bringing with it a growing relief. Beside the road we passed many houses, separated from each other as in the earliest of times: a dog bark and a shout away. It was practical. If their neighbour's house burnt down, then theirs would be saved from the flames, but they were near enough too to lend a hand if catastrophe struck. That was the theory anyway.

11 A DIFFERENT REALITY

The Daugava slipped westwards through Latvia towards the Baltic Sea, with me on its bank lying on my stomach in the grass, refreshed from splashing its cool, tea-stained water onto my arms and face. Occasionally, a fish would jump and my eyes would dart to the ripples already sluggishly elongating as they were caught in the river's flow. Half submerged in the muddy edges, fresh water mussels siphoned the current. The sun back-lit the hairs on a cow's ears as the animal waded through flank-high grass swinging dandelion fairies loose with its pendulous udders. A horse brayed, then clumped into sight, flaying its nostrils and kicking up dust from a drover's path as it lumbered in front of a heavy oak cart, pilloried by a large wooden yoke.

'This is what it's all about,' Rohan's voice said from behind me. It was the best part of the day: when we had time to be still. And we never felt closer. 'What were you thinking of?' she asked.

'How it used to be...before the roads came to our countries. When all you had was your cow and your chickens and you worked in the fields. I've been thinking, about those chickens...'

'You don't like eggs.'

'That's not the point. I'd learn to like them.'

'And you never want to stay in one place for longer than a year.'

'I know. But I wish... '

'Can you drink this water, do you think?'

'It looks clean enough and there seems to be plenty of life in it,' I said.

She knelt down, dipped her hand in and brought it cupped to her mouth. 'It tastes sweet.'

I followed her lead and leant forward to take a long draught. Later I read in the Western press that the rivers of the former Soviet Union were some of the most badly polluted in the world, but most we came across were alive like none I had seen in the West. And where else would you see so many flowers in the fields and hear birdsong as we did? Certainly not in the lands of its critics, where everything was doused with chemicals, and which were now even intent on genetically manipulating their crops—so they could spray even more, and kill off the insects and flowers they call weeds, and contaminate both the waterways and us for the sake of the worst perversion of the capitalist world: a quick profit at any expense.

Rohan is whistling now, quietly content in hanging out her washing on the tops of bushes. And I am lying again beside the water, with the sun beside me, slowly sinking into a bath of its own peach and strawberry hues. It comes to me that I have taken the time to lie in the grass a scant few times in my life. I must make the most of it. The next thing I knew, years would have passed and the grass would have withered and died and been covered by snow, and the seasons would pass once more, and again, and the time I am here would seem as quick as a bird call. So I lay and listened to the plopping of the fish and the far-off braying of a donkey somewhere and my girlfriend's whistle and the clatter of pans as she kicks them by accident with her pathetically-torn road shoes, and above it all I smell life. I smell baked earth and cooling grass, and the chocolate-minty smell of the river. Life is a process of dying and renewing yourself, and there are certain circumstances that allow you to do that; and the best of them is travel. The journey is one of those frequent opportunities in life to take stock and to renew. Remove yourself from your normal occupations and you are free of them; you can shed your old skin and become anyone you want to be. You can try on a different personality. No-one will ever see you've changed, except when you come back, of course. It's like falling in love, when your personality thaws a little, and allows for a little change in shape, before it refreezes again.

But you can't change, of course, without reflection. The real traveller is active, not passive. He moves about but actively reflects on life and what is happening to him and lives each moment as it arrives. So many tourists go away and let new experiences wash over them like plankton in the sea, without grasping them and allowing their imagination to flower—you can travel down to the end of your street, and experience it differently every time, as long as you are aware, and have new eyes to see. And you must be there, in the present, like the Buddhists who close their eyes and walk all day barefoot on the warm ground just to feel it under their feet and know they are alive.

✳ ✳ ✳

Daugavpils was a drab, Soviet creation: a Russian outpost—10 per cent Latvian. It had once supplied the whole of the Soviet Union with bicycle chains.

We had lunch at a local gostinitsa—a simple establishment serving grilled pike and a mush of carrots and peas. The meal was smaller than I was used to cooking up myself, so I ordered the same again.

'You know how to eat,' someone said from behind me.

I turned around. A fat man in his fifties was mulling over an empty glass. His head was bald and looked like someone had taken a chisel to it. His eyelids sagged. A finger of cigarette ash tensed for a moment, before collapsing onto his knee. A half-smile curled across his lips as he heaved himself out of his chair and stuck out a podgy hand. Janis was an immigration officer, though being his day off he'd left his uniform at home. He asked if we had a hotel, then offered us a place to stay. Just down the street. His mother would like it.

We left our bikes chained to a drainpipe in the backyard and followed him through into a fusty stairwell, our panniers slung over our shoulders. His mother, a horse-toothed woman, was gnawing at a husk of bread in the living room while tufts of spiky hair on her chin dabbed up the crumbs. Swabs of green eye shadow exaggerated her pale eyes, and cut half way up her forehead were two thin painted arches in place of eyebrows. She showed no sign of welcome. Janis didn't even explain who we were.

I looked around, feeling uneasy, like Hansel surveying the witch's oven. The flat was cramped with heavy, gingerbread furniture, difficult to squeeze between and lit by only a single low-watt bulb. I sat down in a moulting armchair. Cats slunk in the shadows.

'We can play chess,' Janis suggested, producing a battered box and a cardboard chessboard. Red-and-white pieces clattered onto a short, chunky table. He arranged them on their squares in a flurry of hands. When he had finished he flumped himself into an armchair opposite me. He always played red. A good defence was preferable to a misjudged attack.

I stroked my chin thoughtfully. Janis drummed his fingers. I moved a pawn. He countered in a flash. More moves followed in quick succession, before two missing bishops, replaced with vodka bottle tops, came smashing through my stoic front line.

'Check mate.' I hadn't even seen his mouth move.

I sat back. His mother, who had been watching the game intently, muttered to herself and turned towards a pot steaming in the corner of the room on a small blackened range, her thighs congealing like curds through the holes in the backs of her stockings.

Dinner came quickly—a gristly meat stroganoff. I picked out the few greying pieces of flesh and joined Rohan in secretly feeding the cats under the table, while our hosts sat handcuffed to a Russian soap opera on the television. When we had finished, I remembered the remains of the bottle of vodka I had been carrying with me since Vilnius. I untucked it from my panniers and offered it around. Rohan's refusal caused Janis to groan under his breath.

'She's a strange one,' the old woman grumbled in turn and bumbled off in search of three glasses.

They downed their vodkas. Quick and neat. Mine went down in stunted gulps. Janis licked his lips.

'Latvians are good at drinking,' he said. 'I have one friend who drinks for one week every month until he collapses. Most people drink. Not only the workers but the bosses drink. And they all drink together.'

He looked across at Rohan, who pretended she hadn't understood. Put out, Janis reached out for the bottle and emptied it into our glasses.

'But I am pleased you are not Russians,' he said at last. 'They have a superior image of themselves. One even asked me once why I spoke Latvian: "You are in Latvia you should be speaking Russian," he told me. Can you believe it?'

'You don't like Russians, then,' I ventured.

'Russians...' he waved a chubby hand dismissively. 'If something doesn't work, like a refrigerator or something, we just kick it and say: "Huh. It's Russian." Even their food is bad. Now we eat nothing that's Russian. Not even salt. It's grey, dirty.' A bottle of Stolichnaya appeared from nowhere. Russian booze was obviously exempt from slander.

'YAAAAAAHHH!' the old woman screeched, jabbing a bony finger at a Russian actress whose face was filling the television screen. 'Gypsy! You see? Dyed hair! And smoking a cigarette!'

'Excuse her. My mother really doesn't like the Russians. When we were children she didn't let us play with them. We kept to ourselves. They were all low-class people. Uneducated. You know, the Russians were farmers and manual workers. Just gypsies.'

He emptied another vodka, his jowls folding like a concertina. 'You know they killed one third of us?'

'Was anyone in your family killed?'

'My father.'

'Oh, I'm sorry.'

'You didn't do it.'

'I know but...'

'My father...he was in the Latvian Movement. He was 17. They came for him in the night and he went to Siberia. He came back. He had mental problems all his life. He threw himself off a building two years ago. Broke his legs. Died later.'

'That's terrible.'

'It was worse,' he shrugged. 'When the intellectuals were deported to Siberia, women and babies were thrown in the trains with them. When they arrived, weeks later with no food and water, they threw their dead babies at the Russian troops. How can you trust people like that? You know they even beat up their wives when they are drunk?'

My head began to doggy-paddle as the vodka seeped in.

'Do you think Latvia is better than America?' Janis asked me suddenly. Before I could answer he had moved on.

'A friend of mine went to Holland and Germany. They kept their old buildings in the air with...' he drew vague scaffolding in the air with two fingers on each fleshy hand, 'Here when buildings are old we build new ones.'

'Sometimes we like to keep the old ones,' I responded, thinking somehow I had lost my step in this conversation. He looked at me vaguely. 'And they had black sheep...and the cows didn't have horns...do you have sugar in America?'

'Of course the Americans have sugar,' I replied.

'No...No...' he said with conviction. He shook his head. 'You have sweetener pills. You do not have sugar.'

I found myself staring at him. The ludicrousness of his observations had surprised me, but his conviction that there could be nothing more than a pale imitation of Latvia outside its borders left me astounded. The problem was, I realised, that he had just as small an inkling of the West as I'd had of the former Soviet Union. We both believed we were free thinkers, but our ignorance of each other had festered.

☆ ☆ ☆

The nights grew shorter. By four in the morning it was light enough to read, and at ten-thirty at night I had to cover my eyes with my arm against the glare of the sun, still well above the horizon. It was difficult to sleep and we crawled north-westwards to the coast in a somnambulant trance, past beetroot-armed women milking cows by the side of the road. There was also more sinister activity. On several occasions we passed trios of Mercedes, doors open, thugs dangling out and looking suspiciously in our direction as we pedalled by. We always turned away, afraid of what might happen if they caught us staring.

One morning I remember wallowing in the shallows of a lake splattered with waterlilies and smelling of fish excrement and mud. I thumped my jeans on the rocks to beat out the dirt and, when I had finished, strapped them onto my pack to dry. Twenty kilometres later I pulled over. My jeans were dry and ready to wear.

'Can you keep an eye out for cars? I've run out of underwear,' I said, quickly removing my boots and shorts. I sat down on the grass verge, naked from the waist downwards apart from my socks. I pulled on my freshly laundered jeans. I felt a sting. It spread rapidly, across my backside and down my right leg. 'Ah...ahh! Ah...ah... ah...aaaHHH!!' I ripped the denim from around my buttocks and hopped around desperately beside the road.

'A car!' Rohan suddenly warned. But by then the pain was so excruciating it made no difference. Instead of covering up I tumbled backwards, the verge clumping against my head.

'Are you OK?'

'Help...' I pawed at my naked thighs as Rohan helped pull off my jeans and rolled me over.

'There are welts everywhere,' I heard her say through the roar of my pain and a truck groaning in my ears.

Out of slit eyes I saw an astonished truckie leaning out of the side window. His tail wind was miraculously cooling. Another passed, with the Latvian equivalent of a wolf whistle. 'Look!' Rohan held out her pinched fingers.

I strained to focus. Whatever it was had been removed from the base of my spine. I spied a pair of pincers and a balding red head as big as my eyeball. For a moment I had no idea what it could be.

'It's an ant,' Rohan prompted.

Of course. It shrank as my eyes adjusted. There were scores of them stuck to the lower part of my body like lobsters, she said. Later we found their nest—in the middle of a flattened, buttock-shaped, patch of grass.

✭ ✭ ✭

In a village outside Riga a skinny man with a whisper-thin moustache and a prominent Adam's apple beckoned us to stop and share some vodka. He was a Russian, but born in Latvia. His father was originally from Kislovodsk near the Chechnya border and his mother from the southern Ural Mountains on the border of Europe and Asia. They had met at university in St Petersburg while studying textiles. In 1952, Stalin's system ordered them to Riga. Production managers were needed for the new Soviet factories.

'Now all my relatives in Russia are dead,' he said as I swigged from his bottle, 'or they've been living here for so many years. I can't go and live there. Where would I live? I'm stateless. Even though I was born here, I am an illegal occupant. They want us all gone.'

Latvia had accused a third of the population—around 600 000 people—of being invaders. They could not vote, own property, join the police, a jury, become a state bureaucrat, a fireman, or hold tens of other positions.

'Even if I go to jail I can not be eligible for parole. Can you believe that?'

'I guess they might be a little annoyed that so many of them were killed in the gulags,' I suggested.

'It wasn't Russia's fault. My grandfather died fighting in Latvia. He was a Russian soldier in the Civil War, the Finnish War and the Second World War. His brothers died in the gulag. My mother-in-law's two brothers died in Siberian gulags. They were Ukrainians, not Latvians. The system killed them, not Russia. The Baltic countries were unfortunate. They had independence between the wars. They got a spirit of freedom and contact with their Western neighbours.'

To him it was an injustice that the Latvians blamed

innocent Russians for everything. They had even falsified history to make them out as evil. The latest version was that the Soviet Union invaded Latvia in June 1940.

'But there was no occupation, no struggle. The union was for mutual protection. Now Latvians are angry because their dreams haven't come true. They still have no video player, nor expensive clothes. They have to blame someone.'

He told us he had been brought up in a mixed nationality school where they took lessons in both Russian and Latvian until the age of 12. Then the nationalities went their separate ways. Even today, his English was better than his heavily accented Latvian. Still, he had many Latvian friends. They all shared one thing in common. Paranoia.

'The problem with Latvians is that they think they are so small that Russia is going to crush them. But that is not true.' He took another swig of vodka. 'You know, in some ways I miss the Soviet Union.'

I thought of Stalin, the KGB, the fact that even if you understood the meaning of 'nationalism' you could disappear, or at the very least be marked down as 'disloyal' on the secret lists. And then there were all those things which seemed more like parodies of themselves: the massive shortage of women's winter boots, costing a month's wages (the very rumour of which would result in day-long queues outside Moscow's stores); or the black-and-white televisions with screens so small that ingeniously thin cubes of glass had to be knocked up and filled with water to make a lens to magnify the picture, while strips of coloured plastic were stuck on the screen to give the illusion you were watching something in technicolour.

'You see, back then people believed in the future...in communism,' he continued. 'There was a target and when we got there everyone would get everything they needed.'

'But what about the gulags?'

'Only in the beginning. How else were we to go forward? With chains around our necks? I never went on any demonstrations. I never felt afraid. I felt free.'

I was beginning to feel as if we had read completely different versions of history—a kaleidoscope of fragmented images, superimposed and blotting each other out. He was 49—one of Stalin's. The cataracts had still not been removed. I tried once more, striking the economic nerve.

'But there were shortages,' I said.

His expression became more serious. 'Of course. There were the shortages. But on May Day, we would buy perhaps a little instant coffee, smoked sausage, some chicken and maybe some red caviar, never black caviar, that was absolutely for Communist Party people...but, no...(his brow furrowed as he tried to pick through the debris of the Soviet system)...perhaps, now that it has ended, I think it is for the better.'

I gleaned more. At 22 he had seen his first pineapple. Two years later he tasted his first banana, smuggled out of the fruit and vegetable storeroom his wife was managing. At 28 he was asked to join the Communist Party. He was driving an old state bus at the time. They offered him a new one and the lucrative monthly trip to Warsaw. He accepted. His passengers—'commercial' tourists—took things to sell: spoons, electric drills, chain saws, anything that was cheaper back home. They turned Polish zlotys into US dollars and at home again into roubles—for a massive profit. He made a killing on his excess diesel. The good old days.

Later on, we looked around his parents-in-law's small rented farm. Its rusticity reminded me of those we had seen in Ukraine.

'I suppose it's not possible to survive off just this,' I asked as I surveyed the smattering of chickens, a milking cow and calf, and plots of cabbage and onions. 'You still work?'

'No. There are no jobs for Russians now. We get by. We buy salt in Riga. Sometimes some fish. We sell a little milk.'

The conversation meandered on to his childhood as we stood watching the calf suckle.

'Were you afraid of us?' I asked hesitantly at last. 'You know, with all that nuclear stuff going on.'

He thought for a while. 'You would always open a newspaper and read: the Americans are going to use nuclear weapons against the Soviet Union. Why? Nobody asked. What about Canadians, Australians, Europeans? We never heard about them. But we weren't afraid. One sixth of the earth surface was covered in the Soviet Union. We had six million troops, commandos, KGB soldiers, people trained in special laboratories to use ESP on the battlefield to kill their enemy. We had three belts of nuclear weapons around Moscow alone, the first around the Moscow ring road to protect the city and the Kremlin, the second from Smolensk to the north and the third from Minsk to St Petersburg. How could I be frightened? I couldn't realise the Americans even existed. I had never seen any. We knew if the Americans started a war they would lose, like the Germans, like Bonaparte. That's how we thought. Everybody who attacked us always lost, from the Crusaders to the Nazis. There were so many of us...and anyway, because the people had nothing, how could we care if we lost it all anyway?'

'But we were scared in the West.'

'Of course you were. Your system hated us. Your propaganda protected your system. It was politically better for your governments to be scared of our bombs. Political games have nothing to do with the people.'

He drained the remains of his bottle and guided us back to the road.

'Enjoy your trip through Soviet Latvia,' he remarked as we saddled up. 'Latvia is not ready for independence. You will see people around here still have a Soviet mind. They let their leaders call themselves Nationalists, or whatever, when they behave like real communists. They drive Mercedes, eat bananas and enjoy going overseas.'

★ ★ ★

The Baltic was dank and weedy. We stopped at lunchtime, intending to cook a meal on a beach, but it glittered with broken glass and smelt of urine. We cycled on, finally finding another a few kilometres further north which was less fouled. Rohan dozed in the chilly breeze. I cooked and tried to detect the shores of Sweden on the horizon. My breath fell in with the suck and slide of the sea. I had an image of us as lice crawling slowly across a large leaf of drying kelp. I realised I missed the hitchhikers along the roads of Ukraine; the crowded bus stops; the women on their porches; the questions and answers; the constant requests to buy our bicycles...I sank into a mild depression. It was so far to go and when I returned home I would be broke again with a child on the way. Waves lapped half-heartedly in front of me. A seagull pattered around my boots, looking for scraps. The mood was still with me as we packed everything away and headed off into a growing wind.

The Via Baltica snaked northwards along the coast, whipped by the twisted saplings lurching in the swamps on either side. Our only companions were the deer that crackled around our tent deep in the forests at night, and which at first had forced me out of my sleeping bag, convinced our campfire had taken hold again and was burning through the undergrowth around us. On the road, the only contact we had was with each other—and with Death, who had begun to stalk us, sitting beside the driver in the truck that rushed up behind us, or in cars that refused to pull out to give us room. Rohan's feelings of foreboding were so strong that occasionally I would hear a swish of gravel behind me as she swung violently off the road to let a vehicle pass. Among these increasingly familiar surroundings—the cars, the reign of the individual, the affluence—the reality of the danger we had put ourselves in had begun to move in on me.

Later, just before the border, I lightened up. A row of hulking wind towers were cutting through the air and humming to themselves as they produced electricity. Like ambassadors from the king they offered up treaties, but I knew those vested interests concerned with the profits from coal, oil, gas and the nuclear would continue fighting, the blood and guts replaced with carbon dioxide and radiation. But while they swished, these giants offered up hope.

Denmark had been the only country to listen to their whispers, building fields of them out to sea, preparing to supply half the nation's power from wind within a couple of decades. That was progress. All the rest were as brutal as the clubs of cavemen.

12 BLACKHEADS ON THE BALTIC

The Via Baltica continued to sulk northwards at 90 kilometres a day. To cheer us up we sang old pop songs at the tops of our voices and, as you always do on a long journey far from home, chattered obsessively about the food we'd eat when it was all over. But the road ignored both our merriment and our cravings, and limped on like a mournful lover, quivering under the weight of the logging trucks.

Endless sea-level plains, the constant head-lamped beams of north road traffic and the hours of repetition eventually began fraying my nerves. I began questioning once again why I was putting us through all this. Once, laying on my stomach in our Berlin attic room with the map in front of me, I had swept my finger across the Baltic States in an instant. Now, as I elbowed my way through the wind on a machine which forced my muscles to clench and strain for hours on end, those instances had been devoured by the reality of the journey. I began to see that I had been blinded by my desire to reach Murmansk by bicycle. My push to achieve some-thing significant and to satisfy my cravings for experience meant I was not entirely enjoying getting there. Catching a train to Tallinn, and then having a couple of days rest to discover whether we wanted to continue or not, seemed better than the alternative of another two long days on the road. I broached the idea to Rohan as I studied the map during a morning break. It showed a railway track a few hours away.

'No-one would ever find out,' I said.

'We would know.'

'But there seems little point in just cycling for the sake of it if it's intolerable.'

'But we would know we had given up.' We sat in silence for a while, watching the cars jostling each other on the road. 'But if you can live with it, maybe we should catch a train,' she said eventually.

But strangely, once we'd swung around to the fact that the goal was not as important as the process of actually being on the trip, and the more assured I became that it was no longer even necessary for us to make it to Murmansk—I'd done enough to prove anything I had wanted to prove to myself—the gloom began to lift.

'Well…why don't we just struggle on to Tallinn and then maybe catch a train to St Petersburg from there,' I suggested.

'OK. I guess we should set off before it gets too late,' she said and kissed me lightly on the cheek.

We floundered onwards and I found myself, as I always do when I'm alone with my thoughts too long, in the grip of other women I have known. Emotions shallow-buried dug themselves up again. Stale indiscretions, betrayals—dreamed and real—washed up and were beached. Swirling, confused images welled up and fell away as I tried to piece together faces and keep them there just for a second. Regrets, dank and clammy, clawed at my bowels. I had to shake my head to scuttle them. Loves lost have the habit of clinging fast like frightened cats when you have too much time on your hands and have run out of other things to think about. To distract myself I tried to concentrate on my surroundings. I noticed the forest had begun to sweep back and forth, exposing glimpses of the Baltic Sea and the bogs and sandy fields of its coastline. The wind picked up. It occurred to me that I had seen no animals along the verges; fattening sheds and intensive farms had locked them away. Around here, thick stands of roadside grass went unscythed, while flashy lawn mowers proudly lined the courtyards of slick petrol stations imported piece-by-piece from Finland.

As the kilometres clicked up I began contemplating other figures, most notably those revolving around the concept of time. It was a short leap from there to working out the probability of my own existence. Bearing everything in mind— evolution, untimely death, and meeting and mating and so on and so forth, the fact that I was alive and cycling across the former Soviet Union was amazing in itself.

At a break stop I got out a piece of paper and pen. To put myself in some perspective I focused on a single period of history—1348, a year synonymous with the ravages of the 'Black Death'. The plague had wiped out a third of the population of Europe: in rough terms, each of my ancestors had had a one in three chance of dying from it. But how many ancestors of mine were around at that time? Given that I was born in 1965, and that each generation emerged after say 25 years, that meant there were roughly twenty-five generations between me and any ancestor alive at the time of the Black Death. I had two parents of course, and four grandparents, and eight great-grandparents and so on back through history...I scribbled away, adding up figures and doubling the result for every generation. I calculated that by the end of the Napoleonic Wars, in 1815, around 64 of my direct ancestors were of the youngest generation walking around; a hundred years before that there were 1024 of them; by the Great Fire of London in 1666 there were some 4100; and by the time the Spaniards were cutting off the heads of the natives in the West Indies in 1515 there were well over a quarter of a million.

I continued feverishly and by the time I had finished I was stunned. The figures showed that around the time of the Black Death well over thirty-three million of my direct ancestors had been born after their parents survived the plague, or had procreated before they were killed by it! The figure was flawed of course, a percentage of each generation would have been cousins who'd mated with each other—their parents were brothers or sisters who shared the same ancestors—but nevertheless, a huge number of them had to have survived the plague to eventually create me. Added to that, the odds of all their descendants surviving and meeting each other, until they passed on their genes to me, were fantastically remote. I was staggered—and even more so when I realised that if every one of those survivors had had more than one child which had gone on to procreate, and so on and so forth to the present date, in all likelihood I had hundreds of thousands of family members alive at this instant—and those were just the ones dating from the past 650 years or so.

My mind flew on. Surely, I thought, if all these people had gone on to do their duty and procreate, then who was I to stand up and say, 'Enough! I shall not have children.' It was the ultimate in selfishness. I owed it to my ancestors and future generations alike to have a child to carry on the genes which belonged to all of them. I looked at Rohan, and at her flat stomach where our baby was growing, and in awe I showed her the figures.

'Umm,' she said, 'I always knew I was taking a chance when I hitched up with you.'

★ ★ ★

We stopped later just outside the seaside resort of Parnu, amid the corpses of thousands of pine trees, their cut ends maturing from salmon to parchment. Heaped alongside them were stacks of silver birch glistening like fairground poles. In Soviet times these forests, which still cover around 40 per cent of the country, were harvested mainly for the local market. The rest of the Soviet Union had its own vast reserves. Now the West was plucking greedily at the vast Baltic woodlands.

Further on, the road chopped up and down like a rough sea. Factories clogged the air with smut and the traffic heaved in heavy black flakes of diesel. For five kilometres I could barely breathe. I couldn't believe that people actually lived here, but beside us monstrous Soviet-grey blocks were strung out between washing lines. One in the midst of construction, had already been graffitied with a swastika. Next to it was scrawled in English: 'Estonia, free country.'

I pedalled harder. My throat and eyes burnt and the clouds above us were stained like a smoker's teeth. A while later, with the suburbs behind us, we rested for a while, getting our breath back. After just fifteen minutes in that place I had developed a cough. It took most of the afternoon and a thunderous wind that hit us head on for my lungs to clear. In the end we barely covered another 15 kilometres despite two hours of hard cycling.

The following day conditions worsened still. The local farmers had cut down the trees to the very edge of the road, allowing the winds to bowl across the bare fields, forcing us to dismount and trudge for hours up a slope that seemed to go on forever, until, almost at the top, the road peeled off its outer layer in great clumps and began slinking around in an underwear of white rock and slag. Once over the crest we mounted up again and sped downwards, forcing a passage through the winds, the dust caking in scales to our skin. At the bottom was a village shop, just about to close for the evening. We pulled up and Rohan went off for a loaf of bread. It was more expensive than we had been used to and she was a small coin too short. The shopkeeper refused to sell it, agreeing only in the end to give us just over half. It made me angry, especially when I heard she'd added on a little for the trouble of cutting it. This would never have happened in the Ukraine, I thought, as we rode off angrily. We were too tired to make the last stretch to Tallinn and camped instead among torn out stumps in a pine forest ravaged by loggers.

✫ ✫ ✫

Tallinn's pigeons clattered around high-hipped terracotta roof tops above oaty façades and narrow windows. A stately, solid-thinking city, Tallinn spun tales as I watched. Medieval workshops, apothecaries and guildhalls shimmered like ghouls from the bones of fast-food cafés. Cartwheels creaked across the flag stones where trolley buses trundled. I heard a clink of armour and the rustle of skirts, the cries of porters and traders, the neighing of horses and the burbling of the crowd. For a brief moment I perceived the smell of damp hay wafting through my unopenable window, and freshly baked bread rolls in the shape of goat horns which had always welcomed the traveller returning home.

Danes and crusaders had squabbled over this outpost of trade. German craftsmen built on the lower slopes, beating a path for the Hanseatic League to trade with Muscovy beyond. Honey, resin and tar flooded out to sea with caskets of hemp, wax, leather, fur and fish bobbing behind. Scandinavians brought swan's down, blubber, whalebones and wool. Portuguese salt was exchanged for grain; and beer, herring and metal for silk, cotton and spices from the east. I even found lamp oil for our primus.

Later, in the Estonian Art Museum, I came across one of the most unusual consequences of Tallinn's good fortune. Hanging on the wall was an altarpiece brought to the city in 1495 and painted by an unknown artist from Bruges. Decorating the lower part of this series of panels were thirty young people, concentrating reverentially on their God. Each face was an individual portrait, the leadership of the Brotherhood of the Blackheads—an unlikely lot of merchants, goldsmiths, chemists, literary men and teachers whose patron saint was the Negro, Mauritius of Ethiopia. Their job was to defend the city from attack, but when they weren't checking the city's fortress walls, or riding into battle in the Livonian Wars, they did what they liked doing best— partying. They imbibed beer in huge quantities, from tall, thin goblets in the shape of deer's feet. The more they drank, of course, the more things got out of hand. Sporadic brawls were commonplace. Rules were needed. If one brother cursed another he was fined one mark—if he hit him in the face the fine was doubled, with another mark for each subsequent blow. If an inebriated brother brazenly chimed the chairman's bell, the fine was a pound of wax for the altar candles. A larger fine, of five marks, was imposed on any Blackhead who 'grabbed another member by the hair or flung beer in his face'. They were my kind of people.

But the Soviet Union had had no time for the descendants of such rebellious and independent middle men. When their turn came they either closed the shops or half-filled them with shoddiness. Factories were starved and offices emptied. Estonia slipped into obscurity until the year of the Singing Revolution. In 1988 a third of the population marched through the cobbled streets of Tallinn with the national anthem on their lips. Sensing trouble, the Estonian supreme soviet announced it would no longer accept orders from Moscow. Then, in one great human chain of hope and tears, some two million people held hands from Tallinn to Vilnius and chanted for freedom. In August 1991 the system tottered in its hobnailed boots, and they had it.

✱ ✱ ✱

Estonian women are generally blonder and primmer than their Baltic neighbours. Elsa was neither: a dark, round cake of a woman. Her low cut blouse billowed around her surging cleavage, while her skirt, hitched high, revealed her stocking tops. Born and raised here in the city, she had been selling tourist trinkets for forty-five years. Not much had changed. Life was as hard as ever. She offered me a lacklustre postcard of an Intourist bus with blurred Russians in short sleeves and yellow dresses. It had obviously been taken sometime in the 1960s.

'It's a bit old,' I suggested, handing it back to her.

'Historical,' she corrected.

Out of the corner of my eye I noticed a blond youth staggering towards us with a half-empty beer glass. He approached the stall and began poking drunkenly at the contents. A map flipped off, landing at our feet. He dropped his glass as he attempted to retrieve it. It shattered on the cobbles.

'Sorry,' he slurred in English and weaved away again.

'He's a Finn over here for cheap drinks,' said Elsa, kicking the pieces of glass away. 'The last ferry goes back at four in the morning. The Soviets let them in too. Even they saw it was good for business. Though I see little of it.'

We stopped at a café on the way home. Rohan ordered a round of tea. A short, blonde woman in her mid-forties was sitting alone in a corner, fondling the pages of a book. She sidled into conversation. Her whole working life she had been a receptionist in a local radio station, she told us. Next month she would lose her job. There was no longer enough money for wages. She didn't know what she would do afterwards. There had been promises of more radio stations and more newspapers after independence, but there seemed to be less. Estonia was falling into itself, relying more on satellite television for foreign news and entertainment. She pulled a small posy of lily-of-the-valley and forget-me-nots from out of a sturdy shopping bag and sniffed at each flower as if she were smelling them for the first time.

'Take these, to remind you of Estonia,' she said.

In a pharmacy we bought more iodine tablets, which we had used to purify our drinking water for the last six weeks on the road.

'Remember, don't take them if you are pregnant,' the assistant advised brightly.

'What do you mean?' Rohan asked, her face dropping.

'They can cause disabilities in the foetus if taken over a continued time. You're not pregnant, are you?' he added with a laugh.

Ashen faced, I thought of salamanders. I remembered back to a schoolboy experiment, when we had added drops of iodine to the water of an axolotl. This newt-like creature usually lives and breeds in its juvenile aquatic form, but when you add a few drops of iodine to its water it sucks in its gills and rapidly evolves into its land-loving equivalent.

'Perhaps the child will turn out to be pretty smart,' Rohan joked nervously. 'A Super Baby.'

'Yeah, maybe.' I swallowed hard. 'Or a Salamander.'

The radiation was dogging us too. Next stop was Sillimae, with its Russian nuclear reprocessing plant and enormous uranium-mining waste deposits heaped up in mounds 160 metres high. Along much of the coastline to St Petersburg the sea was radioactive. The locals lived in corrugated-iron-roofed huts and drank water from their wells. They knew the ground water was irradiated, but unlike us they were too poor to buy mineral water from the local shops. I wondered if you could even trust that—and if in the end it was too late for all of us.

That evening we walked down to the harbour for our last look at the Baltic. Oil and cigarette butts brooded on the surface. A lonesome seagull squealed plaintively. Along the coastline to our west was Paldiski Nuclear Base, the main training base for the Soviet nuclear Baltic fleet. A closed city, it had two land-based training submarines complete with fully functioning nuclear reactors. Only eight months before our arrival in Tallinn, the Russians finally finished encasing each of the reactors in a concrete sarcophagus—not before Russian troops were suspected of criminal smuggling operations involving radioactive material. Earlier, hundreds of tonnes of radioactive water and metal had been abandoned and thousands of truckloads of contaminated dirt secretly dumped around the site.

'It's funny,' Rohan said quietly, looking down into the murky water from a concrete platform. 'They don't seem to like the sea. It's really cheerless.' The Baltic was slovenly, good only as a dump and a line of transport: a well-used railway line with sprats. If it summed up Tallinn's languished psyche then I didn't feel like hanging around to fish any deeper. It was four days' ride to St Petersburg along a concrete slab highway. The quicker the better.

✳ ✳ ✳

Early next morning we steered eastwards on a hard shoulder. The day progressed. The road thinned. Mosquitoes harangued us in their thousands whenever we stopped, swarming around our faces in a cloud, biting through jeans and a second pair of trousers I had taken to wearing underneath to give me some protection. My skin began to blister through the holes in my watchband and on the crown of my head as they searched out places uncovered with repellent, and as we cooked they fell in squadrons into the frying pan. In the end I became vindictive, capturing the fattest ones swollen with my blood and pulling off their wings and legs and throwing them to the mercy of the ants.

★ ★ ★

Sillimae chattered with Russians, mostly school girls in
frilly red-and-white uniforms and babushkas who'd lost
their husbands in the Great Patriotic War. The outskirts
reeked of burning oil. Abandoned train carriages littered a
bogie yard that once made the wheels for the whole Soviet
Union. Chimneys and slag heaps of shale followed us to the
Narva River.

We reached the border by late afternoon. I was worried.
Following a series of rampages, Russian psychologists had
advised that 60 per cent of the country's border guards were
too unstable to carry guns. In the latest incident, a border
guard in eastern Siberia had shot and killed his five colleagues. Ours though could hardly raise a yawn. With one
look at the scruffy packs strapped to our bicycles and at our
sheepish smiles, they waved us towards their colleague in
customs to handle. There, an official flicked through our
passports, then gestured towards the frame of a metal
detector. We pushed the bicycles up a ramp and through. The
machine screamed. I looked bemused. So did the guards.
Starched lapels and an over-large cap were called for. This
time we were forced to sit uncomfortably in wooden chairs in
front of a heavy desk. Our visas were examined. A call was
made on a bakelite phone.

'Got any cigarettes?' the officer asked finally in Russian,
replacing the receiver.

I told him I hadn't.

'Pity,' he said, before gesturing for us to leave. 'It's cold in
the north,' he called out as we walked through the door. Then
he turned away again, shaking his head and pulling out a
packet of Marlboros.

13 ELECTION DAY

The heat was spectacular. Bathers waddled in the Narva
River, or fished bare-chested on its banks. Women tended
their onions and potatoes in bikinis, their husbands swigging
vodka from bottles in the shade. I felt like I had come home.
With the breakup of the Soviet Union, Narva had claimed the
water works which until then had serviced both towns.
Ivangorod sold water to its twin, but the debts were adding
up. Water only periodically reached the apartment buildings
where most people lived. When the taps occasionally
spluttered into life, buckets and bottles were filled and put
away like wine. No one doubted that soon the water would be
cut off all together; that you'd have to melt snow in the
bathtub and raw sewage would limp into the river.

The water crisis highlighted the real difference between the
economic systems of the two countries. The Estonian
authorities had ensured that water meters were installed in
homes and businesses and that its citizens were billed
individually. The central planners in Russia, on the other
hand, hated the idea of dispensing with free government and
social services and collecting utility bills based on market
prices. It was unfair, it tantrumed, especially since the
waterworks were built in Soviet times. Now it had just been
taken away.

But it was more than just squabbles over economics. The
whole feeling about Russia was different. As we crossed to
the other side of a bridge which spanned the two towns we
were met with waves and smiles, and an offering of vodka. In
a space of five minutes, as we leant against our bike frames
chewing on a loaf of bread and sipping from our water

bottles, five separate people came up to ask us where we were from.

'Do you realise they are the only people who have shown any interest in our trip since we left Belarus?' Rohan commented, shaking her head.

There was little traffic on the roads as we forged on, and the cars that passed burst with people. Hitchhikers thumbed for lifts. Queues of baggy breeches and frumpy dresses waited for buses. Old men and women sat by the roadside once again, with their buckets of potatoes and jars of milk and cheese—they made me think of my grandmother far away. Here in Russia the old work until they die. And then they die in their community, not locked away in some retirement home. Here, if you want water, you get it from the communal well. If your cow is hungry you graze it on the communal grass. The old people sit by the roadside and natter about the state of the nation and their rheumatic knees. My own grandmother, meanwhile, her husband long since dead and the rest of her family too scattered and busy, sits alone in a sitting room waiting by the phone and marking the passing of the days solely by the date on the television guide. 'Nobody comes to see me...nobody rings...your dad never calls. Haven't heard from your sister...' Constant refrains of rejection and loneliness. The comfort of a nice armchair, a warm room and enough tinned food to stock the larder is cancer compared to vitality of life.

Sometimes in our breaks I close my eyes and imagine I am 80 years old. My bones are heavy and my breathing difficult. Then I'll throw myself back in time, to become me at this very instant beside the road. I marvel at the strength in my body, listen with eyes closed and try to guess where I am. I study an expression on a face—Rohan when she was young and glowing from the exertion and the wind. A money spider prickling my skin as it crawls up my arm. Clouds blustering across the sky. A smile. The balminess of skin, salt and grasses. Clangs, chirps and whistles...It lasts for moments. Then, consistently, I forget I am alive again.

* * *

The road sign grumbled 'Leningrad' in faded white letters. I posed for a photograph beside it. The next, a little further on, called out 'St Petersburg' in a hesitant voice. Either way, both had their distances wrong.

We began casting our eyes covetously ahead of us, looking for dignified spires. The picture I had of the place we were approaching was a composite made up of fragments of paragraphs and half-remembered images. I tried to condense them in my mind, but ended up with little more than a vague, alluring splendour. Rohan saw it as it had appeared in *Anna Karenina* and Gogol's *St Petersburg Tales*: a place of grand boulevards, beautiful women, lap dogs, high fashion and fur hats. The road wriggled in expectation. Hobby gardens grew slowly smaller. Dust massed listlessly in the centre of the road. A car, aggrieved at our presence, honked its horn as we struggled up an incline. Another sign tolled us into St Petersburg, but only the gradual increase in cars—the colour of intestines, iodine, or fizzy orange—showed we were getting nearer to the centre.

About an hour later a derelict city taxi appeared, its driver scratching his head despondently as he examined his flat front tyre. The road dawdled on, widening and withering away again as it went. It began to spit with rain and the wind picked up as a highway finally reared its head.

The rustic gradually gave way to the rambling. Bright wooden shacks were repealed in favour of fretted concrete and bricks streaked with cement. Walls rose in place of fences. Pot holes hastened towards us like old friends. Then, suddenly, the city gulped us in and retched us out again among colossal gashes of repetitious housing blocks. We pushed on, battling over tram lines, past trolley buses strumming the sparking lines above our heads and into the depth of a honeycomb dashed apart and covered in dirt and shifting with a mass of workers. This was a part of the city which tourists rarely saw. The outcome of wars and neglect, a crude and graceless place, a shuffling, rogue crow pecking

blindly at the bright plumes of the forebear we glimpsed
ahead of us in the pale northern sky.

Some time later we burst like fugitives into a square
teeming with bodies. We needed to make it through to the
other side, but the crowd forced us to abandon our plans and
instead cycle around the long way in search of Nevsky
Prospekt and the pulse of the old St Petersburg. We weaved
through the traffic and over an ornate bridge spanning a
canal. Marlboro Man lassoed a steer ahead of me, while
behind us the red star of Russia gazed down upon six lanes
of traffic and a horde of pedestrians in overcoats. I soaked it
all in: the mash of restaurants, shop fronts and banks,
shameless mounds of marble and glittering, voluptuous
palaces. Finally, breathless, we crossed the River Neva and
arrived at Finlandia Station, from where Lenin, returning
from exile in April 1917, cried out: 'The people need peace.
The people need bread and land. And they give you war,
hunger, no food, and the land remains with the landowners.'
I reached up and touched Lenin's leg. It was cold. Rain
dripped from the end of his nose and ran down the
declaration he held in his hand.

Not long afterwards we were sitting in a hostel room beside
a Dickensian red-bricked prison, with towering walls and
two rows of barbed wire and metal fences. From our window
we made out prisoners waving pale hands between broken
wooden slats shading the bars of their cells. A note was
lowered by a string from one to another. Young women, their
mouths smeared in lipstick, roamed the square beneath us,
or sat on a children's climbing frame, furtively semaphoring
news in well-practised hand signals, and wailing Russian like
alley cats. A prisoner shouted back. A guard patrolled a
watchtower. It rained harder.

✳ ✳ ✳

The morning was dull and cool, the street full of agitators. It
was the day before the first democratic presidential elections
Russia had ever seen. Fascist flags and neo-swastikas hung
limply in the drizzle, their sharp eyed owners scanning the

crowd for sympathisers, their knobbly scalps bristling as they paced back and forth in tall black boots. Meanwhile, communist pamphleteers handed out greying, faintly printed booklets with powdery hands. The men were scrawny types with berets on their heads and hammer and sickle insignias pinned to their lapels, who stroked their wispy beards and looked nervous, like communists all over the world. The greatcoats of their female companions hung from stout shoulders to boots more used to tramping the snow than summer streets. Tightly curled hair was stuffed into crocheted hats. One held out a leaflet to me with a leather glove.

'Comrade. We've been betrayed,' she croaked. 'They have pulled the legs from underneath us—after all that we struggled for, fought for, went to the camps for...'

My Russian is good enough by now to catch snippets from worried conversations around me. A bomb has exploded on a late night train in Moscow—Yeltsin is behind it. And did you hear? Our comrade Chechnyans found abandoned nuclear missile launchers still in the bunkers. And now they have nuclear rockets too, smuggled by Ukrainian bandits. That's why Yeltsin is calling for peace...

✳ ✳ ✳

The crowd is barging towards the deep, deep cellars of the underground, while we peel off to buy bus tickets from a street vendor. I pick out individuals from my place squashed up against a peeling wall as Rohan counts out her roubles. Each face scowls from the swell of North Sea-grey as all around them the decrepit, smelly, ugly, irritable other that smears itself across the city gets in their way. I smell the scent of violence in the air. Trucks, trolleybuses and cars whine so loudly that my ear drums threaten to burst. A bus pulls up. We squash on and our tickets are snatched from me and passed over heads by hand after hand, to be clunked and holed and sent back again. Ahead of us, the driver sits in a cabin with a military-style cap and pinned to the carpet in front of his brow are medals and badges, a hundred hammers and sickles, red stars and Cyrillic letters. His bus.

Only his. He grinds it onwards through puddles and grime, the staunch opulence of St Petersburg steamed up through the windows, and various makeshift shades of white, blue and red Russian flags flap from streamers strung up across the road; old Dutch colours in a different order, appropriated by Peter the Great who held its navy in high esteem.

We are expelled in front of a bank and join a queue of nine hanging around its firmly closed doors. It reminded me of a Russian joke; the one about a man queuing for vodka. After a while he turns around to his neighbour and says, 'Bugger this, I'm off to shoot the president.' A little later he returns. 'What happened?' asks his neighbour. 'There was an even bigger queue,' the man responds bleakly.

'When is it open?' I asked hesitantly to no-one in particular.

'It's open now,' confirmed a angular-faced youth in English. He had recognised my accent. 'You are a foreigner, I suppose.'

'Yes.'

'Tourist?'

'Sort of.'

'It is a bad time to visit our city,' he said abruptly. 'The people are scared. They expect a bomb.'

'They don't look very happy.'

'They have to choose a president.'

He fell silent, then putting an arm around my shoulder he guided me away from the others. 'We have a problem. How do we choose when they are all bad?'

'Sometimes we have the same problem in my country.'

'Umm.'

'Why are the bank's doors closed?' I asked after a short silence.

'They are open, but not for us.'

'What do you mean?'

'We must wait. You see, we are only small people. The doors open eventually.'

'How long have you been waiting?'

'Not long. Maybe an hour.'

He looked at me carefully. His eyes, a mournful brown, had a lost look about them as if he was no longer sure of why he was here. I had sensed a similar affliction elsewhere in St Petersburg. From waiters to people in the street, they would break off their sentences midway and sigh: '...but what can we do?'

'You must be careful here,' the young man said. 'I was in a restaurant the other night. People are dancing and drinking vodka. I see a man ask a woman to dance. Another man enters and tells him to leave the woman alone. He says no and tries to hit him. The second man...he is more accurate. He has four friends. You know them, of course...'

He seemed perturbed and looked around to check no-one was eavesdropping. 'Well. It is very crowded restaurant, but the man put his Italian shoe on the head of the other man, he make unconscious and stamp very hard many times. When he is dead, the four men take his body out of the restaurant and it never seen again. The police come later. The restaurant staff clean up. It is not news. The criminals probably drink expensive champagne afterwards and laugh. Capitalism builds on the bones of its victims. It is true. Everyone pay protection money. One man I know buy a BMW and it disappear the next day. He go to police and they say they can do nothing. They say, "Go to local mafia boss." So he ask a kiosk seller who is the mafia boss and he find him easily. The mafia boss tell him it not happen on his territory. But, "I make some inquiries," he say. A day later the mafia boss say him that the man who sell him the car was one who arrange to steal it back. "We can have him killed for US$1000," the mafia boss tell my friend. "Usually it cheaper, but the man you look for has already offered us $500 to kill you. But because he is bad man we will take your money first." My friend have no money. He leave St Petersburg. Now in Siberia.'

At that, an armoured security van pulled up. Two heavily-built men in flak jackets got out, their arms crooked over their holsters. Another, a weaselly character dressed in a flared white suit, climbed out of the front passenger seat and ran towards the bank door. The guards followed, jerking their heads like roosters as they checked the coast was clear. The weasel rapped sharply at the heavy wooden door. He slipped inside followed by his entourage. It was another half-an-hour before it was our turn.

Inside, the bank was small and dark. Four wooden chairs rested their backs against a brown concrete wall. Three clerks sat behind a wooden counter, with three desks piled up with triplicates behind them. Rohan counted out a few US dollars. I took a seat. There was another sharp knock at the door. I turned to see it opened for more goons. One, thinner than the others, walked over to Rohan. The clerk who was serving her, a bouffante woman with a puckered smoker's mouth, waved her back. The goon took Rohan's place, while the others sat next to me, one picking at his teeth, another running his hand over a Kalashnikov.

Large wads of money were tipped from a sports bag and shoved towards the clerk until they bricked her in. She counted each note in turn, there were thousands of them, all large currency. It took nearly half-an-hour until they were triple-checked. I didn't want to know where the money had come from, I just wanted to be out on the street again as soon as possible.

Afterwards, while taking stock of a city map in a park, we were hexed by gypsies. Two old women swirled upon us in lacy dresses. Black eyes turned to menacing coals as we refused them money. They insisted. We turned away. One spat loudly in our direction and a curse slithered out from between rotten teeth. We were unnerved immediately but stubbornly refused to turn. We walked away regretting it already.

* * *

It was a sensitive time. Just 80 kilometres west of St Petersburg in the closed city of Sosnovy Bor were the four Chernobyl-type nuclear reactors of the Leningrad power station. The trade union had threatened to close down the reactors; the plant's union head had been on hunger strike for six days, and 7000 workers were sitting in to demand three months' back pay. Operators were so hungry they were collapsing over their instrument panels. In desperation some had turned to crime. In the past few months dozens of power plant workers had been charged with stealing, racketeering and possessing drugs and ammunition, and police had detained more than a hundred employees found drunk on the job. You had to suspect a major accident was on its way— they had occurred at the Leningrad plant in the past, most notably two separate explosions in January and February 1974, when three people were killed and radiation leaked into the atmosphere. Then again in November the following year when, in a scenario chillingly similar to the Chernobyl disaster, an experiment ended in an explosion which completely destroyed a reactor and set fire to nearby buildings, releasing in the process between thirty and forty times the amount of radioactivity from the bombs dropped on Hiroshima and Nagasaki.

These days the nuclear waste storage situation is so dire that hundreds of tonnes of radioactive waste water has been secretly pumped directly into the Baltic Sea, and unsorted radioactive waste has been spotted left lying around the plant in plastic bags. The threat to St Petersburg was feared to be so great that local scientists came up with a revolutionary plan to defend the city against a nuclear explosion at Sosnovy Bor. They designed a radar-based system designed to locate and shoot down clouds of radioactive material, claiming radiation released from disasters as large as Chernobyl could be destroyed in as little as fifteen minutes. They proposed a belt of artillery rockets and aircraft to blitz the radioactive cloud with chemicals, which would rain down to earth in a cotton-like foam. The foam could then be shovelled up and buried. Not surprisingly the project was shelved because of lack of money. Or perhaps because it was insane.

The achievements of the Soviet Union were measured in smoke stacks, tractors, slag heaps and power generation. In Russia, like elsewhere, atomic stations remain surrounded with an almost sacred aura of mystical and ultimate power. I wasn't surprised to learn that nine new reactors were planned for the site.

✶ ✶ ✶

Rohan, who had doused herself in Russian literature, was finding it hard to eke out the St Petersburg of Tolstoy and Chekhov as we wandered through the streets over the following days. The gaiety and horse-drawn carriages were long gone; whiskers and starched collars a thing of the past. There was no taking tea in silk dresses, no top hats or liveried footmen nor bespectacled clerks in frock-coats. But at least the great authors had taken us with them through the extravagant splendours of Tsarism, and with their help we could see life as it had been behind the façades now obscured by vehicle soot and telephone wires. The greatest of what remains is undoubtedly the Winter Palace, a Russian Baroque extravaganza which shone white and gold from beneath brooding rain clouds the day we visited.

Sometimes I feel disconnected from a place, and the sense of awe that I thought I should experience doesn't arise: I feel no reverence for it, and instead of soaking in its meaning and beauty I find myself thinking about what I am going to do next. This happens when I have no connection to the place; when I encounter it cold. Chinese temples—with all their colours and dragons and swirling symbolism—do this to me. I can't access them; I don't know what it all means. And even if someone explained it all to me, I imagine I would still be shuffling on my feet in simmering boredom, and end up wandering away as untouched as when I had arrived. To get the most from a place you need to approach it with a tie-in from your past. You must have always wanted to go there, to have read about it and imagined what it would be like. Or, it must have touched you culturally, like Bethlehem once did to me. (I am not a religious man, but after hearing about the place and its meaning throughout my life, when I finally visited by chance I was blown away. The awe I felt at being there stays with me to this day.)

I'm not saying the Winter Palace did this for me, but the adjoining Hermitage galleries certainly tried their best on Rohan. The art collection—started by Peter the Great and continued by subsequent Tsars and Tsarinas right up to Nicholas II, and later filled with requisitioned paintings from aristocratic collections during the Revolution—kept us entranced for hours. We passed quickly over the Indonesian sections, and objects from China and Tibet—after all they meant little to us and failed to resonate—and while Rohan studiously gawped at the works of Matisse and the Cubists, I gazed into the eyes of Allied and Russian generals and leaders as they looked down their noses at me from the days of the Napoleonic War.

Rohan had lived with art all her life, and now she was up close to some of the greatest masterpieces Europe had ever encountered. 'There are just so many of them in one place,' she exclaimed, flushed with exhilaration. 'If only I could paint like that.'

'If only we could have been around in the time some of them were painted,' I said. I could see myself with a face full of side whiskers in a time when St Petersburg was at its social prime.

'Problem is we'd be just peasants after a handout of bread.' We ended our excursion surrounded by hoards of precious metals and stones amassed by the Tsars, before passing a few roubles around to the beggars still haunting the main gates.

★ ★ ★

On our final afternoon in St Petersburg a freak show ended our chance of a child. The rain had nudged us into the Museum of Anthropology and Ethnology and the anatomy theatre where Peter the Great's bottled 'curiosities' had drawn a crowd of excited school children. A severed head peered blindly from a pickling jar. Foetuses exhibited elephant noses, additional arms, or clung to each other in a Siamese embrace. A new-born baby floated above a tail where the legs should have been and two others shared the same head. We were as ghoulishly attracted as the youngsters were. I managed to find a gap and moved closer. The babushka in charge of the group jabbed me violently in the ribs with her elbow and hissed like a swan.

'Get back,' she huffed, 'you are blocking the view.'

To her, educating the children in her charge was far more important than the contemplations of an individual; even more so because it was obvious by my speech that I was a foreigner. She jabbed me harder. I shuffled sideways, but obviously not far enough, as I was treated to a barrage of insults, but I stood my ground for a moment more to get a better glimpse of a young child suspended in a bell jar. Its head was twice the normal size, and flat, as if someone had sat on it. I felt sick. In the last couple of days I had found myself staring at children in the street with a stupid smile on my face, and casually inspecting toys and picture books in shop windows. Now, the sight of what could go wrong hit me like a crack on the skull. I shuffled backwards, sucking school kids into my draft like a sinking ship.

That night, Rohan tossed and turned for hours. By morning she had willed her period to come.

14 NORTHLANDS

A middle-aged woman lay in the gutter on the Murmansk Road with blood on her temple and her stockinged toes curling in a puddle. A crowd had gathered round. A man had removed the front passenger seat from the car that had hit her. He was trying to push it under her head to give her some support. Another man, younger than the first, pointed at his cracked windscreen aggressively.

'She just walked out into the road,' he was saying. 'Look what she's done to my car!' It seemed an inauspicious start to our long trek north.

After that conditions deteriorated rapidly. The rain which had made us late in starting became heavier. The wind picked up again, flinging dirty spray from car wheels into our faces. As the city thinned, what had started off as a four-lane highway turned into a rough track and we were forced to cycle for safety on the sharp, jagged shale at the side of the road. Visibility got worse. The clouds turned sootier and began to rumble threateningly. We struggled onwards for hours, and still the flow of cars continued, mixed in with rusting, hulking buses packed with bodies, ignoring the lengthy queues huddled at bus stops every kilometre. I had no idea where all these people were coming from. It was like a mass exodus. By now we were well out into the countryside, with unbroken tracts of trees on either side of the road, and no towns that I could make out. Perhaps they were rushing back to the city in time to vote after a nice weekend in their country dachas, I thought. But I couldn't shake off the feeling that they were fleeing southwards away from an accident—a major disaster we were flying straight towards. Finally, I had to pull over and ask someone.

'It's the football,' he said. 'The European Cup. Everyone is going to the city to drink with their friends and watch it on TV. It's a big game.' Paranoia was getting to be a habit of mine.

The cars thinned out as the evening progressed. Somewhere to the left of us was Lake Ladoga, which acted as a frozen life line for St Petersburg during the Second World War, when the city was beseiged and up to a million people were killed by starvation and shelling. Later the Soviet Navy and the local Atomic Energy Institute tested construction materials for nuclear reactors and chemical warfare techniques on some of the islands, despite the lake being St Petersburg's main source of drinking water. Birch trees now shivered in the marsh land in wiry clumps, and again and again we dismounted to search for a dry spot to camp. But as soon as we had wandered away from the drone of traffic the mosquitoes would sniff us out and settle in their tens of thousands, lapping up the insect repellent on our skin as if it were honey. Once, and I will never forget it, I looked down at my body to see it had completely disappeared. In its place was a black, seething mass of abdomens, thoraxes, wings and legs. Not one scrap of clothing or human flesh was visible. I ran as fast as I could back to my bike, trailing a cloud of ravenous insects behind.

We trundled onwards too exhausted to speak, almost asleep over the handlebars. When we didn't care any more we erected the tent right there beside the road, on a carpet of squidgy moss, relying on the approaching darkness and a thin screen of trees to keep us undetected.

The next day was again cold and dreary, and we braced ourselves with vodka bought in St Petersburg. I began to believe it would never stop raining. I felt misery come on like a chill. To keep up my spirits I tried to think good thoughts. When I would return I'd take up an instrument: the trumpet perhaps. I'd learn to make pots. I'd buy a turkey to guard the house I had yet to save up even a deposit for. Travelling encourages positive ideas: the knack is to ensure that the plans made on the road are not shaken off the moment one returns home, as they almost inevitably are, like apples from a tree.

At lunchtime we rambled down a woodsman's track and stopped in a clearing. I boiled up some dried leek soup. Rohan huddled close to the primus thawing out her fingers. We really needed to rest, but a ferocious blitzkrieg of mosquitoes and wood ants picked up our scent and forced us back onto the saddle before we could even finish eating. I emerged from the forest thinking fondly of living rooms, where one can sit in perfect peace, where nothing moves, except perhaps your fingers as you turn the page of your book. Not like in the Russian countryside, where every inch of ground and air is crawling and swarming with chopping mandibles and wiry appendages. For the first time in my life I realised perversely what a pleasure it must have been to cut down the trees, to drain the swamps and claim the land from the insects. Later, I noticed I had begun to crush flowers beneath my feet, uncaring, and for the first time I left tin cans buried by the side of the road instead of carrying them with me.

The day passed. And another. We hardly saw a soul. Whole forests dwindled in height, then reached for air again in a last ditch attempt, then drowned. The gypsy's hex made sure that when it was time to camp it was again impossible. We cycled on for an hour longer, then found a resting place on a patch of ground surrounded by mouldering tree trunks and spears of bracken. I lit a fire. An Arctic tern wheeled overhead. To get into the tent we had to slap and wave towels about each other to fend off marauding swarms of mosquitoes. Then, all zipped up, we sharpened our eyes to hunt down those who had cracked our defence. Later, cackling hysterically, we took to pulling off their proboscises in revenge as they probed for blood. But still they massed between the fly sheet and the cotton interior, banging their heads angrily against the fabric, sounding like rain.

* * *

Katoshka is playing up, slipping gears, becoming more unruly by the day. Its panniers have ripped badly right down the sides, and are spewing out their contents of dried milk, toiletries and mugs and plates across the ground at irregular intervals, forcing us to stop and retrieve our belongings and then crouch in the wet while Rohan stitches them up again. The rain keeps coming and the distances on the signposts are testament to our madness. Then, just as the tears are about to break out, the clouds vanish and the sunshine comes, warming our weary bodies.

The countryside opens up with the weather. Strung out alongside the road are simple pine huts with tin roofs. They are surrounded by fields of wild flowers purring with bumble bees. The air is so crisp with pine you could reach out and snap it.

Our shaggy appearance has turned us into wolves out from the woods, lean and hungry. Russians who pass us on the road jerk their heads away anxiously, as if we were sure to pounce should we catch them looking. Others regard us shyly from behind their windows, or rush from the safety of their public bus seats to huddle against the back window and leer at us until we are nothing but specks.

One evening we camp beside a river, on sandy soil which takes tent pegs well. It's drizzling when we wake up, amplifying the sound of cars on the wet, sticky road. Taking off we find the mosquitoes have taken to riding with us, established like stains on our backs and panniers, and biting only when they feel like it.

* * *

A ground-to-air missile pointed us towards Petrozavodsk, and a run-down mansion posing as a hotel where a huge Saint Bernard struggled with his chain in the portico, chomping viciously at the air.

'Victor, shut up,' a gruff voice called out from a second floor window. The dog fell silent and began wagging its back end stupidly.

'We want a room,' Rohan called out.

'You have money?'

'Yes, a little.'

'A little is not enough.'

'Oh. How much do you want?'

'Dollars.'

'We have roubles.'

'How many?'

'Look. How much is a room?'

'I don't know. I will ask my wife,' he said finally.

We overheard vague mutterings from somewhere within. After a while his head emerged again.

'Fifty American dollars,' he said.

'That's far too expensive.'

'Where are you from? Finland? You have the money. Take it or leave it.'

We cycled on, stubbornly after a bargain, in a town which directed us to its centre past a tank on a concrete plinth and a railway station crowned with a glossy red star.

Hotel Severnaya was on Lenin Street. We stumbled into our room, clapped out after a day that seemed to go on forever. Rohan feebly offered to find a kiosk and some vodka. I was to take the first shower.

Inside the communal bathroom a man was washing his feet in a sink. I pushed on the door to a shower cubicle. It was locked. I pushed on another. It refused to budge.

'There is no water,' the man said, bundling up his mud-smeared soccer kit. 'There was no water last year when we played in this town either.'

I fronted up to the floor lady. 'There's no water.'

'Nyet.'

'Why?'

'There's been an accident.'

'What kind of accident?'

'With the boiler.'

'What happened?'

'It broke.'

'When?'

'Today, they say'

'When will there be water, then?'

'Tomorrow. Next week. Next month. Maybe,' she replied brusquely, turning away.

I hummed to myself as I walked downstairs.

'Why did you sell us a room without telling me there was no water to take a shower?' I asked the woman at the desk.

'I did not know. I have only just started my shift.'

'But I met someone who said there were no showers a year ago either. And why are all the cubicles nailed closed?'

'It is the infrastructure,' she pronounced, thrusting her chest out, knowing I'd seen through her. 'Too many visitors expect water for showers. The boiler is too small. We used to charge for showers, but people were resentful. So we decided to stop them. Now no-one complains. There is always shortage in Russia.'

'Thank you.'

I returned to our room. There was a tiny sink in the corner with a single tap. I turned it on. Water gushed out. It was hot. I shook my head and sighed.

✷ ✷ ✷

In the restaurant the air was thick with cigarette smoke. Trestle tables were done up with white cloths cluttered with bottles of champagne, plates of half-eaten salads and paper-thin slices of sturgeon and trout. The place was heaving. There was no place to sit. We should have come earlier, a waiter said, when we asked if he could squeeze us in. I noticed a balcony above us. A man was leaning over munching on something between swigs from a bottle. Over an empty dance floor and up a swirl of iron stairs we found a bar. I ordered two bottles of beer and a large packet of crisps to share. A little while later Rohan went back for seconds.

I scanned the room from my perch up above. The band struck up a Russian pop song. Women with heavy make up and tight glittering dresses hobbled out to dance. There were plenty of tuxedos, but only one man dared to be seen among the boogieing females. He was older than the rest, drunk and clinging onto the neck of his partner, his face in her cleavage. The song ended and was replaced by a slower tune. The women stood shuffling their feet as they waited for a partner to pick them out. The prettier ones were snapped up first and shuffled around in awkward clasps. Others, rejected, slunk away. When the tune was over, each pair broke, returning to their separate tables with barely a word between them. As the night wore on the women flirted from far off tables, throwing meaningful glances across the room.

I went for a walk, following the balcony around from the bar. A large recess held rucks of gamblers and bored croupiers. The players, heavy set and hatchet-faced, wore chunky rings and arm-fulls of tattoos. They bet $50 a time. I leant on the railing to watch for a while. Suddenly, I felt a weight against my shoulder. A bull-necked drunk had listed sideways. I turned my head slightly, noticing the ruddy cheeks, a violent scar and the beer glistening on a thick moustache. Stuck in the waist of his trousers I saw the handle of a pistol. I froze. He coughed again. A cigarette fell from his fingers to the floor. The smoke crept towards me. I desperately wanted to take a drag. He coughed. I shifted my weight. His head jerked, swayed for a moment, then flumped back down onto my shoulder. I had given myself up for dead by the time his two companions pulled him up and staggered away with him.

'A pretty dull night,' Rohan said when I returned. 'All in all.'

✶ ✶ ✶

We mounted up early the following morning and rode with the wind behind us. Clouds hung in the sky like cauliflowers might. The road ran with us towards the Arctic. Trees shrank. The bog expanded. As we rode on I found I was only half-pleased that Rohan was not pregnant. I was thankful that we had not brought a child into this world that was deformed because of my desire to achieve something at all costs, but after all those long days of coming to terms with her pregnancy, I felt it had been taken away from me too suddenly. I had a feeling of emptiness. When I broached my feelings to Rohan she swamped them with a surge of her own. The nightmare was over, she gushed. For weeks she had felt the child glowing inside her like a lump of plutonium. How ever could other women live like that? Those poor women. Millions of them. She would rather live by candlelight. Only later would she admit that deep down she too had felt a sense of loss.

We camped each night beside the road, boiling up our rations as quickly as we could before diving for cover into the tent, maniacally slapping down insects as they whined into attack from the air. In those isolated times the BBC World Service was as comfortable as an old jumper. We stopped at lunchtime in time for the news and listened for hours during those long bright evenings, cuddled up together in our sleeping bags, until we fell asleep, or the batteries ran out.

Once, as we were cycling along looking for a place dry enough to camp, a car pulled us over. A man leaned out waving a bottle of vodka. His white fringe stood out brilliantly against the rest of his brown, swept back hair. He looked friendly enough. He offered us a night in his shack.

Alexander was a painter. He lived in St Petersburg, but drove up here whenever he had saved enough of his pension to pay for the petrol. This time he had been here for a week. He liked the desolateness of the place. It was the essence of Russia, partly tamed. He could paint from the heart here. He planned to build up a collection and put on an exhibition.

'I want to work hard,' he said thoughtfully. 'It is like a sport. I paint and paint. Then I will reach my peak and I will paint masterpieces. I want to learn how to paint masterpieces very quickly. I train by copying Van Goghs at the Hermitage in St Petersburg.'

His wife had slipped away with a sailor years ago. His children had gone more recently, his daughter to the United Arab Emirates to work as a computer operator in a private medical clinic, his son to Moscow. All Alexander knew of him was that he made money. He had forgone his education to make hard cash in changing times.

'You know, I have a passport too. I can leave any time I want,' he said pointedly. 'I don't have to stay here but I want to. Too many people are leaving. Now all our mathematicians and computer programmers have left for the USA. They think badly of Russia's future, but I always think good about it. I have hope. I don't want to think in another manner. Many people here think people are destroying industry,' he continued at length. 'The politicians don't think so, but it is true. They think they will build a new beautiful future with capitalism, but we've destroyed our industry, our agriculture, our basics. A child, if he destroys a toy he is playing with, still thinks he is playing as he is destroying it. Our society is like that child. People now don't understand their position in life—why there is no pension, why food is so expensive, why there are no jobs. Why? Why? Simple people don't understand it. In Russia everything is bad quality now and production is getting less and less. We used to hear all the time about our industries, how they are growing, now they forget about it. We only hear about the struggle for power.'

Communism was no better. It tried to change human nature. It was an idea. It should have stayed that way. It was a primitive system, but it was the Russian People's system. Space, that was different. Space, ahh, yes, space. That was the only good idea. People agreed with space. It made them proud. Everyone was so happy when the Sputnik went up in 1957. It was a holiday for everyone.

Before he started painting Alexander had been an engineer in Murmansk, working on nuclear ice breakers. I probed for details, but he fended me off.

'Is it still really a secret for you?' I asked.

His face broke out into a smile and he laughed. 'It must always be a big secret.'

'Did you have any problems at the navy yards?' I pressed.

'Yes we had problems. At first the technology was really advanced—very modern. But then what could we do at the end of the life of the engines? We didn't know where to put them.'

'So you dumped them in the sea.'

'Like the Americans did. They are as bad as us. But you won't hear about that.'

I recognised the familiar wooze of vodka on the brain. I looked over to Rohan. She had fallen asleep, warmed by the fire which flickered across her face. I leant closer to Alexander. 'Were you scared of us?' I asked hesitantly. 'I mean, of the nuclear weapons.'

'I was going to ask you the same question,' he said.

'Well, were you?'

'For a long time I lived and worked in St Petersburg. Of course I was scared. Seventy per cent of the people there used to work in the armaments industry. We all knew you would bomb us. We had to defend ourselves. We were the only ones working for peace. It was the socialist way to want peace. I used to be scared of nuclear weapons when I was a little boy. I used to remember the pictures of the victims of Hiroshima and Nagasaki and what the Americans did to them, and I would have nightmares that it would happen to me. It is funny. I asked my children recently if they thought the same, but they answered that there are far more important things to worry about.' He paused. 'But I think we're still not free from the past,' he said finally. 'Perhaps we're even lost to the future.'

15 THE GULAG ARCHIPELAGO

Valudin added water to his vodka, swirled it around the dirty, chipped mug and washed it down with a spoonful of cold, mashed potato scraped from an old gherkin jar. He topped up his glass again and tossed the empty bottle into the White Sea, then dragging on a reedy cigarette and scrunching up his weather-worn face, he inhaled. A string of saliva stretched from his lower lip to the dog end as he pulled it from his mouth, spanning the distance like a sagging bridge, before snapping wetly down onto his chest. Nadia giggled and self-consciously smoothed her hands down her leather jacket.

'I'm no communist,' the young woman announced. 'It's not for me.'

'Yes. It's obvious you've done well under Yeltsin,' Valudin said as he studied the gold rings on her fingers.

'Of course I have. Look what else Yeltsin gave me.' She opened the clasp of her leather handbag and pulled out a tiny pair of scissors, still encased in their clear plastic cover. 'From Germany.' She waved them in front of her. 'I'm a hairdresser. Now I can cut straight! That's more than I could do with scissors made in the Soviet Union.'

We were seated in the cabin of an old wooden fishing boat—a ferry to the Gulag Archipelago. Somewhere out to sea, beyond the mist, was the island of Solovetskiye, the home of the first of the Arctic prison camps. Valudin's younger brother, Anatolie, had beckoned us to come aboard after spotting us worming through the battered landscape towards the sea front. 'Tourists? Good. Come and drink. And then we take you to the island.'

We had little left of the money we had changed in St Petersburg. It would be difficult enough to buy enough food to get us to Murmansk if we didn't find some way to access our credit cards and travellers cheques. A day trip to the island seemed out of the question. It was bound to cost more than we could afford. But Anatolie seemed to be reading our minds.

'Don't worry about money. We take you. We leave in ten minutes.'

That had been four hours ago, and there was still no sign of the boat leaving. There was little for it but to keep downing the drinks.

We had arrived in the town of Kem the evening before and had checked into a hostel just as a heavy fog descended. It was freezing and we were both gagging for a hot shower, but the hose only dripped, icy cold. We warmed up on vodka instead, and cooked a meal of gluggy pasta on our primus in a corner of the room.

Morning had brought frost and a chill wind. It was too unpleasant to even contemplate cycling, so we left our bicycles chained up in the hallway and were carried off, armed with a loaf of bread and a chunk of cheese, by a local bus to the seaside. We rattled on through flat and featureless country to the final stop beside a village of coarse shacks. A tar road treaded with sand from the tyres of heavy trucks led us past chunks of abandoned masonry towards a sea the colour of wet concrete and heavily contaminated with nuclear waste. Just three years earlier hundreds of seals along this coastline had been found to be suffering from blood cancer. The incident followed the grounding of millions of dead starfish, shellfish, porpoises and more seals three years before that. Now, rubble, splintering telegraph poles, piles of sand, cranes and rusting railway carriages littered a churned brown foreshore. I spotted a fishing boat tied up at a wooden jetty. A Russian flag hung dejectedly from its mast.

Valudin was darker and stockier than Anatolie, but they were equally sozzled. Of the two, Valudin was the better dressed. His boots were newer and his muddy trousers thicker than his brother's faded jeans. He wore a red-and-white jumper, slimed and spotted with oil and trailing woollen strands at the cuffs. The brothers shared the same piercing blue eyes. I guessed Valudin, who was draped across the wheel rolling a cigarette, was in charge.

Nadia was just visiting. A local girl made good in the city, she had fled to St Petersburg two years before and had shacked up with the manager of a tourist hotel.

The mate, an old sea dog, scuttled into the cabin, his herring-bone moustache quivering beneath a large pock-marked nose. Dirty checked trousers, galoshes and a faded black jacket covered his wiry frame. Anchors embossed his buttons. A green woollen hat sat limpet-like on his head, the escaping hair drifted across his forehead. Squinting comically, he tried to focus, then threw himself forward to collect Nadia's hand. He brought it to his mouth, opened it like a clam and slurped a wet kiss.

'Don't suck up my rings,' she shrieked, pulling her hand away.

'Thessse are nothing like I could buy you if I wanted to,' he hissed. 'Nexssst time you are here I will take you out for a danssss, or a meal. Jusss call me.'

'Thank you, I will,' she said, fighting back her laughter.

'Good. Necssht time you're here we won't drink cheap vodka, we'll drink chhhampagne.' He raised a make believe glass in his hand.

'Champagne to Russia,' Nadia toasted.

'To beauty,' the fisherman replied, listing to starboard and foundering against the cabin door.

'To vodka,' proposed Valudin and Anatolie simultaneously as they raised their mugs.

'Yesssss. To vodka,' said the fisherman, before stumbling out of the cabin.

I took another cigarette from Anatolie and smiled weakly, wishing desperately that my Russian was better. Then we sat down to smoke and contemplate: there was still no sign of moving off anywhere. Half-an-hour of back-slapping and drinking later I was getting a little concerned. Given the time, it seemed unlikely that we could make it over to the island and back in the same day. God knows what that would mean. A night wandering the Arctic wastes? Camping down somewhere in an abandoned shack? Valudin picked up on my contemplations and dismissed my worries with a conspiratory clunk of our cups.

'Will we come back today?' I gestured.

He flapped his hand, sprinkling me with ash from his cigarette. Why were we worried? We could stay the night at his mother's house on the island. They would bring us back to the mainland in the morning.

I wasn't too happy about it, especially with Muttley and Katoshka chained up in the hallway back at the hostel. I regretted not locking them in our room, but, desperately wanting to go to Solovetskiye, I reluctantly agreed to go where fate took us.

Soon, another man—this one sober—strode aboard. He was short and serious, and decked out in an ankle-length, navy blue coat. He had a red CCCP badge pinned to the brim of his cap. Eight other passengers followed, women and children and old men. I turned in time to see the sea dog scampering down into the engine room with a bottle of vodka in his hand. Valudin and Anatolie stubbed out their cigarettes and motioned that we should join the rest of the passengers below deck. With Nadia leading the way we bundled out of the cabin and clunked down a set of wooden steps into the hold.

Shafts of light squeezed weakly through two small port holes. A wooden table dominated the room's centre. Benches loomed out from the panelled walls. Everything percussed in sympathy with the engine.

Our fellow travellers pulled off gloves and mittens and warmed their hands on the hot metal pipe that ran at head height around the room. A middle-aged woman, chunky as an ice block, with felt boots, thick ankles, a tundra hat and a rumpled yellow raincoat, jabbed out her hand. I reached over to grasp it in mine, expecting a crush. I was surprised at its gentleness. Her young daughter, dressed in a fluffy purple hat and a Finnish jumper with reindeer prancing across her chest, spat sunflower seed husks upon the table and flicked them, bored, into a spittley hill. The woman reached into her over-sized handbag and produced thick, crenellated wedges of brown bread and some butter and cheese. She quickly turned them into sandwiches. Her daughter grabbed one roughly, without a thank you—my experience generally with Russian children had shown them to be notoriously spoilt and ungrateful. The woman urged a sandwich on us too. I took it gratefully and handed half to Rohan. Tea was poured into plastic cups.

She was from Murmansk. Did we know it? Ah, we were going there. It was colder in Murmansk than here. This was nothing. It was only around 6°C here. You can catch a fish up there in Murmansk and it will be frozen in ten minutes, and that's not even in winter time. Natasha, my daughter, learns English in school, she counts from one to ten. Count, Natasha, count in English...ah, she's shy. It's too hot in here... She puffed out her cheeks to emphasise she could hardly breathe, but kept her raincoat on nevertheless.

I smiled at the daughter and was unnerved when I got no response. I tried again later, but she just stared coldly, while her mother fussed around her, making sure she had enough food, a meal for a fully-grown man.

I didn't speak to Nadia again. Her individualism was swamped by the crowd. It occurred to me fleetingly that this phenomenon could explain why Stalin could bring himself to order the deaths of so many he had never met.

The boat nosed out to sea. It was warm below decks and the constant hum of the engines sent me to sleep. I woke up to Anatolie shaking my shoulders. There were whales alongside the boat. I rushed upstairs. A family of five ghostly Belugas rolled like dappled grey barrels through the swell. I could hardly believe it, but I heard them calling to each other in a liquid, musical trill.

'They sound like canaries,' I said, wondering if I should give up on the vodka.

But Rohan put it down to the whine of the engines, or the wind in my ears. Later, I found out that Belugas do actually sing to each other. I guess they try to cheer each other up, like cyclists in bad weather.

It was late evening by the time we arrived at the island. We embarked under a heavy sky and onto a large greying jetty, strewn with loose planks and logs. The sea rose in a curtain of damp mist, blurring edges. On one side a headland staggered under its weight of trees. The town looked bleak, all russets and greasy with small windows. We followed Anatolie to a bus parked nearby on a thickly rutted track.

'Jump on,' he said.

'How much does it cost?' Rohan asked.

'It's free. Don't worry about money. Come on. It drops us off at my mother's house.'

'One of them thought he saw you on the road, cycling,' Anatolie said turning to me.

'Oh really.'

'I told him he was stupid. I can see you are not peasants.'

'But we are cycling,' I said. 'To Murmansk.'

He looked at us and laughed. It was a good joke. We would need huskies to pull our bicycles. We wandered on with Anatolie chuckling to himself. He only stopped when he met a friend, pushing a wheelbarrow full of chopped wood. The break was the chance I needed to look around. The island certainly had a wildness about it. It reminded me of northern Scotland, all combed-back grass and rabbit-chewed shrubs to your ankle. Beside the road lay a pile of logs, and behind, a woodcutter in a dark home-spun overcoat and cap rested on a long-handled axe. He scrutinised me carefully before acknowledging my self-conscious smile. Further on was a wooden storage shack, which leant towards another with a black tarpaulin dome and a pig nosing at the muck in a stall. A stretch of grass

ran away in the background, leading to a formidable wall
made from enormous boulders washed with orange lichen
and a stout tower crouching beneath a pointed turret. My
eyes were drawn even further back, over the wall and the
wet roof tops of the buildings hiding behind it, and
towards my first glimpse of Solovetskiye monastery itself,
a chalky white con-glomerate with nine grey sultan's hats
spired with fretwork crosses. My attention shifted to a
puny figure walking across a threadbare rise. He turned a
corner and disappeared. The air was so still I could hear a
voice calling down on the quay. I shivered slightly and
pinched my coat closer around me. The smell of wood fire
drifted into my nostrils.

Anatolie's friend nodded goodbye, and we continued our
trudge, down a path and into the reception hall of a
lopsided building, where mats thick with boot mud lay in
front of closed doors. Three flights up Anatolie inserted a
key into a lock, twiddling it impatiently until it turned. We
entered a cramped kitchen with bare floors, scantily
furnished with a sturdy peasant table, two chairs and a
heavy cast-iron range.

Mother turned from her stirring. A large woman, she
wore an apron flecked with blue flowers over a home-
knitted jumper, her thick legs bulging through woollen long-
johns above thick-soled socks. A drop of green juice
dripped onto the linoleum from a wooden spoon she held
in a huge, rough hand.

Anatolie introduced us in a flurry of drunken gestures, the
woman listening with remote soberness. I shuffled
uncomfortably on my feet, my movement catching her
attention. I noticed a small tomato plant on the window sill.

'Will it grow?' I asked hesitantly.

'It will grow,' she said. 'So, you have a voice.' She motioned
for us to come nearer to the range. I followed her gaze into a
large steel pan, bubbling with peeled potatoes. They would be
ready in five minutes, she said. Would we like tea? We
nodded gratefully.

She removed a second pan, smaller than the first, from the flame. A viscous green ooze congealed as I watched. I caught a whiff of something bitter.

'It's for my cancer,' she said without waiting for me to ask. It was made from herbs collected in the forest. She took two spoonfuls in the morning and the same again with lunch and dinner. It worked. She was in remission. She placed a kettle on the hob. Whatever, I thought.

I suddenly remembered the two small loaves of bread we had bought for lunch. She accepted them with a stony countenance and motioned for us to sit down. The kettle top chattered with escaping steam. We ate a frugal meal of our bread and tomato jam, and forked from a plate of potatoes sprinkled heavily with salt. It was delicious. We washed it down with the sickly sweet tea from bone china cups.

I looked at my watch. It was past nine in the evening, though outside it was as light as midday. I felt the skin hanging heavily on my face. The further north we rode the longer it seemed to take to recover from the road. But Anatolie was determined. He wanted to take us on a tour of the monastery.

Outside a gale had risen and icy spray whipped across my face. Buildings moaned, and seemed to sway in the wind. Anatolie screwed his eyes up and looked out to sea. He shook his head. It didn't look good for the next morning's trip back to the mainland. I didn't want to think about it. I knocked a mosquito to the ground instead and picked it up to examine it closely. It was enormous, four times the size of the ones that had chased us since St Petersburg. I placed it in my jacket pocket. It's stuck in my diary now. I still can't look at it without scratching.

As we approached the walls the enormity of the construction became evident. Rohan took a picture as I stood next to a boulder. It was almost the same height as me. Its suitability as a prison was not easily overlooked. Political prisoners of the Tsars found themselves stranded here, and shortly after the revolution the monks themselves were imprisoned too—Lenin had created the Solovki Special Purpose Camp, the first in the Gulag Archipelago.

It was here at Solovki that the gulag system was created and refined: where camp directors discovered the minimum amount of calories needed per day by the average prisoner; the number of guards needed for each one hundred inmates; where to aim during executions. It was neither the biggest of the camps, nor the most brutal, but a letter signed by inmates in 1926 and sent to the Central Executive Committee of the All-Union Communist Party gives us an insight:

'It is difficult for a human being even to imagine such terror, tyranny, violence, and lawlessness. When we went there, we could not conceive of such a horror...People die like flies, i.e., they die a slow and painful death...If you complain or write anything ('Heaven forbid'), they will frame you for an attempted escape or for something else, and they will shoot you like a dog. They line us up naked and barefoot at 22°C below zero and keep us outside for up to an hour... they force the inmates to eat their own faeces...'

No-one is sure exactly how many people died in Solovki before it closed in 1939, but it's worthwhile noting that from the 16th century to the Revolution there were a total of 316 people incarcerated here, while on the night of 28 October 1929 alone 300 people were executed. Estimates put the final death toll at the hands of the communists at Solovki between 10 000 and 100 000 people. Inmates even reported German Nazis visited the camp in 1932 to swap experiences.

I tried to sense the terror, the hopelessness, the brutality that was part of this place for so many years, but I couldn't get past the incense, the tolls of the great black bells, the scaffolding and the hope and excitement which enveloped discussions about the monastery's grand future as the religious icon of the north.

After our return from the island, researchers dug up a mass grave containing the remains of more than 9000 political prisoners in a remote grove of craggy fir trees near the small town of Medvezhyagorsk—an innocuous little place we'd passed through six days after leaving St Petersburg. More than a thousand of the victims came from Solovki. Among them were Catholic priests, members of the Ukrainian and Jewish intelligentsia, the head of the Russian Baptist Church, four Russian Orthodox bishops and a gypsy 'king'. Documents showed the executions took place over three days in late 1937, during the Great Terror, when the KGB murdered nearly a million people.

* * *

The gale had blown itself out and the morning was calm and clear. We set off to explore after a breakfast of jam and bread. Just past the monastery the path split in two, one arm leading towards the quay and the other inland. At the intersection a friendly calf nuzzled its horns into my palm as I scratched its bony head. It followed us for a while as we tramped towards the forest, before it lost interest at last and dropped its neck to nibble on some grass. A little further on pine trees replaced the last of the shacks. The silence so common to remote northern islands was broken only by our boot steps, and a faint clicketty-clack of an engine far behind us. Gradually the noise of the engine grew louder, until its resounding mechanical clamour forced us both to clap our hands over our ears.

'What the hell is it?' I yelled.

'It sounds like a tank,' Rohan shouted back.

'Get off the road!'

A huge red box swung towards us from behind a line of trees. I blinked. A bell rang, once, twice. We barely had time to jump to the side of the track before a fire engine, royal red and gleaming brazenly, was upon us. It slushed to a brattling halt in a puddle, spinning a coat of wet mud across my thighs. A finger tapped silently at a side window. I saw Anatolie's gormless smile below his messy thatch of hair. He clanked open the door and jumped out beside us. His eyes flashed madly. He looked like he had slept the night in a barn. He yelled for us to get in. Before I realised what I was letting myself in for, I was sitting behind the two brothers with Rohan crawling in beside me.

We jerked into motion with Valudin at the wheel and Anatolie as second-in-command. I didn't have the faintest idea where we were heading. I could only guess that they had commandeered the fire engine in a drunken moment. My fears that we had just become accomplices in a daring heist were compounded when I noticed five brass rings inset in a shelf in front of me. Jammed in one was a fireman's hose nozzle. The other four each held a bottle of vodka.

'Where's the fire?' I shouted, determined to get to the bottom of it all.

'We don't know yet,' Anatolie called back as we bumped past the trees and down the track. 'We're off to find out.'

He laughed maniacally and grabbed a bottle of vodka, turning it upside-down and whacking the bottom sharply against the dashboard. The top popped off, sending liquid splattering across his knees. He reached down between his feet and came up again with a chipped glass, and dusted it off with a corner of his shirt. He filled it up until it swished over the sides and passed it back to me. Without hesitation I gulped it down. I needed a drink.

'Where's the fire?' I asked again after my third.

'Fire? There's no fire. It's a party,' Valudin replied. 'Anatolie was only joking about the fire.'

'Oh. Where's the party?'

'Here!'

'In the fire engine?'

'Are you not having fun?'

'Of course.'

'Then it's a good party!'

'Are you real firemen?'

'Of course.'

The glass came back to me again after doing its rounds. Then again and again. Eventually, the fire engine slowed and lurched to a stop beside a wooden shack. Valudin switched off the engine.

'We have brought you here for the boat,' he said. I nodded.

Anatolie jumped out and opened the back door. I climbed out ready for anything and followed him giddily over to the edge of a small pond. Nestling in some reeds by the edge was a blue wooden paddleboat.

'Get in. Get in,' Valudin blustered. 'Both of you. And take a bottle of vodka with you.' He handed me one over. 'Paddle hard. It's training for Murmansk.' He sniggered.

I climbed in. Rohan joined me with a look of apprehension.

'We will be back soon for you,' Anatolie called out as he set us adrift and pushed us out into the pond.

'Where are you going?' Rohan called out.

Valudin stuck a finger into an empty vodka bottle and pulled it out with a plop. 'We need to fill up?' he said, and staggered away.

'I think they must have a still somewhere,' I said, gently paddling around in a circle.

'They probably fill the water tank with it and jet it out of the hose to fill the bottles,' Rohan said with a grin. The engine let out a fearful roar.

After ten minutes of paddling we'd had enough. We moored our little craft to the bank and wobbled back onto dry land. Taking the bottle of vodka with us to sip en route, we set off back towards the port, expecting at any minute to hear the boys approaching. But we never did.

✷ ✷ ✷

Back on the boat Valudin was nervous. He apologised briefly about forgetting to pick us up. The party had continued at a friend's house, he said. Then he disappeared as quickly as he could. The man with the CCCP cap nodded as he came aboard, scrambled below decks to the engine room and closed the door firmly behind him. There was no sign of Anatolie. I was confused. The camaraderie between us all had vanished as quickly as it had come. I wondered if somehow I'd offended them.

In the passenger hold we were met by a stranger, a pug of a man in a brown suit and white waistcoat too smart for island hopping. He stared at us, deadpan. I grinned back nervously. He acknowledged my gesture in an accent rougher than we had heard before. Rohan didn't trust him from the start: it was as if he knew he had the power to throw us overboard.

I attempted another smile. A corner of his mouth twitched in response. CCCP appeared. He looked nervously at the stranger. Then at us.

'Dollar,' he demanded, rubbing his fingers.

'What?'

'Dollar. Fifty dollar.'

'What for?'

'The boat. Two people. Fifty dollar.'

'But Anatolie said we could go for free.'

His eyes flicked across to the stranger, who was watching the scene unfold with interest.

'I am the captain. I have to make a living. I have to pay for petrol. Anatolie had no right.'

'But I thought they owned the boat. We didn't know you were the captain. We only have about fifty dollars left in cash to get to Murmansk.'

'That's not my problem.'

I felt trapped and disappointed. It seemed as if it had all been a con to get us to the islands. But no, I refused to believe it. I was sure the change in attitude had something to do with the stranger. Rohan put on the best of her sorrowful faces. 'But it's the last of our money. We won't be able to eat.'

But it was no use. There was no way out. I handed him our money. After we had paid for the hostel room we would have just 15 dollars left to get us to Murmansk. It seemed unlikely that we would find anywhere to change a traveller's cheque or use a Visa card. And we had at least another 450 kilometres ahead of us and very few supplies.

There was silence. The captain looked embarrassed. Finally, he shrugged his shoulders. There was nothing he could do, he seemed to say. He turned on his heels and crashed the door shut behind him.

'I have been following your journey,' the stranger said suddenly, in broken English, startling us both. News travels fast about two foreigners on a bicycle. He had passed us on the road, somewhere outside St Petersburg. What did we do? Was I a journalist?

'I'm a student,' I lied.

He sneered knowingly and fished in his pockets for a pen and a piece of paper. He handed them to me. 'Draw your route for me.'

I compromised by writing down a few place names. Then I cut to the quick. Russia's Federal Security Service, the successor to the KGB, were intently paranoid about networks of spies invading the country. It had just accused the British embassy of running a spy ring out of Moscow. I had heard on the radio that nine British diplomats were to be expelled.

'KGB?' I asked.

'Me!' he said, taken aback. 'No no no. I am sailor.'

As if to prove his cover wasn't blown he peeled off his shirt, revealing tattoos of an anchor, a red star and a hammer and sickle. I asked him what city he was based in.

'A closed city,' he said.

'Which one?'

He refused to answer, instead drawing a submarine on the paper.

'Nuclear powered?' I asked.

The game took a chilling turn. 'What do you know about nuclear submarines?'

'Nothing,' I said a little more unsure of myself.

'Why are you cycling to Murmansk?'

'Sightseeing,' I said in English.

He shrugged his shoulders. 'I don't understand.'

I was silent. He stared at me. I kept his gaze.

'You will never make it,' he said finally.

'Why not?'

He thought for a while, then rolled his hand through the air in gestured mountains. 'You'll be lucky to do

20 kilometres a day.'

'I hope 60 or so,' I said.

'We will continue to follow your progress,' he concluded with a sneer. 'Very closely indeed.'

I gulped.

16 TOUCHING THE NUCLEAR

I had begun to grow a beard, but after three days my chin itched so much I was forced to shave it off. The problem was the irritation remained, stuck somewhere in the back of my mind. Then, on that last night in Kem, I finally realised I was missing something. But what? I didn't understand. I should have been content. I had all I wanted—the freedom of the road, a companion I loved...

Rohan grimaced. 'What's this with the red circle around it?' she asked pointing at the map. 'It's not another power station, is it?'

I sat bolt upright, pulling the blanket off us both. 'That's it!' I announced somewhat dramatically. 'We have to get closer!'

Directly ahead of us was Kola nuclear power station, the first plant in the Soviet Union to be built north of the Polar Circle. This time there would be no running away at the gates. Rohan sighed. 'Not again.'

I couldn't sleep much that night. The itch was gone, but it had been replaced with nervous energy that kept me thrashing around until at last Rohan threatened to push me out of the tent.

I bounded into the telegraph office next morning, with Rohan dragging her feet behind. I wanted to ring the station to tell them I was coming. After all, it would be rather impolite just to turn up to a nuclear power plant and insist on a tour.

Behind the desk was a single phone. To the left were a couple of simple wooden booths. There was just one line north, to the exchange at Murmansk. My call would be redirected from there to the town of Polyane Zori and on to the power station. We sat down to wait.

Half-an-hour later I was summoned over to the desk. The line was busy. The operator would try again later. Would we like to wait? We agreed to stick around. Two hours later we still hadn't managed to get a line. Outside the weather was sunny and the morning was wearing away. I made a snap decision: we would just turn up and see.

On the outskirts of town we met up with an old comrade— the railway line north. It winked at us, catching the sun on its brows. We stopped beside it for Rohan to stretch the cramp from her back. I bent down. The track was cool against the side of my face. I held my breath and listened as hard as I could, but all I heard was a dog yapping in a yard somewhere.

We urged ourselves forward as the road climbed up a hillside like a steeplejack, then went to ground again. For a while it gouged onwards through a valley shaved with open fields and scattered woods, then took to shuffling undecidedly this way and that, until at last it tracked back up the slope again to get a better fix on where it was going. We followed it down the other side and into a bog, then got out our utensils for lunch while it waited, rimmed on either side with ditches shimmering with cotton-tipped reeds.

I built a fire from crinkled twigs. The flames took well and the soup was bubbling in no time. I finally doused it out with the dregs of my tea. Rohan scampered off into the bushes, holding her stomach. She came back pale and uneasy, blaming it on the water.

★ ★ ★

Night disappeared along with the trees. At five in the morning the sun was so strong it would force us awake with its heat. And when we should have been fast asleep after hours on the road we would wake to each other's slaps and knees in the back as we flailed and rolled and tried to cover our eyes against its glare. We rode on like zombies, sometimes too tired to speak, our legs somehow turning as we folded like fortune fish over our handlebars.

The swamps began to drain into hollows as the first flurry of the northern hills welled up. At the first lake of any real size we filled up our water bottles and dared each other to take a dip. It was icy cold, but we lathered up anyway. After spotting my wolfish reflection on the surface I even dragged a blunt razor across my face. It was our first real wash in two weeks. Further on we spotted more trees. They hobbled towards us like cripples, mangled and coppiced by the winter winds. They grew shorter by the hour, until most barely reached above our heads. In the end they gave up altogether and we left them behind, the last just fallen stumps.

Three days out of Kem we found ourselves camping in a pasture of buttercups and marsh marigolds. By now, our supplies were growing as thin as our faces. Our panniers revealed just two packets of dried pasta and three soups between us. Feeding on little more than antibiotics to clear up her stomach, Rohan's mouth watered as a phantom toasted cheese and tomato sandwich floated just in front of her handlebars hour after hour. As for me, I kept myself going with Sunday roasts and Indian curries, drool escaping from the corners of my mouth.

The following day we found a service station. I gulped down a bottle of fizzy orange and bought up their supply of bread and beans. It would last us a couple of days. The owners boiled their own drinking water, but said they'd run out. We were directed down the road to another lake. It was swimming with tiny freshwater jellyfish. I filled our bottles up anyway, avoiding as best I could the largest creatures. I hoped I'd get the chance to boil the water before I got too thirsty.

Further north, Arctic forget-me-nots, harebells and horsetails clustered on the roadside verges. A falcon sporting a black moustache soared overhead. We began to climb again. Saplings hurried down to meet us. Further up the pines grew loftier. At lunchtime we dozed in a wood on a sea of lichen: brittle shaggy branches, pixie cups, and frilly-leafed lettuce, the colour of ivory and reindeer horn. A sandpiper peeped in warning as we set off again.

Out on the road once more it dawned on me that this was the first time in my life that I was on *my* time. I woke up when

I wanted, left when I wanted, rested and cycled when it pleased me. Rohan had fitted into my lack of schedule nicely, until we were like women whose periods coincide. Watches had been abandoned long ago. It was left to the BBC World Service to inform us we were getting up later and later each day. If the trip had continued much longer we would probably have found ourselves stirring when the birds came home to roost.

We flew on, sweating despite the encroaching bitterness in the air. The hills flung away to our sides and we cycled through a sodden hash of moss glittering on either side with a hodgepodge of lakes and soaks. In the distance I spotted a rise of tenement blocks which marked out Kandalashka, an industrial city washed up on the northern tip of the White Sea. Bus stops began appearing out of nowhere. The forests looked chewed at the edges as if giant rats had been at them. A military aluminium plant fugged clouds of black smoke from its chimneys. The crows that had heralded our passage through the countryside took off. Trees had their limbs lopped. Plants were trained. I picked a discarded newspaper off a bench. General Lebed was warning he would position nuclear weapons on Russia's borders if NATO tried to expand its influence eastwards.

Forty kilometres later we rode into Polyane Zori. At a shop on the outskirts we restocked on bread, a tin of corn, a packet of spaghetti and both tomatoes. Nearing the centre it began to rain. We surveyed the town from beneath an awning. Washing hung from lines behind closed windows stacked on top of each other like plastic egg cartons. There were no balconies: there was little point with a dreadful view over railway yards and factories. When the rain eased I took a picture of a red Lada parked beside a housing block. On one side of the building, bricks had been painted dark brown to resemble a half-built wall. Above it the four-storey upper torso of a grim-faced man was picked out in black. He held a trowel in his hand. In the other he held an atomic element like a six-sided star. Around the corner was a slogan which preached: 'An Atom is a Worker, not a Soldier.'

✶ ✶ ✶

It was change-over time. Workers clanked open one-way revolving gates then pulled up their collars and buttoned their coats. We cycled towards the power station's main reception area like emissaries from a foreign state. Open mouths greeted us as we dismounted and casually began removing our helmets, gloves and capes, and stuffing what we could in our panniers. We propped Muttley and Katoshka against a reactor wall and took a look around. On both sides of us stood striped chimneys. The plant's buildings were box-like, peeling with white paint and rust. A tannoy blared in Russian. For a moment I thought the words were directed at us, but no-one pounced, so we walked as confidently as we could through the main door.

It was as gloomy and Formica-clad inside. People milled around. I spotted an office with an open door.

'We are tourists,' I announced in Russian. 'We want to see the reactors. We have our bicycles outside.'

The woman behind the desk looked at me incredulously.

'I tried to phone. Do you speak English?'

'Nyet.' She eyed us suspiciously and picked up the receiver of her phone, gesturing for us to sit. It was a long wait.

Eventually, a man arrived. He was the spitting image of Robert De Niro down to the mole. He grinned pleasantly, his cheeks dimpling. 'I have been expecting you,' he said in perfect English, folding his arms. 'I had a phone call from Kem to watch out for two foreigners on bicycles.'

My mind rushed back to the incident on the boat back from Solovki. I feigned ignorance. 'Oh really,' I said. 'I wonder who that was.'

He raised his eyebrows mockingly.

'Can we have a look around?' I asked, changing the subject.

'Of course. We have nothing to hide. I am the public relations officer.'

I gawped. 'Things have changed, my friend,' he said with a chuckle. 'Come on.'

He led us out of the office and down a corridor, before ushering us into a small hall. Diagrams of the power process were tacked to wooden partitions. On a table was a scale model of the station itself. Our host started rattling off statistics, as if he were selling us a vacuum cleaner.

'We started building Kola nuclear power plant in 1963,' he intoned. 'It has four VVER-440 reactors, going online between 1973 and 1993. The plant now supplies 65 per cent of the electricity to this region. Seventeen hydro-electric plants supply the rest. Kola employs 3050 people, 500 working directly with the turbines and reactors. There are two canteens, twelve buses to ferry the workers to Polyani Zori...'

My eyes glazed over, though my hand kept writing mechanically in my notebook. Later I would review what I had written. The Russians were working on a new power station with three reactors. It would have a containment field, lots of nuclear safety facilities, radiation monitors around the plant, a special system for storage of nuclear fuels. Construction work had already started not far from Kola, but was proceeding very slowly because of lack of money.

A St Petersburg research institute had also developed an underground nuclear power plant, the reactors similar to those used on nuclear submarines. They would be located in four air-tight, fifteen-metre-long tunnels. There was also a proposal for a floating nuclear power station, with two reactors similar to those found on nuclear submarines.

'...seven to eight train loads a year of new nuclear fuel, every reactor has 309 fuel rods and 37 control rods to shut down the reaction, the water temperature is 300°C, during one year we change 400 fuel rods...'

I dropped my pen. He paused while I picked it up. 'We have a special pool for heavy water. It offers very good protection from neutrons. For three years they stay in this pool and are then put in a special container in a train and sent to Chelabinsk in the Urals or to Siberia where they are reprocessed and made into new fuel rods. There is a very small part of plutonium waste, we send it to a special breeder reactor owned by the army. We had nine breeders before 1991 and now only three. They use the plutonium to make nuclear bombs...'

My eyes wandered over his unremarkable, brown suit and down to his meaty hands. Suddenly I felt a yawn well up. The PR man stopped in mid sentence. Then he lowered his voice.

'But you are not here for this,' he said.

'I'm sorry. I didn't sleep well last night...'

'Come. We will sit down.'

He strode towards the partitions and squeezed through a gap. Behind it was a small table. He pulled up some chairs and sat opposite us, resting his gentle, crinkled face on top of the backs of his clasped hands. His eyes, I noticed, were a remarkable blue. He looked tired, even resigned. He lit up a thin, brown cheroot.

'Listen carefully,' he said, exhaling smoke as he spoke. 'We have a problem...' My ears pricked up. '...with the waste. The storage ponds are already full. Now we are putting more fuel rods in, twice as many as the pools were designed for. It is a very serious situation.' I couldn't believe I was hearing this. It wasn't very good PR.

'Here, our nuclear waste is distilled out of the water and it's made into glass and stored at the plant,' he continued. 'But we need a big nuclear storage site, perhaps on the island of Nova Zemla—or Death Island as we say—in the northern sea, where we tested our nuclear bombs, or near Archangel, or maybe a place here in the Kola peninsula somewhere. Everybody of course says we need it, but not near us. Of course, eventually it will be put where the people have the least power to officially object.

'We have no problem with the reactors though...' he continued, '...only with money.' Then, in almost the same breath, he went on talking casually of radiation leaks, about a tornado which tore down transmission lines, and how the KGB had visited and warned that the plant should be closed as soon as possible.

'I read back home about how you cut off power to the

nuclear submarine base in Murmansk because they hadn't paid their bills,' I said.

'Ah yes. I was here. The officers flew down and put guns to the director's head and forced him to turn the power back on again. You see, they needed electricity to power the reactors' cooling systems. Another few hours and there would have been a critical situation. Now, Yeltsin has prevented us from cutting off power to major state-owned industries who owe us money.'

I nodded my head encouragingly, my hand aching from the speed of my writing. 'We have an interesting system in Russia. Every month we have less and less money. We don't get money for our electricity because plants are bankrupt, but we still have to pay our own costs—for the fuel, wages, modernisation, equipment, for the shut-down program, and to the organisation in Moscow which controls all nine Russian power stations. In June we got February's salary and last week, now July, we get March salary. We can't strike. We must work, work and make energy, but we have no money. Only people who have many children and have normally only a small salary are paid every month. Others must eat on a small advance.'

He knew he'd fully engaged our attention now. I was just waiting for him to come right out with it and admit the whole place was about to blow at any minute.

'I will tell you a story,' he continued. 'We have in Russia a factory which makes stainless steel. They have no money to pay for electricity, but they send steel to a factory that makes cars. The car is a Russian Muscovitch. They send a car to us, so we have lots of cars and no money. Last year we got 400 cars. So for six months I have no money, but I have a car. We have to barter for vodka, even for equipment for the power station.'

'Why do you still work here with all these problems?' Rohan asked. 'Aren't you worried about the danger?'

'A reactor operator earns good money, maybe six times more than a doctor or a teacher and four times more than a waiter. That's good money. Every year people who work in the reactor have eighty-two days holiday. A man who works here for ten years gets a pension at forty-five and a woman who works here for six years has a pension at forty. And we get extra money for experience and because we live in the north. Very often everybody wants to work here. I have been here since the start—for twenty-one years.'

On the way in we had passed a series of greenhouses. I'd wondered at the time why they were there.

'What were they all about?' I asked.

'Ahhh,' he smiled. 'They were the pride of Russia. They were there to show how safe we were. We heated them with water pipes from the reactors and grew tomatoes and lettuce and cucumbers. This area was very much a winter garden. We sent hot water to the beef and pig industry, but it became very expensive energy and now must be closed down. Did you see the ponds? I'd take you there, but the rain, you see. I don't like going out in the rain. But the ponds...we used to have a farm of American rainbow trout in the water that came from the reactor. We would harvest 30 tonnes of fish every year and we sent it to Murmansk and other towns. Then a private company bought the farm, but the fish food became too expensive, so the production became smaller every year. There are no fish now.'

We cycled away in a downpour that got under our skin, with my faith in the failure of the system more unshakable than ever.

17 HOLED-UP IN THE ARCTIC

The forest wrapped itself around us, womb-like and comfortable in the rain. Twigs cracked under our wheels, the pungent smell of pine resin, thick black humus and crushed mushrooms arose from our footsteps. When we were far enough in to be sure of our invisibility from the road, we rested the bicycles against a tree trunk each and wandered off in opposite directions in search of the perfect campsite: dry and flat, with an area sufficiently cleared of overhanging branches for a fire. Within a few minutes I had found a likely spot, but as I swept my booted feet in arcs around and about I was met with uncampable reefs of tree roots and stones.

Rohan's voice called thinly through the forest: 'Have you found anything?'

'It might do at a pinch, how about you?'

'Yeah. I think it's perfect.'

I followed her hails until I arrived at a clearing caged by young pines and portalled by a couple of stumps that would do for chairs. The ground was smooth and thick with a coat of springy dry moss. We set to, unloading our panniers; Rohan furrowing for the tent pegs and torch, while I debated over a possible meal. I cooked just outside the tent awning: a spaghetti curry, which at other times would have made us wince at the thought, all topped off with tinned corn and tomato, piled up so high on our plates that each could have satisfied three normal-sized appetites.

With our stomachs full we retired to the tent, zipping out the forest and snuggling down for a well-earned rest. As I was wrapping my jumper sleeves over my eyes to block out the irrepressible light, a long, lonely howl of a wolf far off was followed by another nearby. Rohan's head shot up and cocked side to side like a chicken's as she tried to gauge exactly where the sounds were coming from.

'Did you hear that?' she asked hoarsely, and was met with another howl, drawn out like a torture on the rack.

There is nothing as frightening as the worst of your childhood tales coming alive. The woods of Europe regress to a primeval state in the dark of the night, when shadows can be anything, and ears sharpen for cracks of twigs which signify axemen or witches, or the evilest of creatures, the thought of which we block from our minds in case they send us wailing like kids again below the covers of our beds. And now, out there somewhere, were man-eating wolves, bigger, shaggier, fangier than any that crept from the page of a book.

'What are we going to do?' Rohan faltered.

'Don't expect me to go out.'

'We can't just lay here.'

'Do you want to go outside?'

'No.'

'Well, then.'

'But what if they attack?' I reached behind me for the torch. It was small, but I guessed it could render a healthy whack on an intruding nose.

My heart was beating like a bird's, and I peered as hard as I could to see through the fabric of the tent and deep into the forest to where the ravenous dogs might be pacing. My ears bristled. My throat dried up. Through the continuing patter of the rain on the tent's flysheet I could distinctly hear something shuffling around outside, far too near for comfort. All of a sudden there came a crash of metal and the sound of scurrying feet. I guessed the wolves had knocked over the primus, and sent the aluminium pot, stuck with the remains of the spaghetti, tumbling.

We sat there in silence like condemned men, hardly daring to breathe, frozen rigid. I'm not sure how long we clung to each other before we began to relax our grip, but by the time we were sure that they must have gone the sun had moved higher in the sky until it poured its rays through the canopy above our heads. Light gave us courage, and in time, we lay back down, and fell asleep.

We emerged into a wind so cutting it sent us piling back into the tent to pull on every scrap of clothing we'd brought with us. The hills of the previous day had led us to the edge of the Arctic highlands—reindeer, not bicycle, country. A night of rain had turned the dried out swamp we'd camped on into a quagmire of sodden moss, which swallowed our feet to our ankles as we pushed the bikes back onto the road. Drips ran down my neck. The frost turned Rohan's fingers blue. By midday the first snow peaks of the Khibiny Mountain Range were casting their shadows across the road. The Soviets had mined them with nuclear weapons, using three explosions to crush a large body of apatite-nepheline ore, used to make phosphate for artificial fertiliser. The bombs had been placed down a shaft and walled up to prevent leakage of radioactive gas into the atmosphere. It escaped anyway, through fractures in the rock.

We moved on, side by side through the constant rain, stopping only to stretch our backs and creak our fingers back to life, passing memorials to crashed motorists. In much of the world a simple posy of flowers, a wreath, or a cross is good enough to mark the site of a fatal car crash, but in Russia it was far more dramatic. Here, cemented into a tombstone, you'll find the victim's photo; a twisted steering wheel; a crumpled bumper; or some other evidence of how the damage was done. It was a sobering gesture to those who used the roads, and for the next few kilometres we always peered more frequently into our mirrors to see what was coming.

In time the trees began to lose their crowns. Then they turned red. We consulted the map. Some 40 kilometres ahead was the town of Monchegorsk: 'beautiful tundra' in the local Saami language. Infamous for its nickel and copper smelters, which had once supplied the Russian army, the giant factory complex, along with another to the west, had killed all the trees for more than 1000 square kilometres. Monchegorsk's town administrators, not wanting the unsightly remnants of vegetation on their doorstep, had torched what was left. Ironically, US and Japanese car manufacturers were now using the plant's products in their catalytic converters—instruments which reduce emissions from automobile exhausts.

At lunchtime we sheltered behind a rock and drank the last of our soups—an almost inedible, and ferociously lemony, court-bouillon bought earlier that year as a treat in a French supermarket. We spent most of the rest of the break with our heads tucked in tortoise-like through the neck hole of our ponchos to avoid the worst of the rain.

When it eased we slotted back into the rhythm of the road, lowering our heads against the wind, with the mountains sliding up on either side. In the end we gave up exhausted, well before our usual time, and found a camp spot between a clump of blackened fingers that just about obscured us from the road. With the tent up I cooked a whole packet of spaghetti, the last but one. I dropped the pan as I was about to serve, sending the whole lot sliding out onto the black, rotting gums of the poisoned earth. There was nothing else to do but scoop it up again with a couple of forks. I pretended to Rohan the black crunchy granules of soot and soil were cracked peppercorns I'd come across by chance in the bottom of my panniers.

It was the middle of summer, but that night it began to snow. Come morning the country around was dusted in a rim of white. Thicker stuff jammed the high passes.

We started off in puffs of our own steam, our fingers mittened in the sleeves of our jumpers. Not long into it a peculiar shriek erupted from above us. We turned to see the full force of a rush of wind dramatically gouge out a hanging valley of snow. The range billowed, then vanished completely in instant mist. The blizzard flung itself towards us, hitting us head on and forcing us into a flailing dead stop. It was followed by another gust, which slapped us in the face with the sting of sleet. In seconds our legs and feet were drenched beneath our capes.

Ahead we could just make out the factory—a city of chimneys. Then the snow rubbed it out. I checked my speedometer. On a steep decline we were travelling at just 7 kilometres an hour when 25 or more would be normal. I was freezing. It flashed through my mind that we had to give up, that we should turn around and cycle with the wind back to the safety of Polyane Zori. It was insanity to go on. My breath was forming in clouds so thick now I could hardly make out my handlebars. Our only other hope was to make it to the factory. Rohan made the decision first. She was by my side, off her bike and dragging her legs like her joints had been nailed together.

Just then the wind dipped, flinging the snow to ground. For a moment I could just about make out some concrete structures not far off the road. I tried to point them out, but my finger refused to extract itself from my palm.

'Come on,' I stammered over the wind. 'We've got to find shelter.'

'I can't feel my feet,' Rohan whimpered back.

I reached out with a free hand and swept her face clumsily towards me. Her lips were a patchy yellow, her eyes fixed and glazed. I was worried. I knew we could easily die out here in the condition we now found ourselves.

We trailed like retreating cavalry across a patch of dirt, clomping past broken bricks, worn-out motors, old transformers, crushed drums, asbestos sheeting, empty vodka bottles and burst pipes. Among the rubble was what appeared to be a concrete insulator shed. It had a roof, a ditch for a floor and three walls—one smack up against the wind. I dropped Muttley onto the ground as the snow pulled in again.

By now Rohan was shivering uncontrollably, her teeth clicking like a typewriter. I held out a useless arm to comfort her. I noticed it was shaking violently too. A thought leapt into my mind: we were suffering from hypothermia, we had to raise our core temperatures or risk falling into unconsciousness.

Suddenly, I found myself sitting down on the edge of the ditch, my legs poking out into the snow. Rohan was resting on a plank, her back against a wall, her legs up to her chest, her eyes staring, open wide. I'd obviously blacked out. I struggled to blink my eyes; my eyelids rolling down as slowly as garage doors. I had an incredible urge to sleep. I tried to shake my head to clear my senses but could barely move my neck. I noticed a tear in the corner of Rohan's eye and I saw it hang there for a moment and freeze. My mind ticked over slowly, like a watch about to stop. I had to get up; it was left to me, finally, to show what I was made of.

Somehow, I made it to my feet, almost tripping over the stumps of my toes. Out in the snow I stumbled over the hidden frames of our bikes. Simultaneously, it seemed, I was standing in silence determining which of the white heaps was mine and fumbling at the tattered plastic bag holding a sleeping bag. I struggled back, zipped it up and helped Rohan manoeuvre herself in.

My slowness was beginning to irritate me. Outside again I hooked out the primus with rigid thumbs, and the last of some lamp oil fuel in a bottle we'd chanced on in St Petersburg. I hunted out a sliver of dried wood for a wick.

With the flames jiggering wildly I climbed into my sleeping bag, my stomach and chest cavities feeling full of crushed ice. The snow continued raging, sweeping almost horizontally across the front of our hideout in tune with the deafening wind. With nothing else to do, I fell across Rohan's body, trying as best as I could to give her more warmth.

With that, I remembered her feet and those silly canvas shoes with the holes in the sides that she'd insisted on wearing. I figured that if I put a plastic bag over each one they would keep her body heat in.

'You're going to have to take your shoes off,' I managed to falter. 'They're wet, you're going to get frostbite.'

Plums popped out of her socks where toes should have been. I poured the remains of the sugar into the water, dropped in the last tea bag and forced the plastic bags they'd been stored in over her feet. Finally I managed to zip her sleeping bag to mine. We took turns with our heads in each other's laps, or with noses poked out of our nylon hatch to sniff fresh air instead of gasping for breath in an atmosphere of damp rabbits in their burrow. Sometime later I poured out the drinks, then took to blowing over the brews to warm up our faces with the steam.

Thinking more clearly now, I poured the last of our water over our final packet of pasta. We waited impatiently for it to boil, then demolished the meal in seconds. It was another two hours until the storm subsided and we felt capable of venturing out.

In a valley behind our shelter the white concrete blocks rose up like high-rise igloos. The city was almost within touching distance. Suddenly I heard voices. Three people were trudging through the snow on the road we'd cycled down, their hands in their pockets and their shoulders hunched against the cold. They took no notice of us, and for a moment we stood there staring at them in amazement, wondering if we had stumbled into another dimension. We could have frozen to death, with hundreds of thousands of people just like them a couple of kilometres away.

We made a dash for it, stuffing everything back into our panniers in relays. At last I strung a cord across both sleeping bags and hitched them to the top of my panniers and we fled towards the city.

☆ ☆ ☆

On Monchegorsk high street an oversized metal worker wielded a hammer. Behind him was the main street and two hotels. At the first, a woman at the desk offered us tea and nearly fell off her chair when we told her we had cycled there. She offered us a room, for the Western price. Rohan clucked, knowing we didn't have enough to pay.

'Look. It's snowing outside. We've cycled nearly 4500 kilometres to get here. Can't you just give us the Russian price?'

The woman studied us carefully, noting Rohan's quivering chin. She picked up the phone. 'I will call my boss,' she said. 'But I'm sure you can stay for Russian price.'

We waited as the woman garbled into the mouth piece, went quiet for a moment, changed the tone of her voice to emulate Rohan's pleas, then slowly replaced the receiver.

'Nyet,' she said quietly. 'It is not possible.'

'What about the other hotel?'

'The same owner.'

'Is there a bank where I can change money?' I asked, remembering our US dollars. We could worry about the train fare back to Berlin when we reached Murmansk.

'Da. It's open tomorrow morning.'

'Will you take dollars?'

'Nyet.'

'Everyone takes dollars.'

She shook her head.

I pointed to the keys hanging up behind her on a nail board. Not even one was missing. 'But you're empty!' I rounded on her.

She shrugged. We walked back into the snow.

I gave up trying to hammer tent pegs into the permafrost when the first three bent in half. I settled for heavy rocks instead.

Luckily we had found a small shop beside the hotel and had managed to buy some biscuits, a tin of tomatoes, two tins of fish and a loaf of bread. We ate everything in one sitting, scooping out tomatoes and fish with our fingers and chewing on biscuits and bread while wrapped up in crunching iced sleeping bags.

Sleep was impossible. Instead we talked, telling each other stories of our childhood we'd both heard before, while outside the sun prowled low among the hills. When we could stand the cold no longer we set off again, through a grizzly landscape of downed trees and power poles, in the tyre track depressions of a truck somewhere ahead of us.

Breakfast time passed without stopping; we forgot about lunch altogether. The city of Onemogorsk drew up. There was no-one in the streets. As the last motley farmsteads frittered away the country reverted to a rink of swamp and tundra.

We spent fourteen hours on the road that day, putting all the weight of our bodies into pedalling, burning up muscle where the fat had once been and ignoring the snow flakes which rested on faces as lifeless as china.

Finally, the first concrete blocks of Murmansk jumped us like highway robbers, their toes causing my neck to creak painfully up from the position it had frozen into. Giant hammers and sickles, workers, warships and doves of peace began looming down from sheer brick walls. Street lamps glowed reluctantly. The few people around looked more like bears in their coats and hats than humans. One, a woman, wore a plastic bag from a Western supermarket over her head, to keep the summer snow off, while sailors in Northern Fleet uniforms with two black ribbons dangling down their backs made their way through the slush with their arms clamped tightly around their chests for warmth.

We could barely stagger into the station's concourse. But the excitement of being there perked us up and soon we were attacking packets of fried Barents Sea Cod like aid parcels, and washing down mouthfuls with peppery vodka.

We had just over $100 put away—not enough, we expected, for the train fare home if we had to pay the Western price, so Rohan asked for tickets in her best Russian.

'Dokumenti', the clerk demanded. She flicked through our passports before passing us onto another woman, glassed-off behind a window with an Intourist sign painted above it.

'Dokumenti!' Our passports were requisitioned again.

'Intourist?' she asked confused, unable to find a relevant stamp.

'Nyet. Stoodyent.'

'Ah, stoodyent. G'dye?'

'St Petersburg,' Rohan lied and passed over a fake student card she'd picked up from a street forger in Bangkok earlier that year. The clerk looked at it for a moment, but the stiff Roman lettering made no sense to her. There was a train leaving for St Petersburg the following morning. From there we could connect with a Polish train back to Berlin. Both had first class carriages. OK?

We thought only briefly of sticking around for a few days, but in the end we felt so relieved to be there, that we wanted to put physical distance between us and the hardship of the journey as soon as possible. The thought of pulling off clothes we hadn't changed in two weeks, and of slumping into a hot bath and sipping champagne was just too much for us to refuse.

'We'll take it,' we said together.

The clerk thrust back our documents and printed out two tickets. They cost just $22 each, including passage for our bicycles. I cuddled closer to Rohan to buffer the chill, happy the decision was made, and not daring to think of what we could have bought over the past few days with the money we had just saved.

'Warm for the time of year,' the clerk said as we turned to leave with the tickets clasped in our hands.

'We nearly froze to death,' Rohan spluttered.

'But I have my coat off,' she replied somewhat bemused. 'It's been a whole year since I have taken off my coat.'

☆ ☆ ☆

From the station you can spot nuclear-powered ice breakers tied up at the dock. Beside them, towering westwards over the Gulf of Kola from where the Nazis came, stands an enormous statue of a Soviet soldier, known to the locals simply as Alosha, but to the bureaucrats as the 'Monument to the Defenders of the Soviet Polar Region in the Years of the Great Fatherland War'. Newly-engaged couples traditionally stand at his feet to drink a good-luck bottle of champagne. We toasted him with a clink of the vodka bottle knocked against bicycle frames. Then toasted ourselves.

We had the whole night, and it would never get dark. It

would be easy enough just to stay in the station, or there was always a hotel if we could use our credit cards. I took another swig, pondering the possibility of making it down to the waterfront and the nuclear base they called Atomflot. I suggested a quick ride, but Rohan was having none of it. She insisted she'd stay and mind the luggage. I said I may take longer then, to get a feel of the place. She wouldn't wait up, she said, and snuggled down in her pannier-padded corner hugging the bottle to her chest.

Within minutes I was charging down Prospect Lenina, avoiding the trolley buses and the remnants of a population which migrates southwards every summer to escape the constant light which they were convinced would make them sick. The suburbs dawdled away, and the cold Arctic air burned my face as I steered a path to the end of my journey. A couple of kilometres outside the city centre I came across the icebreaker base. A checkpoint was manned, but the guard seemed unsure about what to do, so I sped past him with a cheery wave.

A concrete path took me towards the sea, coming to a halt at its edge. An icebreaker towered up beside me, barnacles already stripped from its hull. The Murmansk Shipping Company used eight of them to plough through the Polar ice to clear shipping lanes of winter ice averaging 2.5 metres thick along the northern coast. It was the world's largest fleet of civilian nuclear-powered vessels, and a good money-earner, charging up to 25,000 American dollars to take tourists on a three-week trip to the North Pole. The company didn't like to publicise the original nuclear icebreaker *Lenin*—after the reactor overheated and killed sixty crew, they simply cut a hole in the hull and dropped it in the ocean. In all, more than twenty nuclear reactors, and at least eighteen Soviet nuclear submarines and icebreakers, have been abandoned and sunk off Russia's northern coast. The most infamous was the *Komsomolets*, the USSR's first nuclear-powered ballistic missile carrier, and the pride of the Soviet nuclear armoury. In 1961, forty-two sailors were foaming bile and sweating blood as they died saving the world from a reactor on the verge of meltdown. *Komsomolets* sank with two nuclear warheads onboard. They are now believed to be leaking plutonium from their place at the bottom of the sea.

I walked to a string which stretched across the dock, cutting me off from a huge container ship, the *Lepse*, with its own concrete sarcophagus slapped together to encase damaged fuel assemblies salvaged from the icebreaker *Lenin*. Nearby signs warned that the *Lepse* was emitting radiation—but they had not been enough to prevent a terrorist attack in 1993, nor the Moscow television crew who walked into the base and made off undetected with radioactive caesium.

I sat beside a yellow icebreaker for a while, trying not to think of all the risks I'd put us through. Then I grew impatient with myself. I didn't want to admit it, but my journey was still not over.

Twenty kilometres north of Murmansk was Severomorsk, where most of the Northern Fleet's surface vessels were based, including its nuclear-powered battle cruisers. But, for me, there was a greater prize. I wanted to reach the largest and most important base of them all—Zapadnaya Litsa. Only 45 kilometres from the Norwegian border, Zapadnaya Litsa was home, among other deadly things, some of the newest additions of the Russian armoury—six Typhoon-class nuclear submarines, carrying 200 strategic nuclear warheads each. Seeing the submarines would tie up my journey from Sevastopol full circle.

According to the map there was little ground left between Murmansk and the base. Unloaded of luggage I figured I could make it there and back and still have an hour or so to spare before the train left in the morning. A light drizzle was thawing the roads and heavy trucks had melted away the snow in lines ahead of me. I had nothing to lose. Rohan was probably asleep by now. It was 50 kilometres or so. What was that compared with the distance I'd already done? I clutched hold of my handlebars, and with the sun wandering along the hills from west to east, pumping out faint rays which inspired early-morning energy in the middle of the night, I flew through the tundra with the wind at my back, covering the first 20 kilometres almost before I knew it. The more I cycled, thankfully, the more distance I put between myself and the snow clouds. The landscape now was barren of trees; there was nothing that reminded me of life. I felt like I was cycling across the moon, with the hummocks of snowy earth welling up and down like waves of rock. The feeling was made more intense by the appearance of a frozen lake, blank and dull to my right, which came up so close to the edge of the road that I wondered if the frost at its edges would reach out and drag me sidewards by the ankles. I was glad when it delved away to begin sparring with a range of eroded hills that clumped towards me, their middles a weaving ridge between snow-bound crests and foggy bases.

After a while I rested in a depression, ploughed out of the earth by some long-melted glacier—the ground a swatch of permafrost and ice needles. I looked at my watch. It was past four in the morning. I had no food, and I was running on empty. I had left the tent and my sleeping bag with Rohan too. All of a sudden I realised the stupidity of my situation. A blizzard could hit again at any time. And I'd be done for.

I jumped back on and pedalled like fury, keeping to the truck trail like an ant following a scent. The road switched and curved and degraded for a while into frozen white stones. Ahead of me something moved.

I drew nearer, ears pricked. Something panted loudly nearby. I flinched violently away from it. Muttley slid in one direction and I spilled over with a heavy crunch into a snowdrift. As I came up for air dark forms skittered black, grey and white around me, ducking and dodging, snorting and flaying snow in all directions. I wrapped my arms over my head and curled up with my face pressed against the road surface as hard and cold as iron. Feet beat like drums around me, then all that was left was a faint creaking of ice and snow.

I looked up. A herd of about thirty reindeer were eyeing me beadily. One of them—and it had to be the largest—snorted angrily and ground a front foot purposefully back and forth like a bull.

I jumped to my feet, almost losing my balance again. The reindeer flinched, but stood their ground. Nervously, I bent down and pulled Muttley from the snow with a clattering of mudguards. As one, the herd took off, bounding over the tundra until they were just speckles in the distance.

Twenty kilometres or so later I cycled up to a guard post standing out starkly against the swaying bilge of drifts which surrounded it. A young soldier, dressed in heavy jacket and fur hat took one look at me and radioed for assistance. He invited me into his cramped little space. It was warmed by an oil heater, but he was still shivering.

'How did you get here?' his arms gestured.

'Bicycle.'

His open mouth said it all. 'I wanted to see the submarines,' I said in English, putting my arm above my head and imitating a periscope.

His mouth stayed open, but at that moment an armoured truck drove up. Two conscripts bundled over to the doorway. One gave a gurgling laugh when he noticed Muttley resting against the side of the guard post.

We were all silent, staring at each other. I was too cold and hungry to care what they did to me by now.

'You want to see the submarines?' a conscript asked in perfect English. I nodded.

'No problem. Next time call. We could have picked you up.' Typical, I thought. I was promised a ride back to Murmansk in the warmth of a truck leaving within the hour. Until then I could look around.

The conscripts drove me down to the water's edge past giant brown storage sheds, with Muttley slung in the back. They let me loose to wander among vessels half-submerged and dead, and others arrowed and sleek and straining at their leashes. Their used nuclear fuel had long ago filled huge coastal reservoirs, and the fleet had been dumping radioactive waste directly into the shallow waters of the Barents, Kara and White seas for decades. There were even reports of boat crews machine-gunning containers full of radioactive material which refused to sink. Radiation is also leaking from the 185 nuclear reactors—submarine, civilian and military—scattered around the region. I've never had much time for statistics, but the fact that the radioactivity dumped off the Murmansk coast accounted for two thirds of all the radioactive waste ever dumped in all the oceans of the world—and I was drinking the local water—gave me the screaming heebie-jeebies.

There was always some unusual twist in a Russian tale though. A new form of trade was taking off in Murmansk. Deteriorating social conditions, low wages, and a lack of funds to carry out maintenance had meant the Northern Fleet had had to come up with ways of raising money to keep their subs afloat. The latest scheme had involved unloading the nuclear missiles and filling the launch tubes with potatoes. The sub then took off from its base on a delivery run to the north coast of Siberia. Rumour has it they made a tidy profit.

But there are more serious implications of allowing elite nuclear units to suffer pay arrears and housing and food shortages. Sailors have been known to actually steal parts of their submarines in order to sell them on. More worrying still is the risk of accidental nuclear missile launch from a Russian submarine. A CIA report warns that some disgruntled Russian submarine crews might already be capable of authorising a launch. It just depends on how far they're pushed.

The safeguards against the unauthorised launch of many submarine-based missiles are weaker than those against either silo-based or mobile land-based rockets, because the Russian general staff cannot continuously monitor the status of the crew and missiles or use electronic links to override unauthorised launches.

Put this together with ageing nuclear communications,

frequently malfunctioning computer networks, deficient early-warning satellites, ground radars which are more prone to reporting false alarms, and budget cuts which have reduced the training of nuclear commanders, then we might all be facing the consequences before we know it. The problems hadn't escaped the notice of former Defence Minister, Igor Rodionov, who admitted in an interview with the *Washington Post* that no-one today can guarantee the reliability of Russia's nuclear submarine control systems. He pointed out an incident in 1995, when a warning related to a Norwegian scientific rocket launched from Northern Norway led to activation of the nuclear suitcase carried by the top Russian leaders and initiated an emergency nuclear-decision-making conference. It took eight minutes to conclude that the launch was not a surprise nuclear strike by Western submarines outside the Norwegian coast. This was less than four minutes before the deadline for ordering a nuclear response under standard Russian launch-on-warning.

✯ ✯ ✯

I watched the conscripts as they stood around smoking. The Russian has a shabbiness about him, as if he was never really meant to wear a uniform. However much he creased his seams and brushed down his over-large cap, beneath it all he seemed as innocent as a child forced to dress-up on a Sunday when he'd rather be out playing. They were at their best with vodka under their belts, and telling stories with flashing glints of patched-up teeth. I liked him a lot, and I was pleased that I could go back to the West with the ghosts of my childhood embodied into flesh-and-blood Tartars, Slavs, Balts and Cossacks. I had seen them all for what they were, not warmongers or fanatics, but people trying to survive as best they could in a country still brushing off the dust of its past, while confused and helpless in a new world that had suddenly jumped up and pulled them from the teat that had both comforted them and kept them subservient. Now they were left with the dark side, which they had pushed to the backs of their minds, as we have done in our society—

with all our own posturing, and arrogant stockpiling, and nuclear tests and meltdowns.

I had certainly been more fortunate than my grandfather, who had never even scratched the surface as he stood on the jetty in Murmansk, while concrete buildings crumbled beneath a leaden sky and crawled up the hills to be swallowed in mist—where it always seemed to be raining, and everyone felt the Russians might turn upon their helpers at any time. But far from expunging the fears that had been latent within me all my life, I also realised that I was more afraid of the nuclear than ever. The future will most probably bring more threats of nuclear attack, and our susceptibility to mistakes, accidents and terrorism was enough to make me certain that we still have the hardest lessons to learn. It wasn't just a Russian problem—every country which relies in part on nuclear weapons and energy faces the same potential disaster, as do their neighbours. The British, the Japanese, the Americans, the French, the Germans, the eastern Europeans—and all those countries like South Africa and Australia that supply the raw ingredients for the fuel—they are all as misguided and to blame as each other.

Then I thought of Rohan, my innocent partner, asleep a long ride away on her bags in a corner of a train station in the northernmost city in the world. And I realised that I missed her already. We'd had blow-ups and harsh words and had stormed off our own separate ways, but in the end the solidity of purpose—and the making up—was worth the disruptions. We had done what others had tried so forcefully to stop us doing, and no doubt we would shine from it. We were like two wheels to a bicycle, and our journey had ensured the frame that kept us together was stronger than ever.

★ ★ ★

A conscript woke me from my musings. There was vodka on offer. For a moment I hesitated before following them back to the guard post and resting my weight wearily against the machine that had taken me from fleet-to-fleet. I took a deep breath and pinned back my ears to listen for the ticking of the submarine's engines. But there was nothing. Just expectation. And the cries of gulls after sprats in the harbour.

EPILOGUE

We returned to Berlin in the height of summer. From the train station we cycled up the very same road we had wobbled down an age ago. The trees of spring had parasolled in such a thick covering of leaves in the time that we were away that we barely recognised Susanne and Kurt's street. No-one was home when we knocked on the door, but it didn't take long for Rohan to find a spare key underneath a pot plant. Inside, the house was the same as when we had left it. There was cheese and beer in the fridge and hot water ready for a bath.

I was consumed with longing to be alone with Rohan. We had lived through fears and anxieties and had seen our self-esteem flourish; with others around the closeness that had developed between us, and which we had come to rely upon, ran the risk of being slowly ground down. As it was, I was so overwhelmed with the swirl of emotions stirred by our being back, that it was a struggle not to break into tears.

We had reason to congratulate ourselves on our courage: we had not been eaten by the natives; the road had failed to do us in; and though Muttley and Kotoshka were battered and scraped, they had prevailed as well. I had learnt to quell the fear of meeting the unexpected, and the dread of finding myself at a loss in the face of unseen events; I had seen the wolves of my imagination for what they were, just shadows. But sadly, I knew that I would have to fit in again, and already I felt the shackles clamping on my gypsy life. Rohan, sensing my unease, and probably feeling it herself, pressed my hand and raised it to her lips without a word.

When Susanne returned with the dog that had left its toothy

imprints in my arm, there was little celebration. While the seasons had moved on, and us with them, she had remained unaltered. To her, the Russians and their ilk were still just savages and gangsters. 'Over there' things were in a state because they were a sloppy race. They lacked German discipline, and anything that went wrong was the fault of each and every one of them. She would never visit the places we had ventured through; she claimed to have seen enough of their inhabitants during the occupation of her Fatherland. In the end I found her rigidity too hard to handle, and I had to lock myself away with the excuse of a headache.

But as I lay in my room I became perplexed on another count. Early on in the journey I had dreamed up the idea of writing a book about our experiences. But books need dialogue, and with just a few words of Russian in my vocabulary it didn't look promising. But whenever I thought to myself along the way that I needed to meet someone who spoke English well enough to fill out the chapters, they would appear. And most of them had some connection with the nuclear. Was I making my own fate by looking out for them? Or was it preordained all along?

As it turned out, fate stamped its mark more indelibly the day after our return. We had just sat down with a beer in our hands when the telephone rang. Susanne got up to answer. It was Rohan's father in Australia.

'Hello, Robert, we were just sitting down...' After a long silence which sliced our contented mood like a cleaver, finally Susanne muttered, 'Tom's dead.'

Tom, Rohan's brother, was a huge chap with the gentlest handshake I had ever felt. He was thirty years old, the same age as I had been when we set off from Sevastopol. His girlfriend had stroked his hair as he lay with his head in her lap, looking up at her contentedly. Tom, with no history of illness, then died in her arms. Just like that. Nobody ever found out why.

Rohan and Susanne paid for the first flight back to Sydney. I would have to wait until I could get on a plane with my existing ticket. Ironically, if we had decided to stay on in Murmansk Rohan would never have made it to the funeral.

In the days alone that followed I had plenty of time to think. I remembered Tom insisting that we should break out of our predictable routines. 'We can't just sit around here watching television,' he would say. 'Come outside and watch the sunset.'

Now, his death, and all the individual tragedies I had experienced in one way or another during our odyssey, served to hit home that life was so fragile, and that you didn't have time to be scared of it.

I was never as sure as I was then that the trip had proved me right in leaving behind the job and existence I had begun to hate. From now on I was determined I would spend more time mapping out my own path, by following the threads of interests which had remained with me throughout my life, but which up to now I had largely ignored. I would endeavour to nurture my love of travel, of nature, and of writing—to combine them, and in so doing map out my own path instead of stumbling past signposts put up by others. In the light of Tom's death it seemed such a waste to spend one's life struggling to climb the rungs of a ladder, only to find out when it's too late that the ladder was against the wrong wall all along. Now at least I could go on—knowing I had taken time out from the settled mediocrity of a secure and comfortable existence to see the sunset.

★ ★ ★

While I was writing this book, Pakistan and India skirmished across their border and tested atomic bombs. Japan—one of the most technologically-advanced nations in the world—experienced its worst ever nuclear disaster. And the Ukrainian government decided, at last, to close down Chernobyl for good in December 2000.

Rohan, by the way, still isn't pregnant.

ACKNOWLEDGEMENTS

I have been helped by countless people in my wanderings and I owe them all a great debt. Our preparations for the journey would have been a lot tougher without the generosity and hospitality of Kurt and Susanne in Berlin, as well as Werner, who so sadly took a last bow not long after our return.

I would like to thank adventurer Charlie Lynn, artist and chef Rob Pigott, and metaphysicist Mike Collins, for their inspiration at different times in my life, and of course Rohan Pigott for her love and putting up with my itchy feet.

Others I need to acknowledge are Jason Goodwin, Jan Morris, Nick Danziger, Eric Newby, Wilfred Thesiger, Peter Matthiessen and Ted Simon for encouraging me to travel in the first place. In addition I would like to mention others who have helped me with comments, revisions and support along the way, including Daniel Scott, Richard Lupson, Jennifer Lane, Anita Heiss, Sally Hammond, Gabrielle Haumesser, John Borthwick, Andrew Conway, Andrew Perrin, Anouska Good, Sophie Church, Nanette Backhouse, Sarah Hatton and my agent Anthony A. Williams.

Finally, to Jo Ludlow, because I said I would, and to Tom Pigott for helping me to follow the project through when things got rough.

I apologise for inevitable errors of omission.

ABOUT THE AUTHOR

Marc Llewellyn was born in 1965 in Newport, South Wales, UK. After completing a Bachelor of Arts in Communication Studies at Sunderland University (England) he took off to Australia, where he completed a journalism cadetship with the *Sydney Morning Herald*. With a Master of Arts in Journalism from UTS (Sydney) under his belt not long after, he left the frantic world of reporting behind and started out on an award-winning freelance travel-writing career. His travel features have been published in *The Australian*, *The Age*, The *Sydney Morning Herald*, *The West Australian*, The *Sun Herald*, The *Herald-Sun*, The *Brisbane Sunday Mail*, *Australian Geographic*, *Australian Way*, *Panorama* and *Travelling Life* amongst others. He currently spends his time jetting around the world at other people's expense and living at various times in Britain and Australia.